INTO THE MAELSTROM

THE WRECK OF HMHS ROHILLA

COLIN BRITTAIN

The History Press

This book is dedicated to the memory of all those who suffered
through the ordeal that befell His Majesty's Hospital Ship *Rohilla*
and its repercussions.

First published 2014

The History Press
The Mill, Brimscombe Port
Stroud, Gloucestershire, GL5 2QG
www.thehistorypress.co.uk

British Library Cataloguing in Publication Data.
A catalogue record for this book is available from the British Library.

ISBN 978 0 7524 9765 5

Typesetting and origination by The History Press
Printed in Great Britain

CONTENTS

FOREWORD

The British India Steam Navigation Company

Aboard the *Cape of Good Hope* the British India Steam Navigation Company carried six companies of the 37th Regiment of Foot (to become the 1st Battalion, The Royal Hampshire Regiment) from Colombo to reinforce the Calcutta garrison in June 1857. So began a history of service to Empire and country which only came to an end with *Uganda*'s involvement in The Falklands Campaign in 1982 and subsequent charters to the Ministry of Defence until 1985.

Between those years in times of war and peace, the BISNC provision of regular and casual troop transports, ambulance and hospital ships was unsurpassed by any other company. Prior to the First World War, ships carried troops to and from twenty-five campaigns and theatres of war, during which the BISNC fleet had grown to 126 ships. After a decision made in the early 1890s not to carry troops in Royal Navy vessels, regular chartering commenced and post-Boer War charters included *Rewa, Jelunga, Dilwara, Dunera* and *Rohilla*. Taken into war service as a hospital ship on 4 August 1914, the latter's career was destined to be only a few weeks long before being wrecked on Saltwick Nab.

Colin has chronicled this event after years of tenacious research into all its aspects, leaving no stone unturned and, indeed, information is still coming to light to record the feats of six lifeboat crews and the succour given by the citizens of Whitby to the survivors, and I am very pleased to contribute to this record of tragedy and heroism.

David J. Mitchell
Engineer Officer 1967–74
British India Steam Navigation Company

AUTHOR'S PREFACE

I have always felt an affinity for the sea, enthralling as it is majestic, and capable of delivering such ferocious power that it can literally break a ship's back, sending it to the bottom. As a child growing up I wanted to be a diver. Today we are spoilt with a wealth of programmes devoted to the undersea world, but to get the sort of warm clear water to dive wearing no hood or gloves and a thin suit means travelling to some exotic destination. I learned to dive in 1985 and recall only too vividly my first open-water dive into Jackson coal dock, which was later filled in and now forms part of Hartlepool Marina. Underwater visibility in this inky black water was 2ft at best and all I could do was follow a buddy line to my dive partner. It was so far removed from anything I had ever seen on television that I wonder how on earth I carried on. Over the years I enjoyed a varied and challenging diving career. When three brain tumours forced me to 'hang up my fins', I was devastated for scuba diving had become part of our family way of life. As an open-water instructor I enjoyed teaching as much as I did being part of a small group of experienced dedicated divers. Having always enjoyed wreck diving, I decided to try and use my existing knowledge and experiences as the basis for a new direction. My first book, *Scuba Diving*, was published in 1999; a dedicated diver training manual followed in 2001, and then I started a book which would take far more of a grip on me than I could ever have imagined, a book that has truthfully seen me through some very dark and painful times.

One of my favourite wrecks, on which I enjoyed many a dive, was that of HMHS *Rohilla*. This large liner was requisitioned as a hospital ship and lost in tragic circumstances at the start of the First World War. During a relatively quiet period I began to write what was initially going to be a short guide to the circumstances surrounding the awful loss of this vessel. But, as I gathered information, it soon became apparent that there was much more to the story than I first envisaged. I felt that I could not do it justice by just writing a simple guide, and my work soon blossomed into a full-fledged manuscript.

The first edition of this book was published in 2002 and since then I have never stopped researching the subject. Often, finding the smallest of references can lead one down a new path. I was exceptionally pleased with the first edition, but since then so much new information has come to light, quite a bit of it from descendants of those who were part of the tragedy in 1914. I am indebted to my publisher for allowing me the opportunity to revise this book.

It is my intention in this second edition to share with you some of the wonderful new information and unreleased photographs, and present a more detailed explanation of how the tragedy unfolded over the course of a weekend. Some past conclusions will be ruled out and assumptions will be found to have a basis in fact. For many years it has been accepted that those who perished numbered eighty-four or eighty-five, but, working with a family descendant, I feel confident enough to reveal that the figure is actually higher than eighty-five.

I have thoroughly enjoyed learning more of the personal history of some of those involved, and been saddened when reading individual accounts given by survivors. With today's advances in social networking and the internet, it is easier to 'talk' with people and in many cases this has been mutually beneficial. I can honestly say that, from the very outset of writing the first edition, I have felt honoured to be able to engage with descendants of those who survived or perished, and to share their stories.

I am sometimes asked for contact details for people with whom I have shared letters, emails and telephone calls. However, out of respect I would not reveal such delicate information; the relatives of anyone involved in the *Rohilla*'s loss need to know they can trust me, especially as some are approaching their wiser years. This may not sit well with some, but then this is not just a pastime for me. If I can help bring two parties together I will, but I won't jeopardise my close relationships with my sources.

In researching and writing this new edition I have included many fine and honourable statements that pay respect to the lifeboat service as it was in 1914, but which apply equally well today. Behind the brave men and women that man our lifeboats, there is a network of thousands who work away in the background supporting the RNLI, incorporating both professional and volunteer sectors. It has to be said that those doing what they can to support the Institution, be it those who man the many retail outlets or the thousands of ordinary people willing to volunteer their time fundraising in whatever capacity they can are as equally important.

Brian Dobie presenting me with the illustration of the *Rohilla* that his son Neil drew for me.

I was pleasantly surprised to receive a large hand-drawn illustration of the *Rohilla*. Well, maybe surprise isn't quite the word I am looking for as I knew the artist was doing something special for me. I just wasn't told what. The artist, Neil Dobie, gets his talent from his mother, who is extremely proficient in all things ceramic and has her own kiln, but what makes this lady special to me is her name – Mrs Rohilla Dobie. I was presented with the wonderful illustration by Rohilla's husband Brian, whom I had only ever spoken to in the past. It must have taken Neil quite a while to complete this illustration and I am really glad to have it.

When working with a story that is very nearly reaching its centenary, some omissions or errors are inevitable. However, every effort has been made to reduce the number of inaccuracies. I would be happy to hear of any amendments or further information that could be used to update my research or be added to subsequent editions of this book.

ACKNOWLEDGEMENTS

I would not have got this far had it not been for the support of The History Press and I cannot thank them enough for the help they have given me. In order to complete this book I have sought help from numerous sources. In the case of those affiliated to professional bodies, I am truly grateful for their patience in dealing with my constant questions and enquiries. I am eternally grateful to those who personally helped in my research and in the supply of material, as I am to anyone who has not been individually listed hereafter.

My grateful appreciation goes to close acquaintances and descendants of those lost on the *Rohilla*: Elsie Naylor, Jan Green, Edna Chadwick, Hilda Elsworth and Rodney Birtwistle. I offer my grateful thanks to Sarah Turner, Ron Dunn and the late John Littleford for the many long hours they spent with the 'lead' to supply the images required to effectively illustrate this book. I am grateful to Paul Hutchinson for his remarkable coloured illustration of Dr Ernest Lomas.

I wish to offer my thanks to the following people who contributed in their own way to the publication of this book:

Alan Holmes – for his assistance with grammatical proofing; Alan Wastell – for sharing his time and expertise to assist me with numerous photographs; Barbara and the rest of the staff at Whitby Library for help in obtaining information from the many microfiche files; A. Vicary – for allowing the use of pictures from his extensive collection held at the Maritime Photo Library; Barry Cox – for allowing me to reproduce illustrations from his book; Ben Dean – for supplying information and illustrations as an ex-owner of the wreck; the late Catherine Smith – for allowing me the use of her postcards, which covered the funeral processions; Charles Collier Wright – for allowing me to use extracts from Mirror Group Newspapers; Colin Starkey – one of the many valuable staff at the National Maritime Museum; David Stephens – for allowing me to rummage through his collection of underwater images; Duncan Atkins – for his assistance in searching through the many original newspapers at the old *Whitby Gazette* offices; Ian Wright – for his picture of the Deadmans Fingers; Jeff Morris – for allowing information from his booklet; Jim Grant – a helpful librarian at the Scottish Maritime Museum; Joyce D. Richmond – for permitting the use of images related to W. Knaggs and wonderful information on Whitby St John Ambulance Brigade; Ken Wilson – for giving me consent to use extracts and illustrations from his book, and to his widow Sheila for her continued support; Lorraine Cunningham – a respected member of staff at Harland and Wolff Technical Services Ltd, who scoured through endless archives in search of missing technical drawings; Lynn Everington – from *The Yorkshire Journal*, who helped secure extracts from the publication; members of Whitby lifeboat station – who allowed me access to the original lifeboat records; Mike Shaw for allowing use of a treasured image from the Frank Meadow Sutcliffe Gallery; Mr Smith for supplying information from World Ship Society records; Peter Barron who gladly gave permission to use extracts from the *Northern Echo*; Peter Thompson Hon. Curator Whitby Lifeboat Museum whose help with lifeboat photographs was appreciated; Stephen Rabson – P&O historian and archivist who gave me permission to use BISNC logos; Stuart Norse and Brian Wead – who gave me information in their capacity as RNLI Service Information Managers; T. Kenneth Anderson for his help in retrieving record information from files at Ulster Folk and Transport Museum; the enthusiastic volunteers at the Whitby Archives Trust who gave me unrestricted access to their files, which are sadly no longer available; the willing staff members of the British Newspaper Library for obtaining copies of papers which covered the tragedy; Andre Dominguez for his input and name correction for the MacNaughton brothers.

Andrew McCall Smith, a great nephew of Arthur Shepherd who shared with me a host of valuable family information; Arthur Walsh, grandson of William Farquharson; the late Chris Lambert, for his background information on Major Herbert Edgar Burton GC OBE; Colin Berwick and John Timmins, for their help and advice regarding the Kingham Hill School tragedy; Wendy and Lewis Breckon, who, as relatives of George Peart, were really helpful and Daniel Peart, for his wonderful history of George Peart; David J. Mitchell, an ex-British India Engineer who shared his expert knowledge of the BISNC; Ian Morris, for his London Pageant photographic work; Jim Barnett, a retired sub aqua diver who has dived the *Rohilla* and whose cuttings were helpful to me; John Cummins, for detailing Thomas Cummins' exploits as the motor mechanic on the *Henry Vernon*; John Mules, for his most valuable help regarding Nursing Sister Mary Louisa Hocking; John Stephenson, a descendant of George Brain; John Todd, a descendant of John Bleakley; John Wilson, a grandson of Frederick Edwin Wilson, Junior Marconi Operator; Mr Pickles, Photographic Curator, Whitby Museum, Pannett Park; Ray and Mandy Harvey, Fiona Kilbane, and Katherine Pennock for providing detailed information on Mary Keziah Roberts and her family; Simon Lowes, whose grandfather, Ernest Parker, was a cabin boy (Ernest and his brother, William, both survived the tragedy); Terry Offord, whose mother sailed on the *Rohilla* when she was a troopship; William McClure, the present owner of the wreck, who supplied information, photographs and his valuable insights; Anne Poole, for deciphering many of the fine handwritten papers I have acquired about the *Rohilla*; Margaret Whitworth, a loyal lifeboat supporter and keen photographer; Betty Bayliss, for sharing her passion for the Whitby division of the St John Ambulance Brigade; Betty Sayer, for her guidance as to the background of Alexander Corpse; Dorothy Brownlee, whose grandfather James Brownlee was the 2nd coxswain of the Tynemouth motor lifeboat *Henry Vernon*, and who has proved to be a trusted confidante and friend; Geraldine Bullock, for her help with information on Harry Claude Robbins; Julie Diana Smith, whose husband's great-great-great-grandfather was Coxswain Robert Smith and was a mine of information (no pun intended); Heather Sheldrick, one half of the folk duo Bernulf and composer of a song about the loss of the *Rohilla*; Whitby Literary and Philosophical Society, Whitby Museum, Pannett Park.

Thanks to the Royal National Lifeboat Institution for allowing me the use of selected photographs including those from Nigel Millard, David Ham, Nathan Williams and the collection of the late Graham Farr.

Thank you to all those who have contributed to this second edition, your help has proven priceless.

All images are copyright of the author unless stated otherwise.

1

ALLIED HOSPITAL SHIPS OF THE FIRST WORLD WAR

Hospital ships were primarily large liners fitted out with the necessary facilities to serve as an efficient hospital. They were registered with the Red Cross and equipped to deal with most cases of injury and disease, and to transport the wounded back to Britain for more specialist treatment or recuperation. They were equipped wholly or in part by private individuals or by officially recognised societies. In 1907 the Hague Conference laid down conditions under which hospital ships would be accorded immunity from attack. In order to be easily distinguished, vessels assigned as hospital ships were given a unique colour scheme: their hulls and superstructure were painted white, a green band ran round the hull parallel to the waterline, broken to fore and aft by a large red cross. As well as flying their national flag, hospital ships displayed the flag of the International Red Cross. To ensure that they were distinguishable at night, the hulls were brilliantly illuminated with long rows of red and green lights along the sides. Identified in this way, it was reasoned that they would be protected from attack under the Geneva Convention; sadly, however, in practice this was not always the case.

The Red Cross insignia, red arms of equal length on a white background, was accepted as the emblem of mercy, and is in fact the Swiss flag with its colours reversed, recognising the historic connection between Switzerland and the original Geneva Convention of 1864. The insignia has two distinct purposes:

- to protect the sick and wounded in war, and those authorised to care for them
- to indicate that the person or object on which the emblem is displayed is connected with the International Red Cross

The emblem was intended to signify absolute neutrality and impartiality; its unauthorised use was forbidden in international and national law.

When the insignia was accepted as the design for the Red Cross, one shipping company, Rowland & Marwood based in Whitby, was required to change its company logo, which until then had been a red cross on a white background, with a blue border. To avoid confusion with the Red Cross, they redesigned their logo by swapping the blue and red around.

Altogether, seventy-seven military hospital ships and transports were commissioned during the First World War: twenty-two in 1914, forty-two in 1915, seven in 1916 and six in 1917. Among this number were four Belgian government mail steamers: the *Jan Breydel, Pieter de Connick, Stad Antwerpen* and *Ville de Lire*. Five yachts were used for the transport of patients.

Among the vessels used were three of the giant liners of the period. The *Aquitania*, built for Cunard by John Brown & Co., had the greatest accommodation with 4,182 beds. The *Aquitania* was launched in 1913 and, after her maiden voyage from Liverpool to New York, begun on 30 May 1914, she made only two more Atlantic crossings before the First World War began. The vessel completed just over two years' service as a hospital ship from 4 September 1915 to 27 December 1917. On one journey from the Dardanelles she had almost 5,000 patients on board, and twenty ambulance trains were needed to dispatch them from Southampton to various hospitals across Britain.

During the war *Aquitania* served as a hospital ship, an armed merchant cruiser and a troop transport, returning to commercial service in June 1919. Later that year she was taken out of service for refitting and conversion from coal to oil. When the Second World War began, she was again called into service as a troop transport, one of a small number of ships to serve in both World Wars. In 1948–49 *Aquitania* was placed on a Southampton to Halifax austerity route, and her last transatlantic crossing was from Halifax to Southampton. After making 443 transatlantic roundtrips, steaming over 3 million miles and carrying almost 1.2 million passengers over a thirty-five year career, *Aquitania* was scrapped in 1950 at Faslane on the Gareloch.

HMHS *Britannic* was the biggest of the three Olympic-class ships (*Olympic, Titanic* and *Britannic*). The *Britannic* had the second largest accommodation for patients, being capable of holding over 3,000, and was in service for just over a year from 13 November 1915. When the *Titanic* was lost in April 1912, the building of *Britannic* had just started, allowing modifications to be made to improve the vessel's safety.

The *Britannic* was launched on 26 February 1914 and was requisitioned as a hospital ship when the First World War began. At around 8 a.m. on Tuesday 22 November 1916, *Britannic* was steaming in the Aegean Sea when she was rocked by an explosion. As the ship began to list, Captain Charles A. Bartlett tried desperately to steer her towards shallower water. Despite the modifications made in construction, the *Britannic* sank in just fifty-five minutes, miraculously taking with her only thirty people out of the 1,100 reported to have been aboard. The *Britannic* was located in 1976 by Jacques Cousteau resting at a depth of 100m. An expedition was made in October–November 1997, during which a memorial plate was laid on the wreck.

Built for the Cunard Line by Swan, Hunter & Wigham Richardson, Wallsend-on-Tyne, *Mauretania* measured 762ft x 88ft. Her maiden voyage from Liverpool to New York was made on 16 November 1907. Although severe storms and heavy fog hampered this first voyage, the ship still arrived in New York in good time on 22 November, no doubt aided by her service speed of 25 knots. A later refit saw a change of inner shafts and a move to four-bladed propellers. By April 1909 the *Mauretania* had made both westbound and eastbound records, retaining the Blue Riband Trophy for twenty years. At the end of 1909, the ship's first captain, John T. Pritchard, retired and Captain William Turner assumed command. The *Mauretania*'s reputation attracted several prominent passengers, including HRH Prince Albert (later George VI) and Mr Carlisle, the managing director of Harland and Wolff. In June 1911 the ship brought thousands of visitors to Britain for the coronation of George V.

When Britain declared war on Germany, the Admiralty sent out an order requisitioning the ship as soon as it returned to Liverpool. On 11 August, however, the *Mauretania* was released from government duties. After the loss of the *Lusitania*, the *Mauretania* was required to return to service. At the end of August 1915, she returned to Liverpool, where she was fitted out as a hospital ship offering room for nearly 2,000 patients. She then left Liverpool in October to assist with the evacuation of the wounded from Gallipoli. The *Mauretania* made several further voyages as a hospital ship and completed her last on 25 January 1916.

The liner had a chequered career, undergoing numerous calls to service and refits before making her final passenger sailing from Southampton on 30 June 1934 – the day the Cunard and White Star Lines merged. The completion of the *Queen Mary* meant that the *Mauretania* was now outdated. After a lay-up the liner was sold to Metal Industries Ltd of Glasgow for scrap, with her fixtures and fittings auctioned on 14 May 1935 at Southampton Docks. The *Mauretania* reached the Firth of Forth on 3 July and was moved to Rosyth for dismantling.

In operations against German-occupied Namibia, the hospital transport *City of Athens* and hospital ship *Ebani* were used, the latter serviced by the South African Red Cross Society. In an emergency the *Ebani* could carry 500 patients. She was staffed by South African Medical Corps personnel and on the termination of the campaign was handed over to the Imperial authorities.

Even when the enemy obeyed the Geneva Convention, the white hospital ships still faced hazards. In the years 1914–17 seven military hospital ships struck mines and were either sunk or badly damaged. In 1917 the Central Powers decided to disregard international law, and hospital ships, no matter how prominently marked, were no longer given their due protection. In 1917 and 1918 eight hospital ships were torpedoed and the resulting casualties were indeed tragic.

HMHS *Asturias*

Built:	Harland and Wolff, Belfast.
Tonnage:	12,105 gross, 7,509 net.
Engine:	Twin screw, quadruple expansion; 2 x 4 cylinders; three double- and four single-ended boilers.
Cruising Speed:	16 knots.
Steel Hull:	Two decks, five holds, with ten hydraulic cranes.
Passenger Capacity:	300 First Class, 140 Second Class, 1,200 Steerage.

The *Asturias* was the first RN vessel to be fitted with a passenger lift. Forecastle and bridge 447ft (136.25m); poop 52ft (15.85m).

History

1906:	Keel laid down, the fifth of the 'A' class ships for the Royal Mail Steam Packet Company.
1907:	Launched.
1908:	Maiden voyage from London–Brisbane, then transferred to Southampton–River Plate service.
1914:	Requisitioned for use as a hospital ship.
1917:	Torpedoed at Bolt Head off the Devon coast, whilst in full hospital colours, with the loss of thirty-five lives.
1919:	Purchased by Royal Mail before once again being laid up at Belfast.
1923:	At the end of a two-year rebuild at Harland and Wolff, emerged as the cruise liner *Arcadian*.
1930:	Laid up in Southampton Water.
1933:	Sold to Japan for scrapping.

HMHS *Rewa*

Built:	William Denny & Brothers, Dumbarton (Yard No. 762).
Tonnage:	7,267 gross, 3,974 net.
Classification:	Passenger Cargo Ship.
Engines:	Triple screws with Compound Parson's turbines, two double- and four single-ended tube boilers operating at 152 psi.
Coal Capacity:	1,506 tons.
Estimated Speed:	16 knots. During trials she managed just over 18 knots.
Steel Hull:	Three decks.
Build Description:	Five holds, eight watertight bulkheads, two hydraulic cranes to each hatch, with main and lower decks lighted and ventilated, ensuring suitability for trooping.

History

1905:	Launched for British India Steam Navigation Co. Sister of SS *Rohilla*.
1905:	Delivered to London. Cost £159,680.
1905:	Maiden voyage to India. First turbine steamer on the route.
1905:	The vessel became a permanent trooper during the season.
1910:	Carried the members of the House of Commons to the Coronation Naval Review at Spithead.

1914:	Became Hospital Ship No. 5 equipped with eighty doctors and 207 nurses.
1915:	Detailed for Gallipoli.
1915:	Left Gallipoli with wounded soldiers.
1918:	While steaming fully illuminated in the Bristol Channel, and carrying 279 wounded from Greece, the ship was torpedoed.

The hit was amidships, mortally wounding the vessel. All the lifeboats were successfully launched, ensuring the escape of those on board, with the exception of three people killed in the initial explosion. The captain had only minutes earlier warned that the alert should be maintained until she docked: 'It isn't over until we berth.' It is highly likely that this vigilance conttributed to the remarkable survival record of those who were later landed at Swansea.

HMHS *Rewa*, a sister ship to the *Rohilla*.

2

THE BEGINNING

Ship number 381 was launched at the Harland and Wolff shipyard, Belfast, on 6 September 1906. She was delivered to her owners, the British India Steam Navigation Co. Ltd, on 17 November 1906, and named SS *Rohilla*.

Formed in 1856 to carry mail, the Calcutta & Burma Steam Navigation Co. operated until 1862, when, after raising more capital in the UK, it became the British India Steam Navigation Co. Ltd. Operating ships ranging from small service craft and tugs to major vessels both passenger and cargo, between its founding and 1972 the company owned more than 500 vessels. The British India Steam Navigation Co. retained its separate identity after amalgamation with the Peninsular & Oriental Steam Navigation Co. (P&O) in 1914, with P&O operating as the parent company, but in 1971 P&O was reorganised into divisions: general cargo, passenger and bulk handling. All ships were progressively transferred to one of these divisions, resulting in the loss of all those individual shipping company names which made up the P&O group. Relatively unknown in the UK, British India had the largest number of ships flagged under the Red Ensign at any one time, reaching 161 in 1920.

Carrying passengers from the beginning, many ships were only 500 tons or so, plying their trade on coastal services round India or from India to Burma, East Africa and around the Persian Gulf. Such was the expansion in trade that within less than twenty years ships on order exceeded 2,000 tons each.

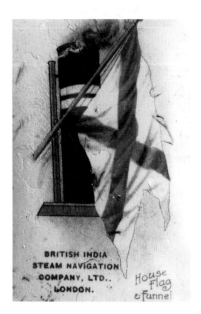

With few exceptions, ships under the control of British India used names which were derived from, or based on, Indian place names, and those places which ended in the letter 'A'. The SS *Rohilla* was no exception to this practice, being named after an Afghan tribe who had entered India in the eighteenth century during the decline of the Mughal Empire, gaining control of Rohilkhand (formerly Katehr, United Provinces, east of Delhi)

The British India Steam Navigation Co. operated fortnightly voyages from London to Colombo,

The British India Steam Navigation Company logo.

Madras and Calcutta. The *Rohilla* was built as a passenger cruise liner and registered at Glasgow. After her completion, the *Rohilla* entered the London to India service, operating from Southampton to Karachi. Those who travelled on the *Rohilla* when she was still a cruise ship remarked on the opulence and attention to detail. The varierty of meals offered on the *Rohilla* were carefully thought out ensuring that the high standards passengers had come to expect whilst cruising were maintained throughout.

Dinner
Consomme Andalouse   Creme Marie Stuart
Fillet of Telapia Sauce
Tartare Bra'sed Sheep's Hearts
Chasseur
Gombos Lyonnaise Leg and Shoulder of Pork
    Apple Sauce

Vegetables
Brussel Sprouts Browned and Boiled Potatoes
White Wine

Cold Buffet
Consomme Froid
Roast Beef Galantine of Chicken
Salad in Season

Wines
The undermentioned wines are ready
    for serving with this meal

White Wine
Witzenberg Hock   HALF BOTTLE   61-

British India White Tailed Kingfisher menu.

Red Wine
Alphen Burgundy   HALF BOTTLE   61-
The Wine List showing a full list of wines in stock may be
obtained from the Wine Stewards

Sweets
Lemon Bavarois
Coupe Bresilienne
OFFICIALLY HELD INFORMATION (LLOYDS REGISTER)

Number in Book:	685
Official Number:	124149
Code Letters:	HJQK
Name:	ROHILLA
Material / Rig:	Steel / Twin Screw Steamer
Master:	Captain David Landles Neilson
No. of Decks:	Three decks, mild steel, part teak with eight watertight bulkheads.
Special Surveys:	Electrical, Light Wireless.
Registered Tonnage:	7,409 tons
Gross:	5,588 tons

PARTICULARS OF CLASSIFICATION

Special Survey:	January 1910
Port of Survey:	Southampton
Built:	1906
Builder:	Harland and Wolff Ltd, Belfast
Owner:	British India Steam Navigation Co. Ltd

REGISTERED DIMENSIONS

Length:	460ft 3in
Breadth:	56ft 3in
Depth:	30ft 6in
Port of Registry:	Glasgow
Flag:	British

ENGINES

Cylinders and Diameter:	Quadruple eight-cylinder engines – 27in, 38.5in, 55.5in, 80in
Stroke:	54in
Boiler Pressure:	HS21894
Horse Power:	1,484hp
Boilers and Furnaces:	3D & 35B, 27cf, G5527, FD
Engine Maker:	Harland and Wolff Ltd, Belfast

The *Rohilla* was well equipped, fitted with the latest Marconi wireless telegraphy, and capable of a top speed of 17 knots. In general, British India ships prior to 1955 shared the same livery, having a black hull with a single white band, and a black funnel with the company's distinctive two white rings, whilst ships after 1955 were painted with white hulls with a black band painted around the topsides. The *Rohilla*, like many British India ships, experienced multiple colour changes during her service, depending on the service operated.

HMT *Rohilla* in port, embarking troops.

Captain David Landles Neilson was given command of the *Rohilla* from the outset. Neilson was born in Tranent, East Lothian, in 1864 and had worked hard throughout his career, qualifying as a 2nd mate when only 18 years old; he was awarded a Master Mariner's Certificate when he was 34. He is recorded as having served aboard the *Dwarka* in 1904 and the *Sofala* in 1906, and spent his whole career with the British India Steam Navigation Co.

In 1908 the *Rohilla* joined her sister ship, the SS *Rewa*, as a troop ship. It would appear that during her troopship service the *Rohilla* was allocated several different numbers. She was initially designated HMT *Rohilla* No. 6, but extant illustrations only show the *Rohilla* bearing the numbers 1, 2, 4 and 6; the numbers signified the route she was operating.

It was expected that, as a troopship in 1908, the *Rohilla* would have operated under the approved troopship livery, a white hull with a thin blue band, white upperworks and a yellow/buff funnel, with minor variations to this scheme being observed.

After serving a tour of foreign service between 1890 and 1908 the 1st Battalion Bedfordshire Regiment began its journey back to England on HMT *Rohilla*. A special card was produced to celebrate both the regiment's homecoming and Christmas: the Bedfordshire Regiment badge was inset on the front of the card with the original regimental ribbon placed down the side, upon which was written 'Hearty Greetings'. There is an artist's impression of the *Rohilla* on the inside, the caption of which indicates the end of a tour of nigh on nineteen years' foreign service. 'Our Anchors weighed were homeward bound' is printed on the opposite page and along the bottom edge the words 'Old Friends Old Times Old Memories'.

A vintage 1908 British regimental homecoming/ Christmas card.

Mrs Selina 'Kit' Offord. (Courtesy of Terry Offord)

In 1910 the *Rohilla* conveyed members of the House of Lords to the Coronation Naval Review of King George V at Spithead, while *Rewa* conveyed members of the House of Commons. In March 1912 John Daniel Vincer was travelling on the *Rohilla* with his wife Fanny Elizabeth and their daughter Selina 'Kit', bound for England and expecting to arrive in April. Vincer was stationed in India with the Field Artillery in the early 1900s and eligible for leave every five years. Kit was born on 3 December 1902 in Belgaum, in the Indian state of Karnataka and was brought up in Meerut near Delhi. Aged just 10 when her family made the passage to England, Kit gave an account of her experience.

As well as the soldiers and their families, a number of general passengers were permitted to travel on the *Rohilla*. Kit recalls there being very few civilians. The family were fortunate to have been allocated a cabin with a porthole on one of the lower decks. It was really warm when the journey began. Leaving port the ship headed out across the Indian Ocean making for the Red Sea.

As the *Rohilla* approached the Suez Canal, Kit was alarmed because as she looked down there didn't seem to be sufficient water for the ship to pass. She could make out the sand and pebbles and 'riffraff' and it didn't seem sensible to go via the Canal. Once safely through the Suez Canal the ship came into the Mediterranean and then made for Gibraltar. It was the stage from Gibraltar, sailing on towards the Bay of Biscay, that really gave Kit cause for concern and which left her with some very vivid memories.

Kit and her mother were on the top deck in deck chairs, enjoying themselves when everything began to move. The ship was rolling badly and the sea was getting higher; the flooding water caused everything to slide from side to side and only the handrails stopped them from going overboard! It became so rough that her father came up and said 'Get down into your cabin, because they are sending out an SOS.' In the end no assistance was needed because the sea seemed to become calm, quite as suddenly as it had become rough. As a result of the weather, the ship had veered off course in the Bay of Biscay, but it was easily corrected as the ship sailed up the French coast towards the English Channel bound for Southampton. Kit was pleased when her mother pointed and said, 'These are the Needles' off the Isle of Wight as they entered Southampton Water for she knew her passage was soon going to be at an end.

The ship slowed down as, like all other large craft, it had to wait for a pilot to guide it safely into the docks. In that time a rope ladder had been thrown overboard and Kit soon saw a head appear, sticking up over the rail. A voice called out, 'Have you heard the News?' The reply was 'No'. 'Well, the Titanic has sunk.' This didn't really register at the time, but the *Rohilla* was docking at Southampton on 15 April, the day that the grand liner *Titanic* sank! Afterwards everything seemed a little less important. Kit and her family found themselves on a train bound for London.

The overall passage from India to Southampton took some five or six weeks, Kit doesn't recall anything about the ship itself because she was very young at the time and all ships looked alike. After disembarkation and boarding the train, Selina heard nothing more about the *Rohilla* for seventy-odd years.

When Kit travelled on the *Rohilla*, it may have seemed a relatively unremarkable passage, but the narrative of her voyage was given in an interview-type session with her son Terry Offord at my request, in 2007 when she was 104. Selina 'Kit' Offord sadly passed away on 11 January 2008 after a two-week spell in hospital. Terry proudly explained that at the age of 105 his mother had lived a very full and eventful life and had never forgotten her voyage on the *Rohilla*. Terry described how he and his mother had visited the site of the Royal Victoria Hospital at Netley near Southampton, which was demolished in 1966 though the chapel is still there, now serving as a museum. They noticed a large picture of a ship on display in the main entrance, by sheer coincidence the *Rohilla*. Terry put it well when he said that it's a small world!

In 1913 HMT *Rohilla* was charged with carrying a number of regiments home to England after a seventeen-year deployment to India and South Africa, including the 1st Battalion Wiltshire Regiment, South Staffordshire Regiment, Gloucestershire Regiment and some Scottish regiments. Colonel Arthur Edmond Stewart Irvine DSO RAMC is known to have travelled on the *Rohilla* and he once had a wonderful photograph album of his voyage.

Netley Hospital chapel.
(Courtesy of Terry Offord)

Colonel Arthur Edmund Stewart Irvine with some of the *Rohilla*'s officers.

It featured photographs of the troops, some of the ship's crew and possibly a ceremony of 'Crossing the Line', commemorating a sailor's first crossing of the Equator and a fine photo of the Drums of the Staffordshire Regiment.

When war was declared, Captain Neilson and his officers remained at their posts, albeit under the command of the War Office. Though they did not know the specifics of the charter, the crew knew that the ship would be entering a period of uncertainty and possible danger. Under the special circumstances of national emergency the captain, officers and engineers remained faithfully at their posts without demanding any increase in their wages. The company, however, had to promise the deck, engine room and saloon hands an increase in wages as they would otherwise have declined to go on what was regarded as hazardous service.

On 2 August 1914, Herbert Savory, the Rear Admiral, Director of Transports sent a telegram to the company informing them 'circumstances of grave national import, which will shortly be announced by Royal Proclamation, have rendered it necessary to requisition the SS Rohilla for Government Service as a Naval Hospital Ship.' The *Rohilla* returned to her builders, Harland and Wolff, to begin the conversion to accommodate her new role. The work continued day and night for the Admiralty gave the builders just twelve days to have the ship ready to sail.

After spending many years voyaging long distances and enduring long separations from his wife Helen and their three children, Captain Neilson believed that plying between

Britain and the northern ports of France, he would at last be able to spend a little more time at home.

Few, if any, of the hospital ships were designed for the task. Most, like the *Rohilla*, *Garth Castle* and the *China*, were converted liners. This type of vessel was ideal for conversion as they had been designed to transport large numbers of people and so had the on-board facilities such as stores, fuel, water, etc., around which to base the medical and nursing requirements. A military 'standard pattern' is likely to have been imposed by the Admiralty for outfitting vessels for use as hospital ships. The wards were laid out in an almost identical fashion and indicate an obsession with cleanliness and order. Large open dormitories last used to accommodate troops were converted into wards capable of carrying around 250 casualties. The lower decks provided the most room for wards and though well lit, there appears to have been little by way of natural light and fresh air. The open portholes allowed limited ventilation and only portable screens provided any privacy. The long open wards were the domain of the troops. It was normal practise to have the cots lined up fore and aft with lifejackets suspended at intervals above them.

The cots were designed with what appear to be three legs at either end. These 'gimballed' cots were intended to lean with the ship as she rolled from side to side so that the patient was kept as level as possible, reducing patient movement and thus improving the recovery process. Despite the many lifejackets, getting cot-bound patients onto the top deck would not have been easy. Hospital ships were generally fitted with a lift arrangement to enable the movement of non-ambulatory patients between decks, sometimes as simple as an

Master of the *Rohilla*, Captain David Landles Neilson. (Copyright John Littlewood)

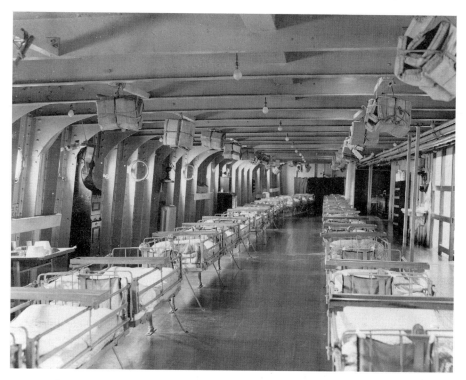

At the far end of the ward there appears to be a curve of what is, most likely, the bow section of the ship. (Courtesy of John Mules)

open hatchway through which injured personnel could be lowered on a square wooden pallet. The use of the cranes and derricks on the upper deck would have been limited to transferring patients on and off the ship.

As a rule, there were six or seven wards for the troops divided to either side of the centreline fore and aft with a 'nursing station' at the amidships end of the ward and two or three wards for officers, which were adapted by converting portions of the saloons or removing cabin bulkheads, some officers also being nursed in cabins. In contrast to the larger wards for the 'other ranks', the wards for higher-ranking officers were far more comfortable. The make-up of the cots would have been similar but with more space between them and curtains to provide privacy to individual berths. It was not unusual to find potted plants strategically placed around the ward. The area that appears to have been the original first-class lounge was most likely used by recuperating and lightly wounded officers.

The *Rohilla* was equipped with two operating theatres complete with X-ray machines. The theatre looks quite stark and brutal by today's standards and it is hard to imagine the injuries soldiers sustained being treated in such conditions. The Admiralty were obviously expecting numerous casualties given the number of vessels requisitioned for use as hospital ships.

The structure for lift assembly can be seen to the left of the photograph whilst the central staircase allows plenty of light to enter the deck opening up the ward. (Courtesy of John Mules)

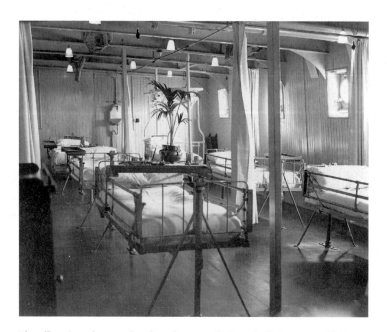

The officers' wards were placed on the upper decks with the luxuries of light and fresh air. (Courtesy of John Mules)

There was not very much room in the theatre to work however. It is likely that in any given emergency, besides the patient, there would have been a surgeon, anaesthetist, with two male sick berth attendants to assist in the procedure and, where necessary, restrain the patient. Female nursing staff, even trained nursing sisters, were still largely kept away from surgery in the services at this period.

The conversion complete and checked by the Admiralty, *Rohilla* was signed off and Captain Neilson took her into the calm waters of Southampton on 16 August, heading west down the Channel and around the Cornish coast. It was not until the ship had passed the Scilly Isles that Captain Neilson was allowed to open his 'sealed orders', which informed him to join Admiral Jellicoe's Grand Fleet at Scapa Flow in the Orkney Islands off the extreme northern tip of Scotland.

The battle squadrons had left Portland bound for Scapa Flow on 29 July. Two days later, HMS *Collingwood* and the rest of the fleet lay in position, guarding the northern entrance to the North Sea, whilst 500 miles to the south on the Baltic and North Sea coasts of Germany, lay the German High Seas Fleet in its heavily defended bases. On the night of 4 August the British ultimatum to Germany expired and the Admiralty flashed the signal to all ships and naval establishments, 'Commence hostilities against Germany'. HRH Prince Albert

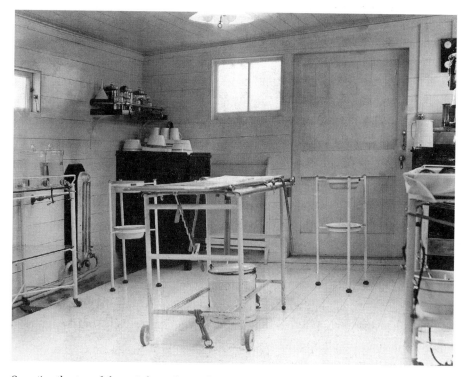

Operating theatres of the period were barren looking places, yet still faced many of the injuries medical staff see today. (Courtesy of John Mules)

was on the bridge of the *Collingwood*, the midshipman of the middle watch, midnight to 4 a.m., and noted the declaration of war in the diary which he carefully kept each day.

The *Rohilla*'s course crossed the Irish Sea, rounding the west coast of Scotland, and on to Wick, the last stop on the mainland where the ship could be replenished after her long journey north before moving on to the Orkney Islands and her final destination. Scapa Flow is a protected anchorage surrounded by a group of islands 20 miles north of mainland Scotland, providing an ideal natural anchorage and an almost impenetrable haven.

Having completed his training, Prince Albert received his first commission as midship man on the 19,250-ton battleship HMS *Collingwood*. Liable to bouts of seasickness he had questioned the decision to enlist in the Navy even confiding such to his mother. He was taught the correct use of the ship's picket boat, not something a midshipman would pick up until he was thorough in all other ship duties. Within months the prince was given the responsibility of running the picket boat, which was approximately 50ft long with sleek lines which seemed to accentuate her cruising speed of around 16 knots. The prince took the name Johnson for security purposes and never revealed his legacy lest people expect special treatment as a confidante of the future monarch.

Unbeknown to the king, the prince had suffered gastric problems which he had apparently concealed, and three weeks after the war had began he collapsed with violent pain in his stomach and appeared to be having difficulty breathing. He was given morphine and poultices applied to his stomach, and though they eased the pain somewhat they did little for his long-term prognosis. He was diagnosed with acute appendicitis and transferred to the hospital ship *Rohilla* and cared for by Fleet Surgeon Lomas until the arrival of Sir James Reid, the Royal Surgeon, Queen Victoria's favourite physician, who travelled up from London by train after being called in by the king.

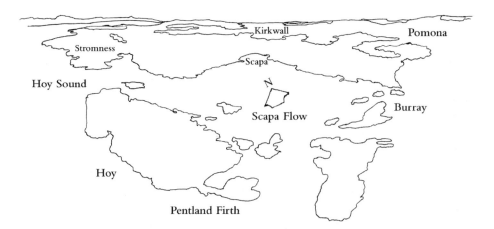

The islands of Scapa Flow. (Copyright John Littlewood)

Prince Albert aged 19 serving
as a midshipman on HMS
Collingwood.

Dr Ernest Courtney Lomas CB, DSO, FRCS was born on 24 December 1864, and educated at Owens College, Manchester. He graduated MB and ChB of Victoria University in 1888, and took membership of the Royal College of Surgeons (MRCS) that year. After filling the posts of house surgeon to the Manchester Royal Infirmary, senior house surgeon to the Royal Albert Edward Infirmary, Wigan, and resident medical officer of the Barnes Convalescent Hospital, Cheadle, he entered the navy as a surgeon in 1891. He was promoted to staff surgeon in 1900 for service in the South African War, became fleet surgeon in 1904 and took the fellowship of the Royal College of Surgeons (FRCS) in 1907. He became surgeon captain on 11 September 1918, and was one of the last remaining survivors taken off the *Rohilla*, before retiring in 1919. During his naval career in the South African War he took part in the relief of Ladysmith, was mentioned in dispatches, and gained the Queen's medal with two clasps, a special promotion, and the Distinguished Service Order (DSO).

At that point, the *Rohilla* was recalled to the Fleet, but Dr Lomas decided it was not safe to move the prince. So the ship left for Scapa Flow escorted through mined waters by two

Dr Ernest Courtney Lomas Fleet Surgeon
RN. (Copyright Paul Hutchinson)

destroyers. When Sir James Reid joined the ship the prince's health had improved somewhat and both physicians agreed it was safe for him to be moved. With the assistance of members of the Barnoldswick St John Ambulance Brigade, who had cared for the prince, he was placed in one of the cots used to transfer patients and taken to the quay at Aberdeen. On 9 September his appendix was removed by John Marnoch, Professor of Surgery at Aberdeen University, with Reid in attendance, reporting to the king by telephone.

The prince's wish to return to duty on the *Collingwood* was fraught with complications. A semi-invalid at just 19, he spent considerable time in and out of hospitals and convalescing at Sandringham or in London in the company of his parents and his sister, while his equals fought and died on active service. While the Prince of Wales left for France, and his position on the staff of Field Marshal Sir John French, Commander-in-Chief of the British Expeditionary Force, the monotony of Prince Albert's life was broken only by shooting forays at Sandringham. In the interim the prince was attached to the War Staff at the Admiralty, where at least he felt he was doing something for the war effort. Sadly, however, it was uninteresting and not what he hoped it would be: 'nothing to do as usual' and 'It seems such a waste of time to go there every day and do nothing' became typical entries in his diary.

In February 1915 his wish to get back to the *Collingwood* was realised, but not for long. 'I have been very fit on the whole since I returned here but just lately the infernal indigestion has come on again,' he told Hansel on 15 May (Henry Peter Hansel was the prince's tutor from 1902). 'I thought I had got rid of it but it has returned in various forms.' By 20 June it had become serious, the prince was no longer able to keep any food down and was described as being very mouldy and wasting away. His godfather, Sir William Watson Cheyne, Professor of Clinical Surgery at King's College London and President of the Royal College of Surgeons, recommended that Prince Albert be sent to a hospital ship for observation. On 12 July, three days after the king visited the fleet (the first time the prince had seen his father for six months) he was transferred from *Collingwood* to the *Drina*. On board the *Drina*, Dr Willan gave a diagnosis of 'weakening of the muscular wall of the stomach and a consequential catarrhal condition', for which rest, a careful diet and nightly medications were prescribed. Albert was, in fact, suffering from a stomach ulcer. It is hardly surprising that he did not make a sustained recovery, given that he had been incorrectly diagnosed from the outset.

Despite the prince's appeals to return to his ship he clearly wasn't well enough. Two months later, it transpired that the prolonged treatment with enemas and self-isolation studying for his exams on the hospital ship was jeopardising his health. The king was advised that a spell ashore at this point would certainly do no harm. The prince was consequently placed on sick leave and sent to Abergeldie in the company of Dr Willan and Hansel. When he returned to Sandringham from Scotland at the end of October he was still unfit for duty.

Anxiety over the state of his father's health after a serious accident in France aggravated Prince Albert's ulcer, making his condition worse. While inspecting a unit of the Royal Flying Corps at Hesdigneul, the king's horse reared up and fell over backwards on top of him, fracturing his pelvis and leaving him in shock and a great deal of pain. Albert loved his father deeply and they had grown close in the few years since he had left Dartmouth, a closeness enhanced by his long periods of convalescence. 'May God bless and protect you my dear boy is the earnest prayer of your devoted Papa,' the king had written shortly after the outbreak of the war, 'You can be sure that you are constantly in my thoughts.' 'I was really very sorry to leave last Friday', the 19-year-old Prince told his father in February 1915 on rejoining his ship, 'and I felt quite homesick the first night ...' 'I miss you still very much especially at breakfast,' the king replied.

Despite the conditions the rest of the country was experiencing, the *Rohilla* still hung onto the last vestiges of her original intended role as the final bill of fare produced for diners on the ship was as lavish as one might expect for a cosmopolitan banquet, not something on a ship of mercy:

S.S. 'Rohilla' 2 October 1914
Hors d'oeuvre. Canape, à la Russe
Soup. Consommé Cultivateur [a type of cold vegetable soup]
Fish. Flétan bouilli sauce Caradoc [boiled halibut with Caradoc sauce]
Entrées. Céleri au jus [Celery with juice/sauce]
Joints. Roast Haunch of Mutton. Red Current Jelly
Braised Duck with olives
Poultry. Roast and Boiled Potatoes

Cabbage

Sweets. Cabinet Pudding [steamed suet pudding containing fruit]

Fruit Tart and custard. Genoise Pastry [a light, dry French sponge cake]

During her stay in the islands the *Rohilla* had only one other patient besides Prince Albert, Pte. RMLI Thomas Anderson RN. His service record indicates he discharged from HMS *Duncan* on 9 October due to a broken leg and went on the books of Chatham Division. The fleet surgeon operated on him to reset the broken bones, and several times more to remove bone splinters. Although the surgeon was satisfied the man would eventually walk again, he thought it would be unwise to move him at that time and the unfortunate rating was kept on board – a move which would sadly proved fatal.

Captain Neilson was provided with all the necessary confidential information relating to the position of minefields between the Firth of Forth and the English Channel. This was new territory for Captain Neilson, who had not navigated the North Sea before, with the alarming possibility of new uncharted minefields and reports of German U-boats. Given the urgency of his voyage and the unfamiliarity of the coastline, Captain Neilson requested the use of a pilot, but his 2nd officer was told that even if one were available it was not standard practise to provide a pilot beyond Scottish waters.

Just after midday on Thursday 29 October, with 234 people on board (the ship's full-time crew, surgeons, nurses, sick berth attendants, general servants and stewards), the *Rohilla* left Leith Docks bound for Dunkirk to pick up wounded servicemen. The past three months had served as training, and on the afternoon they left Queensferry everyone had taken part in the boat drill when each man was assigned to his station and inspected by the first officer and the fleet surgeon. With everything in order, they were finally heading off for action.

It had been heavy weather since leaving the Firth of Forth, but the ship was able to cruise at 12.5 knots at the beginning of the voyage. The *Rohilla*'s course was set to take her off St Abb's Head on the eastern coast of the Scottish Borders and then down the east coast of England. Under wartime restrictions all navigational aids such as lights and signals were blacked out, posing additional risks to shipping. Such is the coastline that, as the storm burst in from the east, the ship was in a perilous situation. It is sufficiently dangerous on this coast on a fine night with no aids to navigation, but with towering cliffs, a rocky lee shore, a night dark as pitch and no guiding light or warning sound, it could soon turn into one of the severest tests any skipper may be called upon to undertake. The lights on the ship shone in opposite contrast, as brightly as they could, to alert any skulking marauder to its identity as a hospital ship.

On the bridge the last accurate position fix was taken at 4.30 p.m. as the sun set. Thereafter, in the absence of navigational aids, all course corrections and position fixing was calculated using a system of 'dead reckoning', mathematical calculations taking account of the effects of time, tidal calculations and wind. By the time they reached the Farne Islands off Northumberland the weather had deteriorated into a full-blown gale, the next set of calculations not due for four hours.

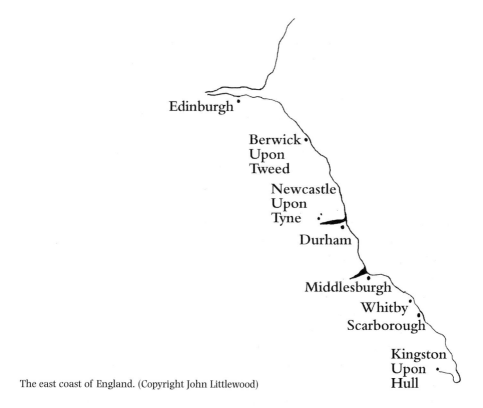

The east coast of England. (Copyright John Littlewood)

At 7.30 p.m. Dr Thomas Caldwell Littler-Jones, a surgeon in the Royal Navy Volunteer Reserve, was on his way to his cabin after the evening tea when he noticed the weather had got worse. At about 10.30 p.m. he felt the ship take on a more pronounced 'roll' and went out onto the deck. He observed a marked deterioration in the weather though everything seemed to be proceeding as expected. He returned to his cabin fully aware that he would get no sleep that night.

The following morning Albert James Jefferies was manning his post in the Wireless Signal Station off the Yorkshire coast which also served as the Coastguard lookout on the top of the east cliff.

Observing what he could in such atrocious conditions, he was quick to realise that a vessel steaming from up the coast appeared to be heading for a hazardous reef system known locally as 'Whitby Rock', just south of Whitby Harbour. Although the hazard was normally marked with a large permanent buoy, the bell had been silenced and its light extinguished due to wartime restrictions. Jefferies tried in vain to attract the attention of those on board using a Morse lamp, to warn her of the imminent danger. When he thought those on the ship might hear, he activated the foghorn at the top of the cliff, but still there was no reply from the ship.

The captain had command of the bridge with Edward Way the quartermaster at the wheel, and an able seaman on either side of the bridge serving as lookouts, though their

The coastguard lookout station was rebuilt after being bombed in December 1914, and added to over the years before being totally dismantled and removed in 2010.

view was very limited. The *Rohilla*'s senior 2nd officer, Archibald Winstanley, had just relieved Chief Officer Frank Albert Bond. Like the other officers on the bridge, Captain Neilson believed the ship was well offshore. The Morse signals were seen by Archibald Winstanley, but they were too quick for him to decipher. He sent for a signaller to decode the incoming message and reported them to the captain.

After leaving the bridge Frank Albert Bond met the bosun's mate, who informed him that one of the lifeboats was loose. He reported the problem to the captain, who told him that he would slow the ship in order to make it safe to secure the lifeboat. At that time, 4th Officer Duncan Graham was away from the bridge supervising depth sounding being carried out at the stern of the ship. The sounding revealed a depth of only 144ft, indicating they were a great deal further inshore than they had thought, and he quickly set off to report his findings to the captain. Second Officer Colin Gwynn had just come on watch to relieve Duncan Graham, but instead was sent to the chief engineer with the message to slow the ship down. The captain ordered a slight change in course to take the ship on a route that he thought would keep her out of danger.

At 4.10 a.m. the bosun and Chief Officer Frank Albert Bond were on their way down onto the deck. Captain Neilson had not yet received the Morse signal or the news that the depth sounding placed the ship in much shallower waters. The *Rohilla* was suddenly rocked by a huge tremor. The captain shouted 'A Mine my God' as a huge shock wave travelled the length of the ship, knocking the bosun and chief officer off their feet. Albert Jefferies heard the crashing sound as the ship struck rocks near Saltwick Nab, just south of entrance to Whitby Harbour, and immediately sprang into action. He contacted Charles Sutherland Davy, Chief Officer of the Coastguard Station at Whitby, whose responsibilities covered the use of the rocket apparatus provided by the Board of Trade.

When he recovered his footing, the chief officer of the *Rohilla* saw the carpenter and sent him to take some soundings before going to report to the captain. Captain Neilson was convinced the ship had hit a mine, believing the ship too far offshore for any other explanation. He had two alternatives: either let the vessel sink where she was, fearful that there would be a huge loss of life, or run the vessel ashore in an attempt to ground the hull in shallow water, where everyone stood a better chance. He instinctively ordered the ship be placed on a course taking her inshore.

Albert Jefferies watched in horror as the drama unfolded before his eyes. The *Rohilla* was heading for the main body of the Scar, a rock ledge that runs out from the base of the cliff for approximately 1 mile. It was just a brief moment before the second, larger impact occurred, fatally wounding the vessel. The shock of the second impact was accompanied by loud grinding and tearing sounds as the *Rohilla*'s metal bottom was ripped open. After a few convulsive movements, hissing seas began to wash over her decks. So black was the night, pregnant with torrential storm clouds, that it was only just possible to glimpse the danger of the rocky cliff by their side.

Saltwick Nab before erosion split it into separate pieces.

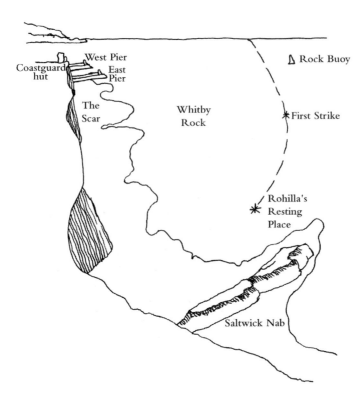

The *Rohilla*'s route over the Scar. (Copyright John Littlewood)

The carpenter reported back to Officer Bond that he could not take the appropriate soundings due to force of water in the engine room. The first seas that struck the ship after the stranding disabled the boats on the lee side with the exception of the emergency No. 1 lifeboat. The speed at which the *Rohilla* was travelling when the impact occurred had the effect of driving her hard aground, causing massive structural damage to the hull, which fractured in two places. Her momentum had driven the *Rohilla* up and over the top edge of the Scar itself, leaving the stern section and about a third of the ship hanging over deeper water.

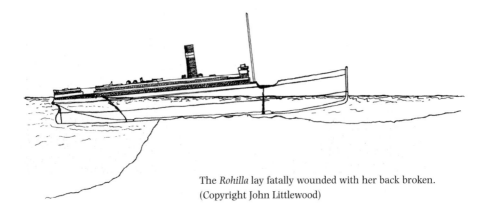

The *Rohilla* lay fatally wounded with her back broken. (Copyright John Littlewood)

Despite being just over 500yd from the shore, *Rohilla*'s position was unreachable and was to have catastrophic effects for the rescue services. Realising those on the stricken vessel were in imminent danger, Albert Jefferies fired maroons to summon the crews of the lifeboats and the Rocket Brigade. After sending a message to the lifeboat coxswain he went to get the rocket apparatus in order and ready to go. Having assembled sufficient men, they used the brief light given off from the distress flares to get some idea of where the ship lay and chose a suitable position from which to fire.

At the height of the gale it was not possible to use the horse-drawn carriage to transport the equipment to the best point at which to fire the rockets. Instead they chose a point level with the wreck at the top of the cliff at Saltwick, and they had to carry what they could. The equipment consisted of a heavy static rescue device which fires a rocket with a light line attached to it. Once the line is secured to the ship a heavier line is then pulled across, permitting the use of a breeches buoy. The device resembled a round emergency life ring fitted with a leg harness and was used to extract people from wrecked vessels one at a time.

When they arrived abreast of the Nab at about 4.45 a.m. it was still very dark and they could only see the wreck by firing distress signals. The location of the ship shocked the men, for it had struck the rock Scar in a most awkward place, in a position 'so close to the shore yet so far from safety'. They deliberated as to how best to serve those on the stricken ship.

The Rocket Brigade tried repeatedly to get a line to those on board.

Their apparatus set up, the Rocket Brigade fired a first rocket in an attempt to secure a line to the *Rohilla* just after 5 a.m. The first three rockets fell short of their target. The sound of the rockets being fired was so loud that many townsfolk believed the town itself was being bombarded, something they had every reason to worry about. It became clear that the height of the cliff only added to the problems presented by the wind. The brigade reluctantly abandoned any further attempts in an effort to conserve rockets, agreeing to wait until first light so that the equipment could be relocated down onto Saltwick Nab, effectively reducing the distance to the ship and giving them a better chance of getting a line across to it.

The *Rohilla* was stranded on the Scar at such an angle that left her broadside to the waves. She had come to rest with the bow pinned over the top of the rock, forcing the stern lower into the water. Waves washed over the decks and spray was thrown above the height of the bridge. As the internal fittings began to rend and tear, water began flooding through open hatches, making any escape even more hazardous. As the engine room flooded the engines stopped, extinguishing all the lights. When the ship hit the Scar most of the crew were below decks asleep and would have known nothing until the initial impact. It is likely that those on the lower decks perished quickly.

Captain Neilson ordered a distress call be issued using the new wireless Marconi radio, but as soon as the *Rohilla* struck the rock the ship's dynamos had ceased to work. The wireless operator, Robert Thurlo Utting, was forced to make use of the emergency set, which initially worked very well but soon failed as the sea mercilessly battered the ship, breaking all outside communication.

Captain Neilson had no choice but to call to all hands to lifeboat stations sure that there were more than enough lifeboats to accommodate those on board. The crew scrambled from their cabins leaving behind all their possessions, many clad in just their nightclothes. In the rush to get to their lifeboat station five unfortunate seamen are known to have been washed overboard; the loss was felt more when it was found that the conditions prevented the use of the lifeboats.

Dr Thomas Jones was in his berth when the vessel struck. Putting on his coat and trousers he made his way out onto the deck. Such was the blackness that he was unable to see where the ship was, but sensing that it was stationary he could not help but fear the worst. He did not see any officers or the captain, but he heard him giving directions in a composed way that seemed to calm his own fears. For a short time at least everything appeared quiet and orderly. Captain Neilson was concerned about the men on the poop, and gave orders that they and anyone else aft were to come forward. Although the men could not pass the after part, he urged them to get as far forward as they could as the seas were breaking over the well deck.

Now and then, as the clouds parted, those on the stricken ship could only glimpse the towering cliffs before them, and the grim jagged rocks that lay beneath them, offering no easy chance of escape. Their only hope of rescue was lifeboats from the shore, but in such ferocious conditions they dared not think about whether anyone would risk approaching them. Fearing that no quick rescue would be attempted, the captain advised everyone to huddle together in an effort to stay as warm as possible.

As soon as the Admiralty learned that the *Rohilla* had gone to ground it had the Admiralty of Patrols establish control, overseeing the efforts to get survivors ashore. The Secretary of the Admiralty was on HMS *St George* at Jarrow at the time. A strong easterly gale prevented any vessels entering or leaving the Tyne. He wired the Hartlepool lifeboat station asking them to send a trawler to Whitby towing the Hartlepool rowing lifeboat. The easterly gale made movement impossible along most of the north-east coastline, however. The secretary of the institution and the two coxswains all agreed that under the present conditions it would be too hazardous for any craft to leave the harbour.

As no vessel could render direct assistance without placing themselves in great danger, the secretary sent Captain Raikes and Lt-Commander Philip W.C. Sharpe, Navigating Officer of the *St George*, by land. They arrived by train at 1 p.m. on Friday 30 October and proceeded to Saltwick Nab.

3

THE BARNOLDSWICK CONNECTION

Fifteen men accommodated on the *Rohilla* upon her departure were members of the Royal Naval Auxiliary Sick Berth Reserve (RN Aux SBR) who belonged to the Barnoldswick division of the St John Ambulance Brigade, a small cotton-weaving town on the border between Yorkshire and Lancashire. Although reservists, they officially joined the Navy when called out on mobilisation. There is little doubt that fifteen men being called up for duty at the same time would have had a dramatic impact on a small community like Barnoldswick.

Local Effects of the War – Sick Berth Reservists Called Up

John Thompson, the local superintendent of the RN Aux SBR, was at home during a lunch break when a telegram arrived from the Chief of the First Aid Department, Chatham warning of the likelihood that his men would be called up to serve their country, that they had to be ready to leave the town on short notice. The following day the message was ratified by a second wire from the same department ordering that fifteen men had to leave at once for Chatham: Corporal Milton Birtwistle, Corporal William Daly, Sergeant Arthur Petty, Privates Thomas Petty, Thomas Horsfield, Walter Horsfield, Albert Elsworth, John Pickles, Anthony Waterworth, Harry Hodkinson, William Eastwood, Fred Reddiough, William Anderson, Frank Dunkley and Henry Barter.

The men were informed of their summons at once, and all presented themselves on the station platform for departure. The news had quickly spread, and a large crowd assembled on the platform to see them off, a crowd whose feelings were in strange comparison to those when the same train steamed out of the station a week before bound for Blackpool and Morecambe. People stood in small groups discussing the events. Some, it is true, were laughing and talking, but others realised the grave import of the summons and waited anxiously for the Prime Ministers statement in the House that afternoon.

The Departure

A faint cheer was raised as the shrill steam whistle signified the beginning of a journey that would have catastrophic consequences for many of the fifteen families. A couple of detonators on the line served to emphasise the very reason why their loved ones were leaving, but also that Barnoldswick could regard its first contingent of defenders with pride and welcome them back in happier times. Here and there a woman was weeping, and even the more optimistic of those gathered realised that their humour was ill timed.

As the train eased its way along the line, very slowly disappearing from view, families bid a sad farewell to their loved ones, and with a heavy heart returned to their homes to ponder the future, a future they knew was completely out of their hands. All fifteen men were bound for HMS *Pembroke* at Chatham, where they would receive further orders in due course, and exchange their Ambulance Brigade uniforms for regulation clothing. HMS *Pembroke* was not a ship as such, but a shore base capable of accommodating over 23,000 service personnel. The Navy insisted that all recruits be registered in a Ships Book and for some time there was a ship named HMS *Pembroke* moored alongside the barracks. Although initially the vessels that bore the name were goods ships, as time passed, any available vessel was used – including, at one time, a prison ship. In 1914 HMS *Pembroke* was an old iron gunboat formerly known as HMS *Trent*. The craft was obsolete yet, despite only been suited for harbour duties, she was on record as having a crew of over 23,000.

After twelve days of basic training, the Barnoldswick men would soon be posted to the SS *Rohilla*, which was undergoing conversion into a hospital ship. All fifteen men would be billeted together in one of the saloons, which had been converted into a large dormitory.

HMS *Pembroke* was not the ship people might expect from its prefix.

William Anderson, one of the youngest of the Barnoldswick naval reservists.

William Edward Anderson was one of the youngest of the Barnoldswick naval reservists aged just 23 and courting a lady named Edith Downes. Shortly after being assigned to the *Rohilla*, he learnt Edith was to attend her niece's christening. William suggested adding a middle name and would have been happy to learn the baby was christened Hazel Rohilla. William lived with his father at 20 School Terrace, overlooking Clogger's Beck. Officially, the address should have been Dam Head Road, but the houses had been known by that name since the Gisburn Road Council School had been built in 1907.

Henry Barter was originally from Worcester. Having moved to Barnoldswick with his wife after securing a job as a railway shunter in the goods yard, they lived in a small terraced house nearby in Skipton Road.

William Daly was one of two corporals in the St John Ambulance Brigade. Born in Ireland, William had come to England seeking work, finally ending up in the cotton mill after a period down a coalmine. He lived with his wife Esther and six children at 32 Westgate. The small houses in Westgate formed what was once the original village centre of Barnoldswick. It must have been quite a squeeze for a family of eight in what was a basic house with just two rooms upstairs and two downstairs. The Daly family were considered 'New Ship-ers' they originally attended the Independent Methodist Chapel. In 1839 a group of members broke away from the Wesleyan Chapel. They were told they would perish if they did not return to the church, which was compared to a 'sound and safe' vessel but they were determined to build for themselves a 'New Ship.' The new chapel has been known by this name ever since. To this day it is the only surviving nineteenth-century non-conformist chapel in Barnoldswick.

Harry Hodkinson was just 27 and living as a bachelor in the family home at 14 Bank Street, he was a keen member of Barnoldswick Prize Band as well as the Ambulance Brigade and was a weaver at Hartley's Crownest Sheeting Mill. He had two brothers who distinguished themselves during the war era: John Hodkinson was a member of the Red Cross; and Arthur Hodkinson a serving member of the Duke of Wellington's Regiment was awarded the Military Medal for bravery in battle. The medal was established on 25 March 1916 and presented to non–commissioned ranks and was seen as equivalent to the Military Cross. The medal ranked below the Distinguished Conduct Medal, which was also awarded to non-commissioned members of the Army. Like the Daly family, Harry was also a member of the Independent Methodist Chapel

The Independent Methodist Chapel plaque. (Copyright Heather Sheldrick)

Sergeant Arthur Petty.

Within the Independent Methodist Chapel there is a large bronze tablet inscribed with the names of twenty men including William Daly and Harry Hodkinson, dedicated 'To the glory of god and in grateful memory of the men who laid down their lives in the Great War 1914-1919.'

Arthur Petty was at work when he first received word that he had been called up to serve king and country. He was well respected around the town. As well as being a cotton weaver, he was a sergeant and honorary secretary of the St John Ambulance Brigade. They were ready for immediate call-up for, like every volunteer, they knew the call might come eventually. Arthur was a non-commissioned officer (NCO) and given command of the assembled party. He was handed travel warrants and orders to report to HMS *Pembroke* at Chatham.

In personal letters addressed to his wife, Arthur indicated how it was that the former liner had served as a troop ship before being converted for use as a hospital ship. In one letter Arthur notes 'it's been hard work, but we feel our responsibility and shall not be found wanting.' He mentioned how many of those from Barnoldswick had suffered badly from seasickness during the short trip from Chatham.

Arthur was one of the fortunate ones to be assigned to the chief petty officers' mess. He wonders in his letters at how they had three Lascars (black men) to wait on them, and notes that 'they walk round our table, as we finish one plate, they take it away and place another before us. I feel like a blooming Lord.' He explained that they received four meals a day consisting of:

Breakfast – a plate of porridge with milk, fish, meat and potatoes, and bread and butter pudding.
Dinner – meat broth with vegetables, pudding (normally sweet bread).
Tea – meat and potatoes with macarones, cold meat, with bread and butter and jam.
Supper – bread and butter with cheese and pickles.

The following letter was written and posted the day the ship left port on its final journey. Unlike the *Rohilla*, the letter reached its final destination.

R.T.A. Rohilla
Thursday, Oct, 29th 1914

My dear wife and child,
I am writing to let you know we leave here for France today, so by the time you get this letter we shall be there. We shall have a few days hard work getting the sick and wounded on board + land [*sic*] them in England, if you keep your eyes on the papers you will see whereabouts the wounded is landed, it might be London, Dover or Southampton. We leave here at 4 o'clock this afternoon + will arrive about Saturday morning, Dunkirk near Ostend so you see we shall not be far off the fighting. I have told you where we are going because by the time you get this letter we shall be perhaps be leaving, so the censor won't object.
My dears you will have got our Elsies parcel by now, I thought about a doll, but it's such a long way + it might have got broke, so I sent her two little brushes so that she could help you to clean up a bit, I hope she will get them, you can let her have them now. So I will write from France if we stop a few days, but don't be anxious if I don't because we shall be busy, so good bye for the present give any love to all, your loving + affectionate husband Arthur
Xxxxxxxxxxxxx

Thomas Petty, at 30, was the youngest of four brothers. He was always busy and enjoyed an active association with the Salvation Army. Tom lived at 11 Coronation Street with his wife Sarah Annie and their three young sons. Apart from his duties as a sick berth attendant, Tom was the *Rohilla's* unofficial barber. He was also one of those lost early on in the tragedy.
Walter Horsfield was decorated with two medals after serving in the Boer War, where he was attached to the Bloemfontein General Hospital from April to October 1900, and then, in the following year, at Deelfontein General Hospital. Walter lived with his parents at 7 Essex Street.

Walter Horsfield.

Unlike his brother, Thomas Horsfield did not volunteer for the Boer War. Instead, he chose to stay at home in Barnoldswick, where he devoted himself to his family and the Salvation Army. He and his wife Julia lived with their seven children at 33 Heather View, a house that enjoyed pleasant views over the surrounding countryside.

Frank Dunkley was born in High Barnet, Hertfordshire in July 1877, but was the local baker in Barnoldswick. He lived with his wife Mary Ellen and their young child in Bairstow Street. Frank was a Royal Naval Auxiliary Sick Berth Reserve as a Junior Reserve Attendant known to be dedicated to the St Ambulance Brigade as well as being a keen member of the YMCA.

A bachelor, Albert Elsworth lived with his parents at 32 Wellington Street. He is known to have been accommodated at the stern of the ship and likely perished in the first onrush of water after the ship hit the Scar. Albert was one of those who had cared for Prince Albert.

Milton Birtwistle was born in Blackburn but lived with his wife Sarah and young son John at 19 Clifford Street, Barnoldswick. He enjoyed a long service in the St John Ambulance Brigade, rising to the position of corporal and was often in frequent demand for the treatment of minor ailments. Milton and his wife, Sarah, were weavers in the nearby mill. Before the ship left on her fateful voyage, many of her crew visited a photographic studio that had a poetic image of the Forth Bridge as a background. At the time of his death his address on the ships register was Sunset View, Barnoldswick.

As an enthusiastic member of the Ambulance Brigade John Pickles retained a keen interest in medical practices and people often called at his home for first aid. John lived at 11 Federation Street with his wife Annie (sister to Fred Reddiough) with whom he had a son, Norman.

John Pickles and Milton Birtwistle took their annual leave in July as the ideal way to escape from the confines of the cotton weaving industry, spending two weeks training with the fleet in Ireland to broaden their first aid knowledge. The additional first aid practice and ship borne duties would have proved valuable training.

Fred Reddiough wrote to his wife from Whitby recounting his experiencing on the *Rohilla*, but did not mention that he was chosen to look after Prince Albert. In his cabin he felt a tremendous shock that seemed to shake the entire ship and threw his personal belongings to the floor, Fred realised immediately that something was disastrously wrong. With water lapping around his feet he hurried to dress, almost severing a toe on a broken bottle. Despite his injury, he grabbed a lifebelt and started out for the main deck as the water level continued to rise. Making his way up the decks, Fred found the saloon passage rapidly flooding, battled his way forward up onto the promenade deck, and then onto the boat deck. As the waves continued to pound the stricken ship he was repeatedly swept off his feet. He managed to take hold of a ventilator, but the waves were too strong, forcing him alongside the ships rails and ever closer to being swept overboard.

The seventh of ten children, Anthony Waterworth, aged 27, was the son of Bella Waterworth, the local midwife for many years. The family lived in North View, close to the cotton mill where Anthony was a taper. Like Albert Elsworth, he had cared for the prince, helping to take him ashore when the *Rohilla* arrived at its rendezvous. Anthony had just come off watch and was still fully dressed when the ship struck the Scar, allowing him to leave his cabin quickly to reach the upper decks, where he found Fred Reddiough getting to his feet.

Making their way along the deck the pair met Canon Robert Basil Gwydir OSB, who was going the opposite way towards the stern and what seemed grave danger. When the impact came Canon Gwydir was on deck, and realising the danger he immediately hurried below to be with Pte. Thomas Anderson, the only patient on board at the time. Canon Gwydir was 48 and born at Longford of a Welsh family settled in Ireland for two centuries. A member of the Order of Saint Benedict (OSB), Canon Gwydir was a prominent figure in the Catholic Church. He was educated at Breewood, Staffordshire and the English College, Douai Abbey in Berkshire. He passed from school to the novitiate house at Belmont Monastery, Hereford, where he received the Benedictine habit and spent the first four years of his religious life. He returned to Douai Abbey and was ordained as a priest in 1891, and

Fred Reddiough.

served his monastery as master in the school and as Procurator, distinguishing himself as a professor in Classics and English, with exceptional intellectual gifts.

In 1899, Canon Gwydir started his career as a mission priest at St Augustine's, Liverpool. Some seven months later, he transferred to St David's, Swansea, where he worked as assistant priest, later succeeding the Abbot of Douai as rector of the mission. As rector of St David's, he was a tireless preacher, writer and lecturer, winning renown in quarters where the standard was critical and high. For a Catholic priest he had the unique honour of being accepted into the 'Circle of Welsh Bards'. He showed great tenderness to the sick and the poor and was prominent in social and educational work. To his friends he was

Anthony Waterworth.

the truest, staunchest of men. In 1914, he became a canon of the Diocese of Newport. He read a paper at the National Catholic Congress at Cardiff in July 1914, and read one before the International Eucharistic Congress at Vienna.

On the outbreak of the First World War, Canon Gwydir offered his services as ship's chaplain. He had always loved the sea and its ships, and was very pleased when he was accepted into the Navy. Leaving Swansea in September, he served in several ships before being assigned to the *Rohilla*.

He wrote back to the mission, his letters cheery, his one regret that there was 'nothing much to do. However, I suppose they also serve who stand and wait.' Canon Gwydir selflessly gave his life to give what comfort he could. His body was washed ashore stripped and bruised like that of the great Good Shepherd, some hours afterwards. Douai's first martyr, Canon Gwydir was the first chaplain of any faith in all the British services to die in the First World War.

When Fred Reddiough and Anthony Waterworth reached the Marconi radio room they decided to rest until daybreak, but at dawn it was clear that it was not safe to stay there.

The Very Rev. Robert Basil Canon Gwydir OSB.

They decided to take their chances swimming to shore. They made slow progress, constantly pounded by high waves. Fred became detached from Anthony and although he was with William Anderson for a short time, they too were soon separated.

4

THE RESCUE BEGINS TO UNFOLD

Coxswain Thomas Langlands, a native of Seahouses in Northumberland, had been a lifeboat crewmember since he was 18. He had a wide knowledge of seamanship and extensive experience of this hazardous stretch of coastline. When the coastguard maroons sounded the alarm, he made his way swiftly down to the west pier where his volunteer crew was assembling at the lifeboat station. Like most stations, there was no motor lifeboat at Whitby, just rowing lifeboats. The wind was gale force and the sea was running at such a level that it was impossible to launch the *Robert and Mary Ellis*. The ramp down which the heavy boat had to be manhandled was so buffeted by the waves that the boat would be dashed to pieces before there was sufficient depth to float her off the carriage used to store and launch the lifeboat. The only thing to do was to wait until daylight in the hope that conditions would allow a rescue attempt.

The *Robert and Mary Ellis* with her crew.

Harry 'Lal' Richardson joking with his wife in 1936. (Copyright Whitby Literary & Philosophical Society)

On the east side of the town John Richardson, a quiet and self-sufficient man, lived in a small fisherman's house where the north-easters rattled the chimneys on winter nights. On hearing the signal he knew that as lifeboat crewmen a difficult time lay ahead of him and his brother Harry, or Lal, as he preferred.

As soon as dawn light began to break, the Rocket Brigade took the whip and line-box down the cliff to Saltwick Nab. With the apparatus in a better position, they fired rockets to get a line onto the wreck. In the unrelenting wind many of the rockets fell short. When a line reached the wreck, it was either caught amongst the jagged steel of the ship, snagged on rocks or cut.

With no improvement in the weather, Coxswain Langlands knew that it was still not possible to launch the lifeboat still sitting on its carriage. The No. 2 lifeboat, *John Fielden*, was kept afloat in the harbour, but in these conditions there was no hope of sailing it out through the harbour from its mooring; they understood that the lifeboat would never 'live' in the seas at the harbour bar, even with the power of its fourteen oarsmen. There was, however, one possible alternative. It would mean undertaking a most formidable task, that of going under the Spa Ladder and through the opening between the east pier and the cliff. The plan was to get the lifeboat to a position on the shore opposite the *Rohilla* before

The *John Fielden* being hauled across the Scar.

launching it into the water, this had never been tried before and the crew could only guess at the difficulties that lay ahead.

The 36ft lifeboat was rowed across the harbour to the east cliff breakwater to be greeted by a mass of people who had gathered, willing to do whatever they could to help. The men soon assembled the many ropes and levers necessary for the task, and then under the watchful eye of Coxswain Langlands, the craft was carefully hauled out of the water, up and over the top of the 8ft-high breakwater. Having accomplished this amazing task the men then had to physically manoeuvre the lifeboat three quarters of a mile over the jagged and slippery surface of the Scar to a point adjacent to the stranded ship.

Despite the damage, it was believed that the lifeboat would still float with all its cork buoyancy. Coxswain Langlands and the 2nd coxswain, Richard Eglon, knew they were the *Rohilla*'s survivors' only hope, leaving them no option but to continue with the rescue plan. The lifeboat crew comprised fourteen men paid just 15 shillings for each occasion they put to sea. Strong family traditions run in lifeboat crews and the *John Fielden*'s was no exception:

Coxswain Thomas Langlands
2nd Coxswain Richard Eglon
J. Eglon
John 'Blooman' Richardson
Harry 'Lal' Richardson
Robert Richardson
Edward Gash
Robert Harland
Thomas Welham

John Dryden

William Snowdon

Frank Clarkson

James Middlemass

John Hansell

Lying deceptively close to shore and with the lifeboat in sight, a quick rescue must have seemed inevitable to those on the ship, but the view from the shore was very different indeed. After dragging the lifeboat to a point adjacent to the *Rohilla*, the men took a long hard look at what lay between them and the survivors. They knew the time to act was now. Aided by local men and woment he lifeboatmen heaved the lifeboat from the rocky Scar into the angry, turbulent water without hesitation, a task made more difficult without the boat's launching carriage.

They set off for the *Rohilla*. Working against strong currents and tempestuous seas, which constantly broke over the lifeboat, it seemed as though the *John Fielden* was making no headway. The wind was whipping off the crests of the waves, sending sheets of blinding spray into the lifeboatmen's eyes. The fourteen volunteers dug in with their oars and everyone watched as the lifeboat moved doggedly forward towards its target.

The only approach to rescue those on the ship was to bring the lifeboat into the leeward side of the ship, yet all around lay the jagged tops of rocks, barely visible above the surface. The lifeboat battled forward, steadily closing on the wreck. With consummate seamanship and bravery the lifeboat and her crew overcame terrific perils and difficulties, managing to get alongside the ship five and a half hours after it hit the Scar.

The captain's orders were for women to leave the ship first, then sick berth staff, stewards, firemen and finally the officers. The nurses were told to muster for evacuation by the lifeboat taking no luggage or additional belongings with them. The five women were first to leave, a most difficult task under the circumstances. Faced with the prospect of having to climb down a dangerously swaying rope ladder into a lifeboat that was constantly buffeted by the sea must have been truly overwhelming. Despite the treacherous conditions on the ship there must surely have been a moment's pause during which staying on the ship might have seemed a safer option.

Nursing Sister Mary Louisa Hocking had followed the captain's orders and stood in awe with the other women as the small lifeboat fought its way towards them. Born in 1887, one of seven siblings Mary Louisa was just 27. She wondered if the tiny looking craft could survive such savage seas. Her family had always had a close connection to the sea, her grandfather had been a ship-owner and at least one uncle was a fisherman.

Mary Louisa had joined the Queen Alexandra's Royal Naval Nursing Service (QARRNS) the year before the outbreak of war, and was appointed a probationary nursing sister; on 17 June, after conducting her initial naval training, she was confirmed as a nursing sister. She joined the *Rohilla* on 23 October 1914, relieving Nursing Sister Hughes, who, given the ensuing disaster, would undoubtedly have considered herself fortunate!

Mary Louisa Hocking QARNNS.
(Courtesy of John Mules)

Mary Roberts (in the small round
hat) sitting on the grass with other
surviving stewardesses from the
Titanic. (Courtesy of Fiona Kilbane)

The QARNNS Service Register records her 'admirable conduct at wreck of the Rohilla' and that 'Their Lordships (of the Admiralty) noted her good services with satisfaction,' the latter commendation being a noteworthy acknowledgement of services rendered in the formal and somewhat understated terms of the Royal Navy.

Also among the women was Daisy Pattison, who was once a boarder at Miss Theedam's School in Brunswick Terrace, Scarborough, 20 miles south of Whitby. Mary Kezia Roberts was another lady thankful for the bravery of the *John Fielden*'s crew, though this was not her first experience of a great maritime disaster. Mary Roberts was a survivor of the ill-fated RMS *Titanic*, signing onto the great ship as a member of the victualling crew on 6 April 1912. Her previous ship had been the RMS *Adriatic* built by Harland and Wolff, Belfast, and launched in 1906, the same year as the *Rohilla*.

The survivor of two catastrophic maritime disasters, Mary declared that of the two the sinking of the *Rohilla* was the more harrowing. In escaping the *Titanic* she would have been put aboard one of the ship's lifeboats in very cold but fairly settled sea conditions, in strong contrast to the circumstances surrounding the *Rohilla*, where she endured unbearable gale conditions, high seas and a ship slowly breaking apart beneath her feet. It seems such an incredile coincidence that both of these wonderful ships were built by the same shipyard. Next to leave the ship were surgeons, the medical staff and John Thomas Knight, a pensioned master-at-arms in the Royal Navy. Although traditionally crewmembers

With great skill and fortitude Coxswain Langlands pilots the lifeboat through the treacherous rocks. (Copyright John Littlewood)

WHITBY DIVISION ST JOHN AMBULANCE BRIGADE
FIRST MEMBERS.   NOVEMBER 1914

The first members of the Whitby division of the St John Ambulance Brigade in 1914. (Courtesy Betty Bayliss)

were the last to leave, three seamen pushed their way forward and dropped down into the lifeboat, a move that provoked much disgust. In the following enquiries these men were later characterised as 'cowards'.

Coxswain Langlands now had seventeen survivors, in addition to the fourteen crew in the lifeboat, and was anxious to get underway. Moving carefully away from the ship, the men used all their strength to row the boat without catching a rock for they could not afford to lose an oar at such a critical time.

The *John Fielden* threaded its way back to the shore where a willing band of local people waited anxiously; as soon as the lifeboat was close enough they moved in to assist the survivors from the lifeboat and then away to safety.

Of those on the shore, the presence of the Whitby St John Ambulance Brigade was most impressive. The Whitby Brigade was formed only about a month before the tragedy, when an appeal was made through the *Whitby Gazette* for sufficient funds to provide equipment and uniforms, without which the War Office and Admiralty declined to recognise any brigade, irrespective of the skills and dedication of its members. William Knaggs began his first aid training when he joined the North Eastern Railway in 1907. He progressed to become an instructor and shortly thereafter, with the assistance of Christopher Hood, commenced civilian first aid classes. William was appointed sergeant-in-charge and soon promoted to divisional superintendent. Dr G.B. Mitchell JP, a local surgeon, was divisional surgeon-in-charge, while Hood served as honorary secretary.

During its inauguration, no one could possibly have foreseen that the newly created unit would so soon be called upon for such a task. Shortly after its foundation the ranks of the brigade had grown to thirty-one members, and the wreck provided their first opportunity to engage in serious work. Not only members of the brigade proper but recruits, who were under instruction for the first course, turned out and proved themselves worthy to represent their town. When the signal rockets were fired from the *Rohilla* on Friday morning the brigade's turnout was very creditable.

Knaggs and Hood took up the direction of the work on the Scar and at Saltwick, respectively, and during Friday morning valuable aid was rendered in the numerous cases where attention was needed as the survivors reached the shore from the lifeboat. It was a member of the division who discovered the first body on the beach. The ambulance men's work won very high commendation from the local doctors, and also from other authorities. Their short history had not prepared them for such a huge commitment and they sent out a call for help. The townsfolk responded immediately and soon food and blankets were being gathered along with bandages and general first aid items. Those with any suitable form of transport were asked to ferry the more seriously injured to the Cottage Hospital, and those survivors not requiring immediate treatment were quickly transported to temporary accommodation.

William Knaggs was later awarded the Military Medal for 'conspicuous gallantry' in attending wounded soldiers under fire during the First World War. Upon return to civilian life he resumed his role as divisional superintendent with the St John Ambulance Brigade, a position he held until his retirement.

During the morning, a message was received from T.C. Hutchinson, manager of the Skinningrove Ambulance Brigade, offering three stretcher squads and equipment, a kind gesture readily accepted.

Mrs Agar and her son, Walter, were among those deserving credit for their part in the rescue. She threw open her door at the Saltwick Nab tea room and kept an open house for survivors and rescuers alike. She did everything in her power to give what relief she could, staying open throughout the rescue attempts.

There were numerous instances of several members of the same family at the fore with comfort and stimulants on the Scar on Saturday. Young ladies who under ordinary circumstances would have hesitated to venture onto the slippery beach, worked to and from their homes bringing blankets and hot drinks, indifferent to the risks involved. Their satisfaction will remain in the memory that, in a locally historic and trying moment, they were not found wanting. Everyone who reached shore alive was attended to, though the helpers themselves were in many cases wet to the skin, and the utter unselfishness displayed was as noteworthy as the work itself.

Many voluntary helpers came forward, lending valuable assistance in any way they could. As man after man came ashore, they were examined by the medical teams on the beach and dealt with very assuredly and skilfully. The workers responded very gallantly to the strain upon them, and the brave fellows who successfully swam ashore were transported

Richard Knaggs one of the founding members of the Whitby St John Ambulance Brigade. (Copyright Joyce Richmond)

away to various institutions, hotels, and private houses in a very expeditious manner. In many cases artificial respiration was the only option open to the first aiders, and several of those who gained the shore owed their lives to the attentions of the ambulance workers. Dr Burton was just one of many local doctors who gave of their service. One survivor was attended to with resuscitation techniques lasting some time; his survival was no doubt testament to the dedication and commitment of those present.

A detachment of scouts who were doing good work for the war service as part a coastwatching scheme which would earn them another merit badge had no idea what lay before them on this rotation, certainly no scout unit before them had ever faced such a dire situation. Yet they valiantly stood their ground performing their duty to the best of their ability. The had gone from patrolling the tops of the cliffs looking for anything dubious to report back to the coastguard officer to a full active role in something no scout training could prepare them for. One of them, Arthur Shepherd, had every reason not to be there as it was his fifteenth birthday. A close watch was kept during the night for as long as was safe to do so, searching along the shore should anyone successfully reach the shore.

Even with added damage to the lifeboat, the crew knew they were the survivors' only hope. Showing true courage, it was agreed by all present that the circumstances permitted a second rescue even though each man knew it was going to be far more difficult than the first. Having taken a severe battering during the first rescue attempt, the damage to the *John Fielden* was more widespread than first thought. The boat had taken on water and was not as responsive as during the first trip, it was clear their progress was also slower. Despite their best efforts to avoid the rocks, the strong wind and currents inevitably buffeted the lifeboat about, the hull scraping against rocks sharp as blades.

The coxswain could see the toll the harsh conditions were taking on his men and cried out, 'Come on my bonny lads, Come on my bonny lads,' spurring them on in the face of adversity. The sea was just as fierce, the wind blowing very hard with spray from the waves, at times rising high above the *Rohilla*. The crew showed true commitment fighting to bring the lifeboat alongside the ship, stowing their oars momentarily out of the way, for should they be lost, the outcome would have been quite catastrophic for everyone.

As quickly as they could the survivors began lowering themselves into the lifeboat, among them Fred Reddiough and Anthony Waterworth. After helping one of the ship's medical officers, who was quite ill, down into the lifeboat, Dr Thomas Caldwell Littler-Jones was ordered to take the last remaining place. Coxswain Langlands had eighteen survivors as well as the lifeboat crew, and could take no more. He knew the lifeboat was in no condition to make a third rescue attempt and it must surely have pained him to give the order to leave the wreck's side, but losing their lives too would accomplish nothing. Those on the shore couldn't help but worry as time itself seemed to stop.

As soon as was practical, the crew lowered their oars and began pulling for the shore, Coxswain Langlands had to use all of his skill manoeuvring his damaged craft through what unbroken patches of sea he could navigate. In such turbulent seas it was difficult to maintain a continuous watch on the lifeboat from the shore, but the battle-scarred craft surged on as if by sheer will power. Using all the energy they had left the lifeboatmen fought against the winds and current. They had the presence of mind to know that, facing backwards, they were at least saved the sight of what they were heading into, for that honour lay with Coxswain Langlands alone. Constantly battling long heavy breakers they all knew they were approaching the shoreline, but that danger was still very real. As the hull of the lifeboat bumped and scraped they knew they could do little more for in no time the lifeboat was surrounded by those waiting on the shore. As the survivors were helped out of the lifeboat into volunteers' arms their thoughts must have been with those left stranded on the *Rohilla*.

When brought ashore in the *John Fielden* Fred Reddiough asked Lena Weatherill, a local girl who lived nearby at Tate Hill, if she had a pair of scissors. She said she could get some, but when she asked what they were for she was shocked by his reply. He pointed to his foot and said, 'Will you cut that off for me.' When she looked down she saw to her horror that his big toe was nearly completely off, hanging by a thin thread of skin. She said, 'Oh no, you will have to have that seen to when you go to hospital.'

Despite his own traumatic ordeal, *Rohilla's* Dr Thomas Littler-Jones felt able to tend to the survivors. Despite his pleas, he was eventually coaxed from the beach by Tindale, who took him to his home to recover, completely exhausted.

The Rev. Richard Allen, who had only recently become a C of E naval chaplain, was one of the lucky survivors. It is thought he may have been on the upper deck, away from the ship's ward, when the *Rohilla* struck the rocks. The Admiralty was unusually unforgiving, and Rev. Allen was not appointed to another ship. As a consequence of the trauma and shock, he was physically unable to serve again, and resigned his commission on 23 December.

Rev. Roland Allen is assisted from the water. (Copyright John Littlewood)

Before being taken to the Whitby Cottage Hospital, Fred Reddiough and Anthony Waterworth asked for a telegram to be sent to their former superintendent, John Thompson back in Barnoldswick. As it was St John Ambulance Brigade business, the honorary secretary, Sergeant Hood, agreed to send a telegram at the earliest opportunity. Postmaster Fred Baldwin received the telegram at the Barnoldswick Post Office in Albert Road. As a member of the St John Ambulance Brigade he knew all fifteen men on the ship. Although it was addressed to John Thompson, he read what was the first official news from Whitby, and made a very difficult telephone call to John. In his office at the gasworks, John Thompson tried to comprehend the message he had just received. No one had thought that these fifteen men could be in any kind of danger as everybody believed hospital ships were protected by international agreement. It was thought that as they were away from the front they were protected from the conditions infantrymen were facing in the trenches and therefore safe.

The second journey had taken much longer than the first and concerns were raised about a third trip. Richard Eglon, 2nd coxswain of the Whitby lifeboat, said it was not fit to launch again. He pointed out that even if they succeeded in making it to the ship and back safely, the tide was such that they would all have to use the cliff ladder to escape the sea.

After conferring with Captain John Milburn, the Lloyds agent at Whitby and other members of the lifeboat committee, it was agreed that any further rescue attempts with the *John Fielden* might result in more loss of life. It was with great sadness that the lifeboatmen agreed they had little choice but to abandon any further attempts. The lifeboat was pulled out of the water and left on the Scar, and they could do no more than watch as the tide rose, the heavy seas pounding the boat to pieces dropping by its side part of the *Rohilla* as if in some form of consolatory gesture.

The Ambulance Brigade members, who had been on duty at Saltwick all night, rushed to the beach when it was seen that men were jumping overboard from the doomed ship. At first there were not enough stretchers, but the work was quickly organised to minimise all difficulties. A party of Grosmont St John Ambulance Brigade members gave splendid assistance reinforcing the Whitby men during the afternoon. The combined brigades were engaged in the grim removal of bodies that had washed ashore despite the difficulties which presented them.

The Ambulance Brigade members were the first to recognise the valuable help given voluntarily where no request was made, and they were especially grateful to Nurse Birch and Nurse Phillips, attached to the brigade as nursing sisters, for their assistance in countless ways. Dr G.B. Mitchell JP, the Whitby division's instructor, expressed delight with the way in which its members responded to the extraordinary demands made of them. The work of the Whitby division seemed not to cease, for they set up a temporary headquarters at T. Rood's Marine Café, which was thrown open to receive the blankets, rugs, coats, etc. that had been lent for the greater comfort of those rescued. Each evening the work of sorting and allotting the articles as they were claimed proceeded. Other doctors who gave of their time and resources praised the brigades' work and unquestionable dedication.

The remains of the *John Fielden* and part of the *Rohilla* lie smashed on the shore.

The following is as accurate a list as can be obtained of the brigade and first aid workers engaged in the rescue operations:

Whitby
W.R. Knaggs (Sergeant), C.H. Hood (hon. treasurer), J.S. Gill, Sergeant-Major Hunt, Bert Hurd, F. Halem, A. Brown, H.L. Hunter, J. Brown, J. Birtle, J. Lyth, T.H. Waters, A. Middleton, G. Puckrin, G. Locker, Wilfred Harrison, G. Breckon, W.G. Barter (Barker), W. Prentice, E.B. Thornton, T.P. Cooper, A.H. Braithwaite, W. Braithwaite, C. Syer, F. Hudson, W.A. Hudson, W.G. Hunter, R.A. Birtles, W. McDonald, A. Coates, H. Frater, W. Parkinson, W. Hoggarth, H. Harrison, William Harrison

Grosmont
J. Harrison (first officer), F.W. Calvert, J. Dunwell, E. Calvert, J. Dunwell, F. Taylor, E. Raw, J. Patterson, J. Agar, E. Martin, F. Morgan, A. Clegg, J. Sigsworth, J. Elwick, H. Harrison, W. Dunwell, H. Stephenson

Skinningrove
Dr J. Donaldson, M. Spafford, E. Bullock, T. Smith, R. Healey, W.J. Wilkinson, G. Norman, V. Davies, C. Short, C. Hauxwell, J. Hutton, J. Rowland, E. Rowland, C. Hall, H. Jefferson, C. Brown, T. Donnelly

The only regret expressed by the Whitby brigade was that during the course of the rescue, their stock of stores and equipment was considerably depleted, entailing additional expense in renewal at a time when the funds available were not sufficient to meet the necessary expenses, given the brigade's recent founding.

Having joined Charles Davy supervising the Rocket Brigade on Saltwick Nab, Captain Raikes and Lt-Commander Philip Sharpe of the *St George* were informed that the Whitby lifeboat had made two journeys to the wreck earlier in the day. It was thought possible that the rocket lines were coming up short because the constant rain had made them heavier, reducing their range. The Whitby men used all their own rockets and obtained fresh dry lines from Robin Hood's Bay. One managed to reach a point close to the survivors. One of the crew, James Mackintosh, crawled perilously out along a boom to try and secure one of the lines, and managed to get the line and secure it to the bridge despite being constantly knocked by high waves. Unfortunately, their hopes were soon dashed when the line snapped. Captain Neilson described Mackintosh as worthy of the Victoria Cross for he performed many deeds of heroism and frequently went overboard to help men in great difficulty.

Davy and his men were unrelenting in their efforts to employ the rocket apparatus. He also requested supplementary rockets from Staithes and other stations. The first day he wired for two dozen, and the next day for sixty more, desperate to try and get a secure line to the ship.

Second Officer Gwynn was asked by the captain to organise a crew to man the emergency lifeboat with the aim of taking a line from the ship to the shore. As the lifeboat was lowered into the water it was thrown by the waves into the side of the ship and irreparably damaged. Nevertheless, the crew left the ship and began the perilous journey. As the line was reeled out behind the lifeboat, it frequently fouled on the rocks, threatening to capsize them. As the boat entered the surf amongst the breakers, three of her oars were broken and the 2nd officer was unable to clear the line when fouled again. In a last desperate manoeuvre, his only choice to save the lives of those in the boat was to cut the line. They had at least reached the safety of the shore.

The rescuers on land were desperate to help the wrecked ship which lay so close to the shore that they could see men gazing anxiously to shore; it was terrible to see man after man drop intentionally into the water in a brave attempt to get to land, seeing them struggle momentarily and then see their bodies cast ashore.

It was hoped that the sea would calm, at least enough to allow those able to attempt the swim to shore. Those on the shore kept watching, looking for anything unusual in the water that might suggest a person. Whenever someone was seen in distress George Peart plunged into the boiling sea time after time to help rescue those who made it near to the shore. In many cases he was overcome as casualties grasped at him, panicking, fighting for life and pushing him under in an effort to get out of the water by any means. A bricklayer by trade, George had the strength and mental fortitude to continue the rescue. His family remarked later that his back was scratched red raw from the fingers of those he was helping, but nobody commented further.

Those on the shore were making lines, fastening themselves with rope so that they could wade out but have the safety of the line should they get into trouble. George could appreciate this, but he also knew that it tied a lot of people into such a small area and chose instead to work with a small group of men who would spell each other off from going into the water but with a safety line. He knew that whenever it was his turn he had to face the icy sea and gale force winds; on the shore there was nowhere to get any respite. Time after time he plunged into the water, sometimes without a safety line because another rescuer was using it and he could not simply stand by without trying to get the poor soul out of the water.

Isaac Haslop was typical of many local individuals who gave what assistance they could. He made for Tate Hill Pier to get cabs and motors to convey those rescued to the many hotels and boarding houses that were willing to receive them. There was little sleep for the helpers who stayed throughout the night, but they were thankful for fresh volunteers on the Scar the next morning. Haslop went to Saltwick, where some nine or more survivors had gathered at the bottom of the cliffs. Here he found L.G. Rowland clearing a way down the cliffs and Rev. W. Bancroft using his great strength to assist in bringing up the men on stretchers. Everyone had to be carried up and both these men did fine service with the

The *Daily Mirror* front page news of the tragedy

George Peart waded into the water again and again bringing many people to safety. (Copyright Lewis Breckon)

ambulance men. Some of these young fellows had never seen a dead body before and yet, after the first strange shaky feeling, they were as bold as lions and seemed as strong as Samson, though it was no easy matter to scale those cliffs. One of the survivors later said, 'Did I come up there on a stretcher? Well, I suppose it must have been.'

As fatigue began to take hold, he accepted he could no longer help people up the cliffs, but he would not leave and eventually settled for the easier task of going with the patients and helping to carry stores where a firmer footing could be obtained. He witnessed another lifeless body wash ashore 4-500yd away and summoned a nurse and an ambulance man to help retrieve the man. Dodging the waves and telling the nurse to mount rocks as waves threatened to wash them over they reached the lifeless body and hauled it ashore even as the tide compelled them to move. Once on firm ground they tried resuscitation, but after trying for some time a doctor declared it hopeless. It was an opportunity to grab what little break they could for they had been out for many hours. But the work was not done. Would anyone jump from the ship at low water in the darkness? They hoped not, for who would see them? But they did, sadly, and only three brave souls survived. Isaac and others were there to forward them for treatment and rest. Haslop worked with Dr Baines and

Nurse Jefferson to make arrangements for where to send anyone rescued. Men rushed to get the saved away to homes where they got rest and fresh, dry clothes.

News of the disaster soon spread throughout the country and many national newspapers reported the unfolding story. The *Daily Mirror* carried a full front-page image of the wreck with a very full account of the tragedy inside.

Across the Atlantic, on 30 October the *New York Times* reported:

The British Steamer Rohilla, which was being used as a hospital ship, ran on the rocks off Whitby, on the Yorkshire coast, early this morning, every one of the vessel's boats, except the last one launched, was smashed by the seas and washed ashore. Lifeboats with extreme difficulty brought ashore two loads of the vessel's passengers, after which further attempts at rescue with the boats were abandoned. During the day people were seen climbing to the rigging of the ship, shortly afterwards the ship broke in two and the stern sank. Tremendous seas are lashing the wreck and it is feared that further rescues are impossible. Rohilla's signals of distress were seen on shore, and soon afterward the bodies of four seamen were hurled upon the beach in a mass of wreckage. The Rohilla was bound from Queensferry to Belgium to bring back wounded from France. She ran on the rocks half a mile south of Whitby, seventeen miles during a violent south east gale and rainstorm. The life savers shot

The Upgang lifeboat and her crew outside the lifeboat station.

lines across the floating forward part of the Rohilla, but communication between the vessel and the shore could not be established.

Countries throughout the Empire as far as New Zealand reported the *Rohilla*'s loss and the rescue attempts being made. On 2 November the *Poverty Bay Herald* reported the efforts of those stranded on the ship to save themselves: 'The lifeboats rescued people, many others clung to wreckage until exhausted, and were swept away. The bridge is the only refuge for those aboard, a number jumped into the sea; many did not make it and were washed up on the beach.'

With the *John Fielden* of no further use and the *Robert and Mary Ellis* in the boathouse awaiting more favourable weather, Charles Sutherland Davy, Chief Coastguard Officer, refused to give up his efforts to utilise the rocket apparatus, and worked the gang of volunteers attending them with great zeal and perseverance trying to get a line across to the wreck, managing to do so at least three times. Captain Milburn and local lifeboat committee members believed that salvation lay in assistance from other lifeboat stations. An urgent message was sent to the Teesmouth station based some 20 miles north of Whitby on the South Gare at Teesside: 'Please dispatch motor lifeboat to wreck of Rohilla at Saltwick. About forty persons remain on board.' The station was equipped with the self-righting motor lifeboat *Bradford* powered by a 35hp Tylor petrol engine. Even in good weather the sailing time was at least four hours, but an attempt would be made should conditions improve.

A telegram was sent from Mr Wilburn of Lloyds in Whitby to John Stephenson, the honorary secretary of the Scarborough Lifeboat, and John Owston Jr. It read, 'Secretary and Coxswain at Scarborough. Can you send Lifeboat with tug. Rohilla of Glasgow, ashore here; 80 crew remain on board. Ashore one mile south of Whitby.' Coxswain Owston and his crew were anxious to proceed, but it was impossible to launch the rowing lifeboat the *Queensbury* with such heavy seas being swept round the piers. In view of the distance to the wrecked vessel it would have been impossible for any crew to row against the tide; the only solution was to tow the lifeboat to the area where the *Rohilla* was stranded. The state of the tide at that time prevented any vessel from departing the harbour, leaving the crew no choice but to wait.

The first news of the disaster to reach Barnoldswick was by means of a telegram from Anthony Waterworth stating that he and Fred Reddiough were amongst those rescued, and it was feared that they were the only two local men to have made good their escape. Neither man knew what happened to the others. Tom Petty's brothers, Walter and Ellison, arrived in Whitby late on Friday evening and asked the first person they met if he knew where they could find accommodation. It was Mr Clough, Chairman of Whitby Council, who willingly put them up in his own house. It was an act typical of the generosity of many of the local residents and the beginning of a lifelong friendship. Anxious relatives and friends of the remainder of the local Sick Berth Reservists engaged at once to try and establish the fate of their loved ones. The only consolation was the news that many people

The stern dropped away into deeper water, taking many crewmen with it. (Copyright John Littlewood)

were known to be clinging to the wreck, and that these might include more of those who had left the town to serve their country. Undaunted, a crowd of people surged around the Post Office awaiting news that would never come.

Spurred on by the amazing feat of hauling the *John Fielden* close enough to begin rescue efforts, and desperate to act, a more daring plan to use the Upgang lifeboat was formulated. The *William Riley* of Birmingham and Leamington was located in a small cove just over a mile north of Whitby Harbour entrance along its west beach, but facing the sea. It was impossible to launch the lifeboat into the surf under such conditions.

A little after noon on the Friday, the Upgang lifeboat was brought out from her station and hauled by road through Whitby and over fields to the top of the cliff at Saltwick Bay, whence the wreck of the *Rohilla* could be seen. Thereafter, one of the strangest ever launches of a lifeboat recorded began. Some of those involved in this courageous plan are named below:

Crew of the Whitby No. 2 Lifeboat *John Fielden*	Crew of the Upgang Lifeboat *William Riley*
Coxswain Thomas Langlands	Coxswain Robert Pounder Robinson
Richard Eglon	G. Leadley
William Snowden	J. Campion
Frank Clarkson	J. Douglas
Robert Richardson	J. Harrison
James Middlemass	James Kelly
Christopher 'Kit' Eglon	Joseph Tomlinson
W. Clark	J. Winspear
John Dryden	K. Wales
Edward Gash	Thomas McGarry Kelly
Robert Harland	W. Carter

John 'Blooman' Richardson	W.J. Harland
Harry 'Lal' Richardson	W. Kelly
Jack Hansell	W. Peart

Edward Verrill (Edot)	Tom Crake	William Thomson
E.D. Verrill (Spinky)	William Ward	Richard Porritt
John Verrill	Richard Humphrey	C. Crooks
Francis Verrill	Alf Codling	Thomas Porritt
Isaac Verrill	Dan B. Harrison	John W. Crooks
Jacob Verrill	Richard Cole	Isaac Ward
Jimmy Verrill (Mugs)	G. Webster	Matthew Thomson
Thomas W Verrill	Will Thomas Ward	Rich Thomson
John Verrill (Knickers)	John Cole (Junior)	John Thomson
G. Ward	John Harrison	G.D. Laverick
Joseph Jefferson	James G Dawson	Jim Tom Theaker
Rich Hick	Joe Unthank	Mark Theaker
Rich Cake	Tommy Unthank	
Each Man Was Awarded 5/- For Their Gallant Effort		

A combined party of six horses and over a hundred people were placed in readiness for this audacious feat. At great risk to everyone, the 36ft, 2.25-ton lifeboat was carefully eased over the edge of the clifftop and down an almost perpendicular 200ft cliff, into Saltwick Bay on the south side of the Nab and the wreck, the whole operation amazingly completed in just two and a half hours.

It was hoped that when the tide receded they would be able to row the *William Riley* around the Nab to the wreck, but it was not possible. Having gotten the boat safely all the way down the cliff, such was the fury of the storm that it was deemed unsafe to launch the lifeboat. The seas continued to pound the shore, much to the disappointment of coxswains Robinson and Langlands and their crew. They remained on duty until dark, but were unable to launch the lifeboat as the sea remained too heavy. The crew agreed that had they launched the boat it would have been impossible to row her round Saltwick Nab. Rescue attempts were postponed until daylight next morning and the crew was to be present at 6 a.m.

As tremendous seas continued their fearful assault on the ship it was obvious to Captain Neilson that the *Rohilla* was in imminent danger of breaking up. The after part was still standing, but the ship appeared to have broken her back. Unbeknown to the captain, the stern was overhanging a deeper part of the reef. The constant pounding eventually proved too much for the ship. Those on the fore part could do nothing as the stern sank, taking with it many of the crew. Just the tip remained protruding above the waves separating it from the bridge and bow section still standing. Hundreds of spectators watched in horror from the cliffs, forced to stand helplessly as the seas slowly took their toll on the ship.

Those on the shore looked on hoping that the sea might moderate as the tide fell away to allow those capable to attempt the swim to shore. William Lindberg and Alexander Coventry seized the moment, plunging into the icy waters of the North Sea. With the weight of their sodden clothes working against them, they fought with each breath they took. Suddenly unknown hands began grasping at them, pulling them, lifting them from the water towards the shore and safety. Safe from their ordeal, they could not thank those that had waded into the icy waters to save them for they had gone, replaced by members of the St John Ambulance Brigade, who immediately began assessing them for any life threatening wounds. They tried to express their gratitude but in no time at all the men were whisked off to one of the many hotels, guest houses, or residential homes around the town ready to open its doors to those who survived without serious injury.

W.H. Dryden of the Royal Naval Reserve had only arrived at his home in Whitby a short time before the ship struck. Though home on leave such was his commitment that he repeatedly went into the water at great risk to his own life, saving at least nine lives. He was eventually pulled from the water and led from the beach, incapable of further effort. Sadly, he was lost just a month later whilst serving on HMS *Hogue* when the ship was attacked by a German U-boat.

Some families lost more than one member on the *Rohilla*. This is true for the MacNaughton family: John, aged just 20, and his father Donald, aged 50, were both general servants. The loss of the *Rohilla* also held special heartbreak for the Hare family, who lost two members serving on the ship. John, aged 60, and his son Thomas, aged 29, were both cooks. By sheer coincidence, at the same time another son was serving on the *Rewa*, the sister ship to the *Rohilla*.

Able Seaman Alexander Corpse RNR was central to helping those who survived the swim to shore. At the time of the *Rohilla*'s loss Alexander was on sick leave from HMS *Queen* after an operation for appendicitis. Alexander was born in Whitby in 1896, he and his wife suffered the loss of their only son Arthur (aged 6 and one of six children) in a tragic accident when he was hit by a train and killed instantly. On hearing of the *Rohilla* he went to the rock Scar and rendered great assistance; despite his own fragile health he continually went out into the water secured by lines from the shore, eventually retreating exhausted to be replaced by the Coastguard Officer Albert Jefferies on the end of the line, who helped bring four more to safety.

Many other courageous people volunteered their services, wading out into the chest-high icy water on numerous occasions to help those who made the swim ashore or to recover bodies adrift in the water. Whitby men notably involved included Robert Patton, George Patton, George Taylor, Isaac Clark, Henry Sayers, John Calvert, G. Clark, W. Beeswick, B. Griffin, F. Osborne, J. Oliver and W.T. Palmer. The following men from Staithes gave valiant service: James Dawson, W. James, John Ward, Matthew Thompson, Richard Porrit, Edward Verrill, Robert Brown, Richard Theaker, James Theaker and Tom Theaker.

Alexander Corpse. (Copyright John Littlewood)

Captain Goodrich of the Devon Motor Cyclists Corps and his detachment stationed at Whitby were instrumental in helping at every turn.

It was not only local men and women helping on or around the Scar throughout the weekend. Bob Patton, a young lifeboatman from Runswick and George Taylor displayed heroism. Patton swam in, saving nine lives and Taylor five. They both worked until they too were almost exhausted, and had to be led to safety. George Taylor was taken to a farm at Hawsker and Bob Patton was put to bed at Dr Wallis' Custom House Hotel. Many more deeds of heroism were performed by young men from Runswick and Staithes only too willing to offer their assistance. While these individuals were notable for their actions, so many more gave equally invaluable service, and it is impossible to list each and every person.

Great courage was witnessed time and time again in men dressed in the scantest of attire, numbed with cold and exhausted by their battle against the raging elements. One poor fellow was full of solicitude for his comrades as he was conveyed to the town in an ambulance. He was one of the first ashore, and kept asking, 'Are they jumping still? Are they getting them? Are they being saved?' He said nothing about himself except that he was very cold. The stretcher party did their best to cover him with what coats and wraps were available. The bravery of the officers who swam ashore was remarkable. One young officer was almost impatient with the workers who rushed to render assistance. 'Save the others, and never mind me,' was his continued cry. Fortunately, he was soon in a fit state to leave and before he left the beach he had the satisfaction of knowing that others who had followed him were saved.

At Teesmouth, the lifeboat authorities had not been idle and at 2.30 p.m. the crew felt ready to start. It was realised, however, that the boat could not reach Whitby in the remaining daylight. The honorary secretary consulted the harbour master and the coastguard as to the feasibility of starting that afternoon. In view of the tremendous seas making up the river they were unanimously of the opinion that to attempt to cross the bar and proceed in the darkness, with all the coast lights extinguished, would be courting disaster. It was decided to despatch the lifeboat the following morning.

Another call was made to Scarborough that afternoon and as conditions had improved at the harbour entrance it was agreed to launch the lifeboat at 3.30 pm. The trawler *Morning Star* skippered by Smalley was tasked with towing the lifeboat *Queensbury* to Whitby. They left the safe confines of Scarborough Harbour knowing it would take them until late afternoon to reach the wreck of the *Rohilla*. Coxswain John Owston Jr. and his crew (Johnson Crawford, Thomas Pashby, Charles Plummer, Wyrill Crawford, William Crawford, William Sheader, Thomas Sheader, Frank Bayes, Richard Dalton, Harry Burton, William Pashby, Joseph Moss and Harry Harwood) readied themselves as best they could for the journey and what lay before them. Hopes of rescue rose as they arrived at the scene at 6 p.m. Both boats took a fearful battering and sustained some damage as they made their way north, but the crew was eager to try and help those stranded upon the *Rohilla*.

It was a black winter's night, making it difficult to find a safe point where the lifeboat could get close to the stricken vessel. In spite of the gales, which continued with ferocity, and the violent seas surrounding the wreck, the lifeboat cast off for the *Rohilla*. The crew made a very gallant effort in the dark, but could not get close to the wreck and were beaten back, carried away north and had to be immediately taken in tow again to get closer to the wrecked ship but were defeated each time. The appalling conditions prevented them making contact with the stricken men. Undeterred, the lifeboatmen all agreed to stand by until daylight and make further rescue attempts should conditions improve. The crew secured the lifeboat to the trawler and prepared themselves for the long night ahead.

Dr G.B. Mitchell, JP, had made a public request in the window of the *Whitby Gazette* office for helpers with lamps and lights of any kind to patrol the beach in the evening, in case anyone attempted the perilous swim to safety. Despite the poor conditions, the townsfolk turned out in their droves, people with lights of all kinds illuminated the dark shoreline until everyone was driven from the Scar by the incoming tide. Many stayed on the cliffs with their lamps so that those on the ship might take some comfort knowing they were still in the thoughts of those ashore. The stranded men must have despaired when the lights on the shore receded on the turn of the tide, especially with the trawler and lifeboat waiting on the other side of the breakers, out of reach. They seemed doomed to spend another night on the battered wreck, as seas continued to batter their only remaining refuge with no release from the gale force winds.

At 7.30 p.m. the Whitby Secretary of the Lifeboat Committee received a request from the Chief Coastguard Officer to organise a night watch on the shore and cliff near the wreck and to supply the men with torches and life lines. Two parties of eleven men each, one to relieve the other, were given the grim task of maintaining watch overnight in atrocious conditions. A line of watchers scanned the incoming waves illuminated by one of the Whitby dredger's strong lights whilst a powerful motorcar lamp, owned and held by R.J.M. Rastall of Ruswarp, helped penetrate the dense darkness lighting up the crests of the waves. Suddenly, like an apparition, two swimmers appeared, side by side with lifebelts. One washed into view on the crest of a wave, and a rousing cheer burst from the watchers. Standing by knee-deep in the water, Colour-Sergeant Stanley Hearn of the Devon Motor Cyclists Corps was already fastening a rope round his waist. He threw down his coat and cap, then with T. Puckrin and a number of privates from the same unit plunged towards the swimmers.

The rope was skilfully paid out and the rescuers battled the waves, floundering up to the waist, slipping on the rocky and uneven bottom, but soon the men were brought half dead from the water to be met by a handful of warm-hearted and attentive assistants. It was a truly gladdening sight to see men brought out of the dark waters into safety. Those hoping their endeavours would be fruitful could now render valuable assistance, the rescued men were taken ashore by any means that could be adapted to transfer the wounded to a variety of locations in the town where warm beds, and warmer hearts awaited them. So long as it was safe to do so, the men of the Whitby St John Ambulance Brigade watched the shore, patrolling for anyone else attempting the swim ashore.

At 11.15 p.m. another message was sent to Hartlepool, this time requesting a trawler depart for Whitby to tow the lifeboat *Robert and Mary Ellis* from the bell buoy, which under normal circumstances is the navigational aid used to warn mariners of the rock scar the *Rohilla* now lay wrecked upon. At around 1 a.m. on Saturday, the Scarborough lifeboat broke free from the trawler and had to be re-secured; the endurance of the Scarborough crew was severely tested in such harsh conditions throughout the long night. After receiving the second request for help, the owners of the Hartlepool steam tug *Mayfly*, Messrs J.T. Graham & Sons, immediately set to work to get a crew together and prepare the trawler for the long difficult journey to Whitby, and at 3 a.m., preparations complete, the trawler left the harbour bound for Whitby.

Daylight brought a small change in wind direction to the south-east, but no respite in the sea conditions, which remained as dreadful as the night before. At around 6.30 a.m. the Scarborough lifeboat made another rescue attempt, again failing to get alongside the wreck. Coxswain Owston Jr. and his exhausted crew had no alternative but to return to the trawler, thereafter leaving the scene for Scarborough, much to the despair of those left on the *Rohilla*. Both boats had remained off the wreck all night and the lifeboat had made rescue attempts by day and night but found rescue by means of a rowing boat impossible. Although saddened to leave men on the wrecked ship, the spirit of the crew was such that they chose to row the lifeboat into the harbour, cheered on by a crowd waiting on the harbour walls. The crews of both boats had spent over eighteen hours at sea, and upon reaching the moorings many had to be helped ashore. On landing, Coxswain Owston Jr. explained to the waiting crowd that 'It was better to have tried and failed than never to have tried at all.'

With no improvement in the weather the crew of the Teesmouth motor lifeboat *Bradford* was moved to act. At 7 a.m. on Saturday morning, the crew, led by John Stonehouse and Jim Thompson, started what proved to be an unsuccessful though plucky effort. Facing strong winds and tremendous waves which frequently swept over the boat, they were seen to be making some headway into what would have been a long and arduous journey, but as they crossed the bar at the river mouth the crew encountered tremendous seas. Wave after wave took its toll on the boat and her crew and, falling into the trough of a mountainous wave, she sprang a serious leak crippling her machinery, compromising the safety of the eleven-man crew and leaving them in a serious situation, for they were now practically helpless and compelled to seek assistance. Fortunately, the tug *Sir Joseph Pease* was following up, having left the Tees on a similar mission. The lifeboat was filled with water and the seas were so heavy that it was felt necessary for the crew to transfer to the tug. The lifeboat was taken in tow and after a difficult journey they reached a safe port just after noon.

The Hartlepool trawler arrived off Whitby to meet with Coxswain Langlands and the Whitby No. 1 lifeboat *Robert and Mary Ellis*, which had been launched in the harbour with great difficulty. With the lifeboat secure behind the trawler, they set off on the short trip to the wrecked *Rohilla*. Leaving the safety of the trawler, the lifeboat set out on its attempt to get as near to the wreck as its crew dared, but could not get any closer than half a mile, and had to return to the trawler. Coxswain Langlands discussed the situation with James Hastings, the coxswain of the Hartlepool lifeboat, and together they agreed that in the present weather conditions there was no hope of getting the lifeboat alongside the wreck. It was escorted back into the harbour, but the trawler agreed to stand off in case their services were required later that morning.

The lifeboatmen of the *William Riley* assembled at Saltwick Bay at 6 a.m. as planned, although dismayed that the sea remained as fierce as ever, but they were committed to making an attempt near low water. The lifeboat was hauled on skids over the rocks and round the Nab to the north side, where she was manned and launched about 9 a.m. By this time more of the wreck had gone underwater and only a portion of the bridge remained clear from the rocks where a boat could lay alongside. The crew struggled manfully for an hour to reach the wreck, but the waves and currents running between the Nab and the *Rohilla* were too strong for them. Time after time they were defeated in their efforts to get close. Eventually they were forced to give up exhausted and bitterly disappointed for on one occasion they had closed on the wreck to within 50yd. The lifeboat was brought ashore and the Rocket Brigade fired from it, but their efforts also proved fruitless. The lifeboat was then hauled round the south side of the Nab into a safe place and the crew and launchers left about 10.30 a.m. It began to look as though the fate of the remaining survivors was sealed.

There was no respite from the storm force winds howling around the survivors or the violent seas that crashed repeatedly over what remained of the ship. The vessel swayed under the continuing impact of the sea, at times almost disappearing when a heavy wave broke over her. Archibald Winstanley maintained his signalling, advising those on the shore that some of the men had perished from exposure.

James Thomas Skyrme, the second son of Thomas and Ellen was born in Pembroke and followed in his father and elder brother's footsteps and apprenticed as a shipwright. He enrolled in the Navy at Chatham as a boy apprentice on his eighteenth birthday on 17 May 1902. His first job at Chatham was working on the finishing of HMS *Abermarle*, a Duncan-class battleship, which had been launched in March 1903. He became one of the ship's complement on 13 November 1903, the day after its formal commissioning. He served on the *Abermarle* until the end of January 1906, during which time he had been promoted to leading shipwright. James had a varied career and served on quite a few ships in the pre-war period, including the battleships HMS *Resolution*, HMS *Bulwark*, and the armoured cruisers HMS *Duncan*, HMS *Shannon* and HMS *Aboukir*. With the state of the world at the end of James's twelve-year service, it was inevitable that he would be enrolled in the Royal Naval Reserve at Chatham on 17 May 1914, however, he was soon back at Chatham on 2 August, two days before the declaration of war. The next entry in

James Thomas Skyrme, whose reference to the tragedy gave nothing away. (Courtesy David Skyrme)

A view of the *Rohilla* as she goes down.

his naval record is the embodiment of understatement. It simply says 'Rohilla 18 Aug 14 to 30 Oct 14'.

The reference to 18 August is curious and may have meant that he travelled by land to join the ship after its arrival at Scapa Flow. Like his fellow survivors, James had very little clothing on: having rushed from his bed and been unable to return, he was faced with extreme exposure to the cold and harsh conditions. Those left on the wrecked ship dared not relax; as comforting as sleep sounded, they knew they could not, for fear of hastening their death. He strung some empty tins around his neck to act as floating aids should he ultimately enter the water.

Captain Neilson knew that they were all in an extremely perilous situation. He had no way of knowing how long the bridge section would stay above sea level and reluctantly gave the order that 'all who could should attempt to swim to shore.' This terrifying choice faced every man left on the *Rohilla*: to stay on board or take a chance in the rough sea? They had seen what happened to the men on the stern, and it seemed likely that sooner or later the remaining piece of wreckage they were on would go the same way. They had also seen swimmers swept away by the current or dragged lifeless and bleeding from the water's edge. Although deceptively close, strong currents and gale force conditions made the swim very hazardous indeed. It must have seemed as though there were to be no more rescue attempts, for Henry Barter and William Anderson made the decision to swim to shore. An accomplished swimmer, Henry was hopeful of reaching safety. Once in the water the strength of the current was such that the two were soon separated. Despite being tossed about in the raging water, Henry almost made it to safety. It was especially lamentable that he made such a brave and considerable effort to reach the shore only to be thrown against the rocks and killed. In the short time before rescuers could get near to his body it had been pitched violently against the rocks, and when recovered it was terribly mutilated. William Anderson had joined Philip Moore the 3rd mate, but it is thought the conditions proved too much for them. William was never seen again; only Philip Moore's body was recovered.

Frederick Edwin Wilson.
(Courtesy of John Wilson)

Frederick Edwin Wilson was born in Brixton, London, on 16 January 1894 and had joined the Marconi Company on 16 June 1914 as a 'learner' in wireless telegraphy. His training complete, he was sent to the Marconi Sea Going Operating Staff and was appointed to his first ship, the SS *Rohilla*, as a Junior Marconi Operator on 17 August 1914, while she was being converted from a troop ship to a hospital ship. At home in Ealing, his parents George and Elizabeth Wilson had no idea his ship was mortally wounded and that his life was in grave danger. In what must have seemed a twist of irony, at 5.10 am on 31 October they received a telegram from the town clerk of Whitby reporting 'Fred Wilson reported still aboard, rescue proceeding.'

At low water more of the rock scar was visible, seemingly reducing the distance to safety. The shore appeared very close, encouraging many to attempt the dangerous swim, but the surf presented the gravest danger. Fred Wilson and Archibald Winstanley, the ship's senior 2nd officer, took to the water at 11 a.m. Fighting with every last breath to stay afloat as the current attempted to drag them off course, the white foam whipped up by the high wind stinging their eyes, making it difficult to see the safest way forward, and all around them razor sharp rocks lay in wait should they misjudge any movement. Suddenly strong hands reached out grasping them, for they had made it safely into the arms of those who waded out to help them.

After an anxious wait that seemed to last an eternity, Frederick's parents received another telegram at 2.21 pm on 31 October saying, 'F.W. Wilson, safe and sound in bed my house. Dr Mitchell, Whitby'. Later, on 2 November, a telegram from the senior operator of the *Rohilla*'s telegraphs said, 'Wilson saved. Marconi Co.'

At the same time, most of the national newspapers and many regional papers were now carrying news of the disaster most often accompanied by a list provided by the Admiralty of those who had survived and those sadly lost. Unfortunately, as is often the case with such lists, the more intermediaries they go through to get into print, the greater the scope for errors to appear. It would seem that Frederick's name was one such example, for shortly after the previous telegram his parents received the last, 'Ignore official list Eric safe confirmed Marconi George.'

The elation of seeing Frederick and Archibald Winstanley make it to safety was marred by the sight of a greater number of bodies being washed ashore. Seeing the loss of so many men was devastating but Captain Neilson knew the longer they remained on the wrecked ship, the less chance they had of surviving. He signalled to shore, 'Have ambulance parties ready tonight at low water. All leaving ship on rafts. She cannot last out much longer.' He called the men together and told them he did not believe the ship could hold out until daylight and that he thought they all ought to leave because if she went to pieces at high water, they would stand no chance. Those that were able, both physically and mentally, set about using any material they could find from the bridge and captain's cabin to construct rafts. Under his instruction, the men left the ship in groups, hanging onto their makeshift rafts; many succeeded in reaching the shore safely. But in the meantime the tide had turned and as the water rose it was evident that the wind had once again freshened, throwing up seas that no

Harry Claude Robbins, master-at-arms.

handmade raft would survive. The captain knew that whilst anything of the ship remained it was safer to stay where they were and the order to float the rafts was countermanded.

Born on 20 March 1862 Harry Robbins, enlisted in the Navy at Portsmouth on 22 March 1878 when ships were still masted.He attained the rank of master-at-arms on 5 February 1895. He accepted responsibility as an officer to stand by his captain, but was unsure of his fate should he stay. He was called up again as a reservist at the start of the First World War, joining the hospital ship *Rohilla*, which was considered 'safe'.

He had the chance to leave the ship early on, but gave it up to help someone else. This time he felt conflicted. Thirteen men still felt the ship would not hold together much longer and sought permission to leave. The captain was reluctant to give permission, but he could see the men had taken as much as they could and had reached their limit. Harry Robbins seized the moment. It later transpired that only three of those who chose to leave the wrecked vessel reached the shore alive and Harry was not one of them. Before joining the *Rohilla*, Harry had enjoyed a varied career at sea and was presented with the Long Service and Good Conduct Medal. He served in military campaigns in Egypt, and was presented with the Egyptian Medal (with clasp Suakin 1885) and the Khedive Star.

The Long Service and Good
Conduct Medal. (Copyright
John Wilson)

Following the death of her husband, Harry Robbins' widow and children lived with his relatives.

The remaining men all huddled together in the captain's cabin, the officer's cabin and the chart room. A head count revealed that fifty men were still awaiting rescue. What was left of the ship had taken a terrible battering and there was barely a dry spot to be had. Like many of the men clustered in the bridge and chartroom, William Eastwood was still dressed in nightclothes. The captain shared out the contents of his wardrobe among those most in need. Eastwood was covered in bruises after his failed attempt to swim for the shore and still wearing wet clothing. Taking pity, the captain gave him the full dress uniform of a captain of the British India Line, which caused considerable amusement in spite of their situation.

At 2.30 p.m., with no discernable improvement in the sea conditions, the master of the Hartlepool steam trawler *Mayfly* made the decision that it was not safe to make a second rescue attempt, and that he was therefore returning to Hartlepool, reaching her mooring at 5.30 p.m. During the rescue attempt, the men of the trawler and lifeboat had been able to make out the men walking about on the bridge of the ill-fated ship, the only part of the

The Egyptian 1885 and the Khedive Star Medals, which were awarded for service in the Egyptian campaigns. (Courtesy of Richard Rosser)

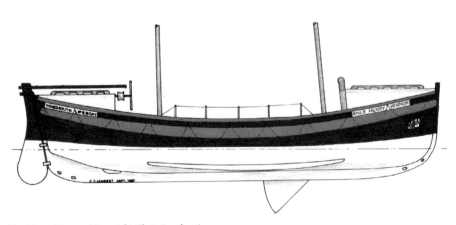

The *Henry Vernon*. (Copyright Chris Lambert)

structure remaining above water. Having briefly experienced the conditions the survivors were enduring, they were determined to try and see if anything further could be done. A consultation was held with the owners of the trawler and a number of other bodies whom they thought might have something to offer. During the consultation, Captain Nicholson of the North Eastern Railway Co. stated that he had received a wire asking for a tug to take oil, but as he had no tug available, the master of the *Mayfly* volunteered to go to Whitby with the oil required. Six barrels of oil were acquired and naval authorities supplied rockets with a view to making an effort to establish communication with the *Rohilla* from the seaward side.

Steam trawlers undoubtedly had a pivotal role to play in the many rescue efforts. J.S. Ellis, owner of the Hartlepool trawler *Gamecock*, telephoned from Scarborough to Hartlepool instructing his skipper to tow the Hartlepool lifeboat to Whitby. They made an attempt to leave the harbour but the small lifeboat was no match for the high wind and seas that washed over her, forcing the trawler to return to the harbour. A torpedo boat was sent from Hartlepool to try the effect of pouring oil on the waves to the windward side of the wreck, but could not get close enough and returned to Hartlepool.

Some of those who had survived the impact had climbed the ship's rigging in an attempt to evade the constant battering from the sea. One soul was reported to have perished aloft, the body remaining 'hung from the rigging' for some time. Many of those clinging to the rigging did so tying themselves where possible to the mast spars as the cold and exhaustion began to take effect. One such individual reported later that he had taken to biting his hands and lips to revive himself when he found himself waning.

News came that the North Shields motor lifeboat *Henry Vernon* had left Tyneside at 4.15 p.m. but it was still a good few hours away and the weather was showing no sign of improvement. Even powered by a motor the lifeboat still had to navigate over 40 miles in atrocious weather, down the same stretch of coastline that had claimed a much larger ship which far outweighed the lifeboat in every sense. Captain Herbert Edgar Burton, superintendent of the lifeboat had command of the boat on this dangerous journey to Whitby with his old friend Coxswain Robert Smith at the helm. Captain Burton had enjoyed a distinguished career with the Royal Engineers after enlisting as a boy in 1878. The *Henry Vernon* had begun its career under a cloud, as the men of the previous rowing lifeboat had misgivings about relinquishing control to a motor.

Some of the Royal Engineers were present as crewmen to accompany the crew of the lifeboat: 2nd Coxswain James Brownlee, Bowman John Robert. Brownlee, Motor Mechanic Colin MacFadyen, Thomas Cummings, Jack Scarth, Archie Craig, John Kay, John Henry, William Storey and David Martin. Two other men started out in the lifeboat, but as there were insufficeint lifebelts for all they had to be returned to the safety of the shore. The lifeboat was stationed at Tynemouth in 1911 and powered by a 40hp Tyler petrol engine, but she still retained her oars and an auxiliary sail. Despite the distance and gale force conditions, the men knew they had to act and so it was that they set out on what was to become one of the most heroic stories in lifeboat history.

The *Henry Vernon* and her crew in 1914.

The crew of the Scarborough steam trawler *Bulldog* assembled at 6 p.m. in preparation to set out for Runswick Bay. It was hoped that the only remaining lifeboat in the area not involved in rescue attempts might yet have a role to play and with the assistance of the trawler be able to get close to the wreck. Saturday night came with a falling barometer and rain clouds gathering to the south-east. When the rain came pelting relentlessly down, the gloom of the people of the town became a party with the elements. They were fast losing hope of deliverance for those in deadly peril just a short distance away from them.

William Farquharson was born in Aberdeen on 16 June 1880. He was a private with the Royal Army Medical Corp (RAMC) during the Boer War. Whilst stationed at Cork in 1901 he married his first wife on 13 April. The following year they moved to Dublin, and William began work at the Guinness Brewery. On 2 August 1914 he signed on with the Royal Naval Reserve and immediately went for training to HMS *Pembroke*, which was to serve as his temporary base during his many postings. Just three weeks later he was assigned to *Rohilla* as an RNASBR junior reserve attendant. Having survived the wreck of the hospital ship, his naval records indicate that the day after the disaster he was back at *Pembroke* and he stayed there until 16 April 1915. His next posting was on board HMS *Campania*, where he was present for the first ever ship-based launch of an aircraft at sea. In all of his postings he was never far from a hospital ward. On 16 May 1916 he was promoted to senior reserve attendant and served from 31 August until 24 March 1917 at Chatham Hospital. His service ended on 21 November 1917 at HMS *Pembroke*, when he was discharged as a result of Fibroid Phthisis, a serious illness often referred to as consumption, or Tuberculosis. William died on 17 June 1962, aged 82, after suffering a cerebral haemorrhage.

A number of relatives left Barnoldswick on the early morning train for the scene of the disaster, unaware that the body of Henry Barter had been recovered.

The St John Ambulance Brigade members and public volunteers maintained a watch on the beach throughout Saturday and a close vigil was kept for the second night in a row as survivors made last ditch attempts to reach safety. In many cases the casualties borne to the town on the stretchers were far beyond what would, in ordinary circumstances, have been attempted.

In the evening a powerful searchlight was brought by a party of soldiers of the Royal Engineers (Tyne Electrical Engineers) based at Clifford's Fort, North Shields. Captain Herbert Edgar Burton, the honorary superintendent of the Tynemouth lifeboat station was stationed at the fort and with the assistance of Brigadier-General Baylay they arranged for a special train to transport the searchlight to Whitby. Lt Mountain had charge of the searchlight party, which comprised Corporal Bianche, 2nd Corporal Drandoff, John Henry Stanford and Sappers Hunter, Edmunson and Guthrie.

Upon its arrival at Whitby the equipment was taken straight to the clifftop, where it was set up with light from Dr Raw's motorcar. The powerful lamp immediately threw a steady beam of light upon what remained of the ship, where the survivors, soaked to the skin, huddled together for warmth and the comfort of still being alive. However, the men were rapidly showing signs of hypothermia.

William Farquharson. (Courtesy Arthur Walsh)

Nobody felt hungry, but thirst was a real problem. It was over forty hours since the last of the food and water had been shared out. Some of the men split pieces of wood and sucked the moisture out, which helped a little. They had grave doubts about how long their position could be maintained. It was agreed that if no help was forthcoming they would attempt to swim for shore at 10 a.m.

The Scarborough steam trawler *Bulldog* departed the harbour around midnight on the Saturday and made best speed possible under the circumstances proceeding to Runswick Bay. After arriving on the scene the *Bulldog* spent several hours in readiness, but the lifeboat did not go out. They were eventually forced to admit defeat and set off on the return journey to Scarborough.

Heading out into the stormy darkness thirty-six hours after the *Rohilla* had been wrecked, the crew of the *Henry Vernon* struggled for over eight hours to keep the lifeboat on course against intensifying seas. Gale conditions increased wave height and ferocity as they passed off Hartlepool, yet still the robust lifeboat motored forward. The motor ran admirably and the boat made the voyage without a stop along a coast that was difficult to navigate, especially since no lights were visible from Tynemouth to Whitby.

After a night trip of remarkable seamanship, the lifeboat arrived at Whitby, entering the harbour at 1 a.m. The lifeboat crew were provided with much needed refreshments and the opportunity to stretch their legs before facing their biggest challenge. All too aware the

Members of the Tyne Electrical Engineers stand by the train with its precious cargo, two of them holding one of the ship's life rings bearing the name *Rohilla* and the city of registration, Glasgow.

A large transportable searchlight typical of those used by the Royal Engineers. (Copyright Nils Mosberg)

survivors were in desperate need of their help, Coxswain Smith and his men were eager to act. The local lifeboat crew explained that the darkness and heavy seas were complicated by the ebb tide, which had created a violent current through the narrow channel between the rocks and the *Rohilla*, making any rescue attempt extremely hazardous. It was therefore agreed to wait until first light.

Captain Burton went up onto the clifftop and used the searchlight to signal in Morse code to the survivors that help was at hand and the boat would come to their rescue at daybreak. Taking advantage of the break, the men of the *Henry Vernon* unshipped the mast and removed all surplus equipment to make more room for the remaining survivors.

The crew of the Hartlepool steam trawler *Mayfly* assembled back at the boat. Having had a short but much needed rest, they began preparing for the difficult voyage to Whitby once again. At 3 a.m. they left the protection of the harbour and were met with heavy seas washing over her decks, threatening to wash the oil barrels adrift.

In Whitby, the crew of the *Henry Vernon* had prepared the lifeboat for the short but dangerous journey. Coxswain Langlands told Coxswain Smith and his crew of the rescue attempts that had been made and the conditions that had thwarted all but those of the *John Fielden*, omitting no detail so that they knew what lay ahead. During the detailed briefing, it was agreed that Richard Eglon, 2nd coxswain of the Whitby lifeboat, would

Robert Smith, coxswain of the Tynemouth motor lifeboat *Henry Vernon*.

make a valuable addition to the crew for this perilous mission, as he was intimately familiar with the rocks and currents in the area of the wreck, experience which would soon prove invaluable to the *Henry Vernon*.

Dr Baines had suggested early on that some oil go to Saltwick for one boat that might go from there. Taking counsel with captains Milburn and Isdale he asked Spaven to let Coxswain Langlands have some. Spaven was only too happy to oblige and promised to leave 4-gallon cans on the steps of his house to be collected when the boat was ready. With the Whitby lifeboat no longer fit for service it was thought the oil would still be of use to the motor boat. When asked if 'the oil will be any use to you', Richard Eglon responded, 'Aye, let's have it.' A car was sent immediately to collect the oil.

Those looking from the comparative safety of the clifftop watched as the *Henry Vernon* crept out of the harbour with Richard Eglon and Commander Basil Hall, the District Inspector of Lifeboats just as the sun rose over the sea at 7 a.m. The wind was strong

The second coxswain of the Whitby lifeboat *Richard Eglon*.

but thankfully not as bad as the day before, though the current was still strong, and was sufficiently rough to render the task ahead extremely dangerous. It was very difficult to get between the broken and jagged steel frames of the ship and the rocks; the lifeboatmen had to fight every step of the way. In the hollows of the seas the frames of the ship would come in like the jaws of some huge monster ready to swallow them.

Under Richard Eglon's pilotage they cautiously negotiated their way through the dangerous obstacles until they were within 200yd of the wreck on her leeward side. The lifeboat then turned seawards in a move that appeared to those onshore as though she was returning to the harbour. It was at this point that the crew discharged the oil from R.D. Spaven's warehouse into the boiling waters. It seemed that such a small amount of oil might have little impact on the tumultuous seas, but the current carried it towards the wreck and, amazingly, within but a brief moment the waters surrounding the wreck seemed to smooth out as if inviting the lifeboat alongside.

The *Henry Vernon*'s crew knew there was not a moment to be lost, for they were aware that the oil's effect would not last long, and the waves would soon rise dangerously again. Coxswain Robert Smith raced for the wreck and, steaming skilfully against the strong current, brought the lifeboat alongside what remained of the *Rohilla* at 7.15 a.m. The fore part of the ship had fallen away and was all but swallowed by the sea, the stern having sunk early on; there was nothing to show of what was once a beautiful and palatial vessel, the only part left being the bridge.

It was too dangerous to secure the lifeboat to the wreck, so Coxswain Smith used the motor with remarkable efficiency to hold the boat in position alongside. The lifeboat crew were shocked at the sight of the poor men, nearly all of whom were dressed just as they had been when they were forced to rush from their berths.

The storm continues to pound the harbour entrance.

James Brownlee, second coxswain of the *Henry Vernon*. (Copyright Dorothy Brownlee)

A rope was passed down from the *Rohilla* and immediately figures began scrambling down with an agility and quickness that seemed astonishing given they had endured the full fury of the elements for two days. Man after man descended until they had all reached the safety of the lifeboat. A number of the survivors had secured empty tins around their bodies in order to stay afloat should they be washed overboard. True to tradition, Captain Neilson was the last to leave the ship, carrying with him the ship's cat.

However, all too soon the oil was beginning to disperse, the sea rising once again, and the lifeboat was buried by two huge seas momentarily parted from the *Rohilla* and those on the cliff watched in horror as Captain Neilson dropped into the water. Still grasping the cat he was fortunate to be within reach of the lifeboat's 2nd coxswain James Brownlee, who helped him back into the lifeboat. The cat must have used several, if not all, of its nine lives.

But the danger was not yet passed; another crisis had to be met before anxiety was allayed. As the lifeboat left the vessel on her return journey, it had to turn broadside into the waves, and met with a succession of high waves forcing her onto her beam ends, which very nearly capsized her. The lifeboat dropped into the trough of a wave, disappearing from view. Those watching from the shore feared all was lost, but in just the briefest of moments, the sturdy little craft withstood the shock, righting herself and rising to the top of a wave, much to everyone's relief for it would truly have been a cruel twist of fate to be lost to the sea after such gallant efforts.

Clear of the wreck, the lifeboat swept gaily out to sea in a wide semi-circle that brought her safely to the harbour mouth. The rescue had taken two hours in the most unimaginable conditions; the motor lifeboat had indeed proved her worth and the gallant crew had succeeded by almost superhuman efforts in rescuing the last fifty souls from the wreck of HMHS *Rohilla*. News of the rescue had spread like wildfire and it seemed as though each and every person in Whitby, many only half-dressed, had rushed to watch the incoming lifeboat and the last survivors from the *Rohilla*.

As the lifeboat slipped smoothly through the harbour entrance and along the riverside, cheer after cheer resounded through the air for a sight that would never be forgotten, nor repeated. The crew of the lifeboat and her thankful passengers waved back for a magnificent reception awaited them. The survivors were beholden to the valiant lifeboat crew, a debt that could never be repaid, and they would forever be held with reverence and admiration.

The bells of St Mary's church on the clifftop above the *Rohilla* were rung to signal the end of the ordeal. Only now would the repercussions be felt. The rescue was a relatively happy finish for the fifty men who had withstood icy tempest, hunger and thirst for fifty hours. The people of Whitby were once more resolute in their willingness to do what they could for the survivors; they rushed to the quayside on the west pier with blankets and warm drinks, but the medical men and women of the town, who had laboured magnificently during the weekend, were there before them, ready to attend to the more serious cases of collapse.

As the survivors were helped up the steps people openly cried, no man or woman could help but be moved by such a sorry procession, for the final fifty survivors were a pitiful sight. Men ran forward to help those unable to walk unaided. Amazingly only a single man had to be carried up; the remainder tottered giddily into the arms of those anxiously waiting to help. The survivors were pale, hollow eyed and gaunt, nearly all barefoot and poorly clad. Some had severe cuts and one had sustained serious lacerations to the feet and legs falling from the rigging.

The casualties were escorted to waiting motor cars and ambulances and despatched to homes and suitable locations around the town. No one had been more assiduous in seeking to alleviate suffering than the members of the St John Ambulance Brigade. At the various places where the survivors were taken the abulance crew gave assistance, tending to their frail bodies. The brigade could not consider themselves free from duty until later in the afternoon, some having had little more than three hours sleep since the *Rohilla* struck the shore.

Throughout the weekend and into the beginning of the week snippets of news about the catastrophe had been received from the scene of the disaster in Barnoldswick. The lack of information regarding local men had prompted those with the means to travel to Whitby. Amongst those waiting on shore to welcome the survivors were some of the relatives from Barnoldswick, who had waited throughout the weekend desperate for the rescue of their loved ones. It was only three short months since the war had begun, and fifteen members of the Royal Naval Sick Berth Reserve had left to take their part in the very necessary ambulance work, of which, alas, there would ultimately prove plenty.

Forty-five of the final fifty men rescued by the *Henry Vernon* are listed below, the remainder having been taken off to suitable locations before being identified.

Captain David Landles Neilson	Master
Abraham Loch	Fireman
Alfred Fox	Ordinary Seaman
Archibald Young	Carpenter
Ernest Courtney Lomas	Fleet Surgeon
Frank Bigwood	Sick Berth Reserve
Frank Bond	Lt RNR 1st Officer
Frank Knight	Able Seaman
George Hastie	Able Seaman
George Summer	6th Engineer
Herbert Wilkin	2nd Baker
Horace Willis	Barman
John Crawley	Saloon Steward
James Thomas Skyrme	Leading Shipwright
James Mackintosh	Steward
James Robb	Fireman
John Armstrong	Signaller
John Bunyan	Greaser
John Craig	Greaser
John Fraser	General Servant
John Pocock	Baker
John Sullivan	Able Seaman
Louis Juliani	Chief Cook
Mathew Turnbull	Chief Engineer
Michael Burns	Fireman

Peter Ferguson	Able Seaman
Robert Rutherford	Fireman
Richard Oram	Ships Doctor
Robert (Peter) Dixon	Fireman
William Eastwood	Senior Reserve Attendant
Robert Thurlo Utting	Wireless Operator
Sidney Gallon	Deck Boy
S. Taylor	Fifth Engineer
Thomas F. Martin	Fireman
Thomas Hare	Hospital Cook
Thomas Hebdige	Deck Boy
Thomas Scott	Steward
W.E. Edwards	Butcher
Walter Sutherland	Shipwright RNR
William Gray	Fireman
William Holland	Officers Servant
William Pattinson	Steward
William Powell	Chief Steward
William Rodd	Purser

James Skyrme's son was for some years the curator of the family bible. Although the bible says that James 'was in the sea for thirty-six hours before being rescued', he is listed as one of the final fifty saved. He would have spent around fifty hours on the wreck and it is entirely conceivable, given how badly broken up the ship was, that he spent some time in the water, a traumatic ordeal by any standards. When James was brought ashore, he was taken with eight others to Seaside Home. James' last few years in the Navy were spent on HMS *Maidstone*, a submarine supply ship operating along the east coast (Harwich, Yarmouth).

When the *Mayfly* arrived at Whitby around 7.45 a.m. they found no signs of life on the *Rohilla* and motored about for some time before sighting a minesweeper. They hailed the vessel, asking if they knew whether the men from the *Rohilla* had been saved. On being informed this was the case, the men were initially disappointed that all their effort had been in vain, but thankful the tragedy was at last at an end. The skipper, R.H. Whittleton, then turned back for Hartlepool, arriving about noon.

During both trips the crew of the *Mayfly* encountered exceptionally heavy weather; they were both physically and mentally exhausted. In undertaking the long arduous journey twice they displayed splendid heroism in the face of danger. The owners of the trawler had every right to feel proud of their crew, who are listed below:

Saturday	Position	Sunday
R.H. Whittleton	Master	The same crew as Saturday, with the extra assistance of captains Cappleman and King, both of whom volunteered.
S.B. Ward	Mate	
E. Butcher	3rd Hand	
M.E. Bennett	Engineer	
H.W. Jefferson	2nd Engineer	
A. Ward	Deck Hand	
H. Lockey	Deck Hand	
E. Butler	Cook	
T. Henderson	Fireman	
James Hastings	Hartlepool Lifeboat Coxswain who acted as special pilot	

With the final survivors safely on shore and the rescue efforts effectively completed, there would now come a time for mourning what had come to pass. Captain Raikes returned to HMS *George*, leaving Lt-Commander Philip W.C. Sharpe in charge of proceedings, it being necessary for a responsible person to make arrangements for the survivors, and funerals for the bodies washed ashore.

Coxswain Smith felt he had not fulfilled his responsibility until he and his crew were safely back home. After taking some time to rest, the crew were back on the quayside preparing the lifeboat for the return journey, replacing all the items they had taken off to make room. Those on the quay were concerned, for Coxswain Smith and his crew were facing the sea for a second long-distance journey. Although the weather had calmed somewhat they still had a daunting challenge ahead. The lifeboat was simply going home so Smith offered the crew the opportunity of travelling by rail, but, when asked, each man declined the offer, insisting they could never do such a thing. Despite the trials facing them there was an air of triumph aboard the *Henry Vernon* for they had endured the journey from the Tyne in worsening weather and had rescued the final fifty survivors when no other lifeboat could. Eager to get underway, they started to say their goodbyes, but it seemed like everyone wanted to congratulate them on their success before they left.

A reporter for the *Yorkshire Post* managed to speak to Coxswain Smith, who gave the following spellbinding but simple account of a courageous and skilful enterprise:

She is a beauty. There never was a better built, and it needed a good one to stand those seas. We were splendidly piloted by the coxswain of the local lifeboat, who guided us safely through the channels and currents. Perhaps Whitby will now look out for a motor lifeboat of her own. I did not take any dead bodies off the wreck because there were none to take. They must all have been washed overboard. I'm glad we have had so good an ending to a bad business.

Clearly delighted with the success of his crew, and with the quality of the *Henry Vernon*, they left Whitby pleased to be on their way but knowing the journey would be long and tiresome. The rest of the trip was like a triumphal procession for they had accomplished two things: proved to the world the efficientcy of the motor lifeboat, and been instrumental in saving fifty poor fellows who had likely given up all hope of rescue.

By the time they reached the River Tyne, they were all exhausted, especially Robert Smith, whose hands were almost numb from gripping the wheel. Nevertheless, he was determined to complete his command of this rescue and get everyone safely home. As the *Henry Vernon* reached the entrance to the harbour, she was greeted by a fleet of merchant ships and warships eager to pay their respects. The lifeboat was escorted into the harbour by the pilot cutter, and received a rousing reception, the steam whistles of vessels in the harbour joining the cheering of the crowds on the quay and on the torpedo boats on the river. Thousands of locals had also gathered at North Shields to welcome them home.

The men were treated like heroes and found a distinguished gathering awaiting them. Captain Burton was the first man to step ashore and he was heartily greeted by his wife

The *Henry Vernon*'s rescue of the last fifty men from the *Rohilla* was an unparalleled success. No other RNLI motor lifeboat had made such an audacious journey in order to carry out a daring rescue.

and daughter, after which the soldiers rushed at him and carried him shoulder-high to Clifford's Fort. The other members of the crew had a similar reception, the burly coxswain Robert Smith being especially well received. Each man thoroughly deserved special treatment for the ordeal he had been through.

Over the course of the weekend there were numerous instances of triumph over adversity, but sadly a great many heart-rending stories too. So many had endured without food or water, facing the full fury of storm force winds and the might of such savage seas. Senior Marconi Operator Robert Thurlo Utting had nothing but praise for all those involved. He explained that:

> ... in the face of imminent danger not a grumble nor so much as a whisper of fear was heard. The men who possessed tobacco shared it with their comrades, and the leaves of some magazines found in the chart room were used as improvised cigarette paper. Those who had pipes in their possession filled them, took a whiff and handed the treasure to the next man, who likewise took a whiff, and so the pipe of good comradeship was passed round.

James McKenzie, who had secured one of the rocket lines, was sadly washed overboard, his body was recovered on the Monday. John Smith, a fireman on the ship was seen entering the water on Saturday and made the shore alive; he was taken to Dr Burton's house, but sadly died the same day from exhaustion. Such was Staff Surgeon Dr Lomas' prominence that the Secretary of State for Foreign Affairs presented his compliments to the Secretary of the Admiralty upon receiving a telegram from His Majesty's Ambassador at Washington about his condition. This was grave: Lomas was suffering severe shock, numerous head injuries and severe confusion, and was indeed unfit to be moved from where he was being treated. Dr Thomas Littler-Jones, a survivor of the tragedy himself, was aware that he would soon be moving on. Concerned about Dr Lomas, he sent a telegram to the Admiralty asking if a nursing sister could stay to nurse him.

By Wednesday morning Barnoldswick knew twelve lives of the fifteen who went to serve upon the ill-fated hospital ship *Rohilla* had been lost, that only one body had been recovered, the remainder missing. With the loss of the *Rohilla* Barnoldswick as a town suffered the greatest shock that the war had yet to impose. Local hardships caused by trade depression, and anxieties about the welfare of loved ones serving their country in whatever capacity, could be borne with some fortitude, but the loss of fifteen brave and well-known townspeople in one fell swoop so soon upon leaving their loved ones was a disaster not so easily overcome.

Of the fifteen men, only Privates Fred Reddiough, Anthony Waterworth and William Eastwood survived. The body of Private Henry Barter was recovered, the rest never found. It is presumed that they were drowned in the storm. It is a sad story, but one that will nevertheless produce a sense of pride through succeeding generations when the story is related in years to come. When war was announced these fifteen men left home, relinquishing their wives and families and all the comforts of home life, and joined the Royal Naval Auxiliary Sick Berth Reserve.

Had the ship run aground on the west side of the piers the matter would not have been so problematic. The seabed is predominantly sand, and the ship would have run until she came to a stop. Rescue would have been far simpler and many more lives would undoubtedly have been saved.

5

THE FUNERAL CEREMONIES

Unprecedented Scenes of Solemnity

Scenes unparalleled in the history of Whitby were witnessed on the Wednesday afternoon following the tragedy, when the remains of ten victims were laid to rest in Whitby cemetery. There was a large assembly near the drill shed on the pier, where the procession gathered together under the guidance of Superintendent Robinson, L. Haslop (Reader to the Mission to Seamen), Sergeant J. Hunt, and others.

The coffins were placed on five drays draped with the Union Flag and surrounded by many beautiful wreaths. From first light people began taking their places along the route chosen for the procession, standing shoulder to shoulder. As the procession came into view on St Ann's Staith, it was clear the solemn occasion was attended by thousands of people of all classes and sects – practically all the inhabitants of the town were present.

Sergeant Gillard of the Devon Cyclist Territorials headed the procession with Scout Bugler Wilfred Gale of Whitby by his side and a detachment of twelve Territorials who were stationed at Whitby. A reed and brass band under A.E. Ainsley played solemnly as the procession made its way to the cemetery.

The townsfolk get their first view of the cortège on St Ann's Staith.

A reed and brass band follows.

People from the district and beyond travelled to Whitby to pay tribute to the memory of those who had perished in such terrible circumstances. As the horse-drawn carriages passed by, each of which had an escort of a scout on either side, it was possible to glimpse the coffins draped in the flag surrounded by wreaths.

It was an unusually long funeral cortège, there being ten men being laid to rest. Two of the bodies went to their final resting place unidentified, none who survived having been able to recognise them; the other eight were John Hare, hospital cook; George Gover, storekeeper; Edward Rose, carpenter; Laurence Nicholson, quarter-master; David Nisbett, able seaman; John Smith, fireman; Sidney Morris and Alfred Page, naval sick berth stewards.

The final carriage was followed by the lifeboat crews with their coxswains, the Rocket Lifesaving Brigade and the combined Coastguard units, under Chief Officer Davy. Twenty-

Horse-drawn carriages bear the coffins with a scout escort across the bridge.

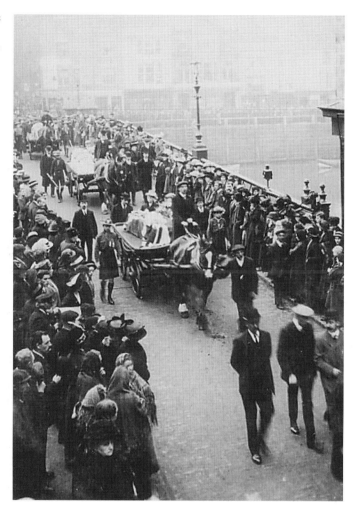

nine wounded Belgian soldiers, who were recuperating in Whitby, were also present. They expressed great sympathy, noting the *Rohilla*'s merciful errand to aid not only British soldiers but also those of their own country. The remaining sixteen of the twenty-six bodies that had washed ashore before the funerals had been taken for interment in their hometowns.

There followed doctors and nurses, members of the St John Ambulance Brigade; local members of the National Reserve under Major E.H. Chapman and Captain E.O. Turnbull; the newly formed Whitby Youths Drill Company under Captain R.K. Jackson; Whitby Boy Scouts with Scoutmaster Vivian Gray and Middlesbrough Boy Scouts – both parties carrying their staves reversed; the local sea scouts; the chairman, members and officers of the Whitby Urban District Council; and local members of the Church Lads Brigade.

Flags were flown at half-mast in various parts of the town, and the parish church bells were solemnly tolled. Wednesday being the weekly half-holiday, the trading establishments

Lifeboat crews with their coxswains follow behind the final carriage as it draws across the bridge carrying its solemn load.

of the town were closed at one o'clock, half an hour before the procession commenced, and at many of the shops shutters had been put up. Throughout the town the procession was surrounded on both sides by the throng of the mourners, the turn out demonstrating how much the tragedy affected the people of Whitby and the surrounding districts. Along the route it was not uncommon to witness a natural outpouring of grief for those directly involved when the ship foundered.

Those able to make the journey to the cemetery did so sometime before the start of the ceremony, fully expecting it to be vastly overcrowded. Several motorcars and other conveyances took members of the crew who were unable to make the journey on foot. Captain Neilson, master of the ill-fated ship, was amongst the mourners; others in the vast

All manner of
organisations and
qualifications were
present in the
cortège including
St John, boy scouts
from Whitby and
Middlesbrough and
the sea scouts.

assembly included G. Buchannan (coroner), Captain Goodridge with the Devon Territorials, Captain Peach RN, Major E.J.B. Buckle (recruiting officer at Whitby), Lt-Com. Sharpe, RN, Captain Isdale (representing the owners of the ship: the British India Steam Navigation Co.), Captain J. Milburn (Lloyds Agent), Brigadier Gilks of Middlesbrough, who was in charge of the northern district of the Salvation Army, and Dr Littler-Jones, a fortunate survivor of the *Rohilla*.

The designated grave was immediately beyond the chapel and was temporarily closed by ropes. A long communal grave had been dug in an open portion of the cemetery, running parallel with the grave containing the remains of Brodie Stein RN, who had been the chief officer of the coastguard station at Whitby for thirteen years. The enclosure was lined

Even after the final coffin had crossed the swing bridge it was some time before the rest of the procession finally cleared the route.

by armed Devon Territorials and local Church Lads Brigade Engineers. As the carriages bearing the coffins arrived at the cemetery they were met by some the vicars chosen to participate in the ceremony, ensuring all denominations were catered for.

The coffins were borne from the carriages by surviving members of the *Rohilla*'s crew, local lifeboatmen, coastguard officers and representatives of the St John Ambulance Brigade and National Reservists. Though there were plenty of willing volunteers ready to help carry the coffins, it was no easy task as every piece of space was taken; the cemetery had never seen so many people in its history.

The Rev. Chancellor Austen, rector of Whitby, read the chief portions, and was assisted by Rev. G.M. Storrar, minister of the Trinity Presbyterian church at Whitby. Also present

The first of the carriages carrying the coffins arrive at Whitby cemetery.

The first coffins are taken from the carriages by surviving members of the *Rohilla*'s crew, lifeboatmen and coastguard officers.

were the Revs W. Bancroft, C. Snushall, R.W. Oakley and Parry-Okeden of the Church of England; the Rev. J.W. Bowman of the West Cliff Congregational church; and the Rev. H.T. Hooper, superintendent minister of the Whitby Wesleyan Circuit.

Thousands stood around the rope enclosure throughout the funeral service. After the coffins had been lowered into the long communal grave, the hymn 'Rock of Ages' was sung, and mourners were asked to share hymn sheets which had been provided as nobody had predicted such a large turnout.

As the band played on, the singing was led by members of the Whitby Bohemian Male Voice Choir, under W.K. Waters. The Rev. C.H. Hart read from the 39th Psalm and, the remaining portion of the burial service being concluded, 'Jesus, Lover of my Soul' was impressively sung.

The Devon Cyclist Territorials, who were stationed at Whitby under Sergeant Crews, fired three volleys over the grave. Bugler W. Gale sounded 'Last Post', bringing the funeral ceremony, which was both very impressive and extremely moving, to a close.

Afterwards, the undertakers Messrs G. Agar, J. Pinder, B. Smith and W.G. Harrison laid many beautiful wreaths from the following known sources:

From the Sick Berth Staff, Chatham; Mrs Heselton; Mrs John Milburn and Olive; 'In memory of the brave men of the Rohilla, from Mr and Mrs Fred Falkingbridge and Freda'; Mrs Lionel Pern; M.A. Young; 'These are they which came out of tribulation' – a tribute to the valiant men of the Rohilla, from Mr and Mrs Louis Tracy, and 'Dick

The specially prepared long communal grave for the *Rohilla* victims.

Tracy'; 'To the gallant men of the Rohilla' – from F Company of the 7th Devons; Angel Hotel; Mrs Hart Stanley Houssellouse; Miss Lilly Richardson and her cousin Ella, Police Station, Kitching, Ruswarp; 'Till the day breaks', in memory, from Maria Kitching, 1 St Hilda's Terrace; the British India Steam Navigation Co. Ltd, London; 'In loving remembrance of Edward Rose, from his sorrowing wife and daughter.

From the Committee of the Soldiers and Sailors Families Association; 'With Sincere Regret, from the Executive Committee of the National Sailors and Firemens Union'; Captain W.M. Isdale, Captain John Millburn and Captain Robert W. Milburn; L. Massey and J. Bootts; Dr and Mrs C.F. Burton – 'To John Smith'; 'Out of the depth have I cried unto Thee, O Lord' – in memory of the Rohilla, from Hannah Elliott; 'With deepest sympathy, from a sailor's mother'; 'In loving memory of Sidney Morris, from all at home'; 'From the Naval Medical Officers of HM Hospital Ship No. 2, Rohilla, with deepest sympathy'; 'To the honour of all those who lost their lives through the shipwreck of HM Hospital Ship Rohilla'; 'With deepest sympathy', Charles King, from the Naval Officers at Whitby; James J. Sellers, from sympathising friends, relations and sons; 'Deepest sympathy, C. Jackson, head of Robin Hood's Bay Rocket Brigade'; 'With loving remembrance from father and brother'; 'With deepest sympathy from Whitby friends'; 'From Commanding Officer, officers, and crew of the SS Rohilla'.

The funeral of five further victims of the *Rohilla* disaster took place the following Saturday afternoon; the internment once more being held in Whitby cemetery, where attendance was

At each of the funerals the townsfolk came to pay their respects to the fallen.

once again impressive. Rev. C. Snushall, curate of St John's church, conducted the service, and the bodies were interred in a long trench prepared for their reception. Among the bearer parties was a company of members of the Whitby division of the St John Ambulance Brigade, who appeared for the first time in uniform, which was favourably commented upon. The hymn 'Rock of Ages' was sung at the graveside and it was pleasing to notice that several townspeople had sent wreaths and flowers to be placed on the graves of the five bodies, none of which, unfortunately, had been identified.

Further interments of the bodies washed ashore at Whitby and Sandsend took place on Monday, Tuesday and Wednesday afternoons. The coffins were laid in the same trench containing the other bodies at the Whitby cemetery, which had been lengthened, and Rev. W. Bancroft and G.E.C. Parry-Okeden officiated at the services.

A Naval Funeral

The remains of two men were laid to rest in Whitby cemetery on Tuesday afternoon, the service conducted with naval honours. The two coffins were draped with the Union Flag and conveyed to the cemetery by the same means as the previous funeral. Preceeding and following were detachments of the Devon Cyclist Territorials. The procession also included a group of coastguards, under the command of Chief Officer Davey.

The bearers were coastguards and members of the Seamen's Guild. As the coffins were laid in the long trench another chapter in the sad story of the wreck was closed. The numerous townspeople at the graveside gave evidence of the deep sorrow felt, though the attendance was small compared to the vast numbers that had assembled at the same place the previous week. The funeral was performed by Rev. C. Snushall, curate of St John's church. The firing party fired three volleys over the grave and bugler W. Gale of the local boy scouts sounded 'Last Post'. A number of wreaths were placed on the coffins by relatives and sympathisers. The funeral arrangements were carried out by Messrs R. Agar & Son and H. Pinder, undertaker. I. Haslop, reader at the Seamen's Institute, assisted.

One of the bodies was unidentified, but it was claimed shortly before the funeral procession left the drill shed, to be that of steward Henry Wilson Weatherstone. A lady and gentleman arrived in Whitby and stated that the body was that of their nephew, who had recently transferred from a cattle-ship to the *Rohilla*.

A short while after the funerals, Messrs George Vint & Brothers were chosen to supply a quantity of the very best West Yorkshire granite from which a large monument was designed and crafted by Thomas Hill & Sons. The finished monument stands 9ft 2in high, 4ft square at its base. The monument occupies a central position over the long trench. An ornamental anchor appropriately rests on the moulding of all four sides at the top of the structure. The long graves are kerbed round, concreted and covered with broken marble.

The cost of the monument, which amounted to £200, was met entirely by the British India Steam Navigation Co. as owners of the ill-fated vessel, who requested that the names

Although of a somewhat sombre nature, the funerals gave Whitby townsfolk the opportunity to express their shared grief.

The impressive monument to the *Rohilla* victims in 1914.

of those lost also be carved into the monument. On the front or south panel reads the following inscription:

THIS MONUMENT
WAS ERECTED BY THE BRITISH INDIA
STEAM NAVIGATION COMPANY LTD.,
OWNERS OF THE HOSPITAL SHIP SS
'ROHILLA,' TO THE MEMORY OF
31 OFFICERS AND MEN WHO WERE
DROWNED IN THE WRECK OF THAT
VESSEL OFF WHITBY. OCT 30TH, 1914.
THIRTY THREE BODIES RECOVERED
FROM THAT WRECK ARE BURIED HERE.
THE NAMES OF FOURTEEN OF THOSE
IDENTIFIED ARE AS FOLLOWS:

A. PAGE
S. MORRIS
D. NISBET
E. ROSE
J. SMITH
L. NICHOLSON
G. GLOVER
J. HARE
J.C. ROSS
H.W. WEATHERSTONE
D. PATTON
M. TARBET
W. BARRON
J. PATON

At the base of the front panel reads the inscription:

I SAW A NEW HEAVEN AND EARTH
AND THERE WAS NO MORE SEA.

On the east panel are the following names:

R. WATSON
H. ROBINS
F.W. MORGAN

H.T. MCBRIDE
A.E. SHUTE

A.H. BURNEY

G. BRAIN

C.H. MARDELL

C.W.M. MILNER

G.E. PARSONS

W.E. ANDERSON

M. BIRTWHISTLE [*sic* for
BIRTWISTLE]

W.J. DALY

A.C. ELSWORTH

F.W. HARRISON

H. HODKINSON

M.A. NEVILLE

A. PETTY

T. PETTY

J.T. PICKLES

J. SELLARS

B. SMITH

H.J. BARTER

F. DUNKLEY

T. HORSFIELD

W. HORSFIELD

The north panel is inscribed with the following names:

The towering centrepiece of the monument created to honour the victims of the *Rohilla* disaster.

J. BLAKELEY [*sic* for BLEAKLEY]

W. OGILVIE

D. TORRANCE

P. RAFFERTY

H. WATTS

J. KELLY

G. CAMERON

F. DAWSON

A. GILLIES

J. GRAHAM

J. HORSBURGH

J. KERR

G. KIRK

W. MUIR

A. MCCULLAM

D. MCDONALD

G. MCGLASHAM

J. MACKENZIE

N. MCCLOUD

D. MCNAUGHTAN [sic for MACNAUGHTAN]

J. MCNAUGHTAN [ditto]

J. QUEENAN

A. REID

R. D. SCOTT

A. STEWART

W. WHITE

On the west panel are the following names:

VERY REV CANNON GWYDIR

ROMAN CATHOLIC PRIEST

P.G. MOORE – 3RD OFFICER

JOHN BROWN – 3RD ENGINEER

WILLIAM PERRIN – ELECTRICIAN

M.J. DUFFY

H.J. CRIBB

A. AMBROSE

J.G. COWIE

J. MURPHY

J.J. BURNS

J. CAIN

J. CURRELL

W. DAWSON

S. HENDERSON

W. MCDONALD

A. MCMILLAN

J. NICHOL

W. REID

A. SCOTT

J. STEWART

J. TINNEY

G.B. GIBSON

W. GIBSON

J. REID

J.J. FOGGARTY [sic for FOGARTY]

Interments beyond Whitby

Some family members of the deceased chose to have their loved ones buried close to them in their hometowns, making their wishes known openly before and during the inquests. The coroner and jury respectfully appealed to the Admiralty to make this possible. The War Signal Office at Whitby received a telegram from the Admiralty shortly afterwards advising that they had 'no objections to deceased Sick Berth Reserve ratings of Rohilla being buried elsewhere subject to the usual maximum expenditure of five pounds in each case'.

Whitby Urban District Council, as it was then, wrote to the Admiralty seeking clarification after being approached by J.W. Thompson of Barnoldswick Town Hall, who knew the fifteen. There were three survivors with only one body recovered and eleven missing. The council wished to know, if any of the eleven washed ashore and were identified, whether they were empowered to have the bodies coffined and forwarded home free of charge to the families. It was the council's understanding that the Admiralty would provide coffins but had not arranged for the carriage fees. In this instance the response from the Admiralty was that 'it concurs generally, but that the £5 maximum expense includes costs of coffins'. Other widows and families of the deceased requested permission to have their loved ones interred in their hometowns and in each case they were subject to the same maximum expenditure. Although a resident of Barnoldswick, Henry Barter was born in Worcestershire. His wife, who left Barnoldswick during the weekend to get to Whitby, had his body conveyed to his native town, where it was interred amidst local outpourings of sorrow and sympathy. The body of Frederick William Morgan, the *Rohilla*'s master-at-arms was retained at the request of Mary Morgan, who wished his body to be interred in London. George Edgar Parsons was interred in a cemetery at Sedgeford, Kings Lynn, Norfolk. His headstone is surrounded with an outer kerb which on the southern (outer) side is inscribed 'George Edgar Parsons SBA, RN, who drowned in the wreck of HM Hospital Ship Rohilla Oct 30th 1914 aged 22 years'. The west kerb reads 'Sacred to the Memory of' and the east kerb reads 'Faithful Unto Death'. A marked grave in the nearby town of Cloughton bears testimony to a seaman (sadly un-named) who lost his life during the sinking of the *Rohilla*.

The *Suffolk Chronicle and Mercury* reported the loss of Chief Sick Bay Steward Albert Shute, whose body was washed ashore. Albert was clearly well known in Harwich and his funeral, on Saturday 7 November at the Devonport cemetery, was a semi-naval one. A number of naval men walked either side of the hearse, and a detachment of naval men followed the coaches. Albert was only 30 when he died, and left behind a widow and two children. As the cortège passed through the High Street, a company of the Bedfordshire Regiment came along from Kingsway at a brisk pace, singing their favourite song 'Tipperary'. On observing the solemn procession, the officer in charge promptly halted his men, brought them smartly to attention, their rifles at the present, and so they remained until the procession passed.

The remains of the Very Rev. Canon Gwydir, OSB, of St David's, Swansea, were laid to rest on Tuesday 3 November at Belmont Pro-Cathedral Priory, Hereford. A solemn dirge for the repose of the soul of the deceased canon had been chanted the previous evening, the Bishop of Newport presiding from the throne. On Tuesday his lordship sang the pontifical requiem mass and gave the Last Absolutions. Among those who travelled to Hereford to represent the congregation of St David's, Swansea, were the Rev. Mother and Mother Claude of St Winefride's Convent, Dr O'Sullivan, Mr and Mrs McInerney, and Mr and Mrs Kelleher. The service at the graveside was performed by the Abbot of Douai.

Canon Gwydir occupied a large place in the public life of Swansea and was highly esteemed, not only by his own flock, but generally by the townsfolk. He took a prominent part in the social and educational work of the town. He was a member of the old Swansea School Board and the Board of Managers of Swansea General Hospital. The people of Swansea expressed the strong desire that his body be interred in their midst, but, in deference to the wishes of his mother, the burial took place at Belmont.

Canon Gwydir is commemorated by a memorial plaque in St David's Priory, Swansea, in the Blessed Sacrament Chapel. Above the screen is the main memorial window, erected by his many friends. It shows the crucifixion with Our Lady and St John; St David and St

An informal photograph of Canon Gwydir with some of the nursing staff.

Benedict are on either side. In the lower panels are the figures of St Illtyd, St Robert, the Arms of the English Benedictine Congregation, Canon Gwydir and St Basil. The inscription reads, 'In token of gratitude and esteem as a memorial of his devoted life in the service of God, and his heroic death in the cause of his King and Country'.

Mr and Mrs George Brain were notified quite quickly that their eldest son George, a naval rating with the carpenters crew, had drowned. Aged just 25, the unfortunate young man had undertaken to swim to land from the *Rohilla*, and his body was washed ashore and taken to the lifeboat station, which was being used as a temporary mortuary. George was highly respected by all on board; the master-at-arms (Mr Knight), one of the survivors, praised his excellent character. The Mayor of Tamworth (F.G. Allton) kindly gave George's father an introductory letter to take to Whitby. Upon arrival, Mr Brain was directed to the lifeboat station where he had little difficulty identifying the body and arranging its subsequent removal to Glascote Heath for burial. George Brain served his apprenticeship at Messrs Musson and Sons, of Glascote, and joined the Navy as a ship's carpenter four years before the *Rohilla*'s loss. After being at Chatham Naval Barracks he was appointed to HMS

The window from St David's Priory.
(Copyright Martin Crampin)

George Brain in the middle of the front row, his cap about to fall off. (Courtesy John Stephenson)

Antrim, and afterwards to HMS *Shannon*. At the outbreak of the war he was selected for the crew of the unfortunate *Rohilla*.

The funeral took place with military honours at the Bolehall and Glascote cemetery. The coffin was draped in a Union Flag and placed on the hearse. The cortège was headed by a firing party of the Argyll and Sutherland Highlanders under the command of Sgt. Farrington, followed by a band of pipers of the same regiment. On the way to the church the pipers played the 'Flowers of the Forest', the music and the solemn march of the men were most impressive. A private family funeral service was held at St George Church Glascote, on Sunday evening, the Rev. R.W. Morbey officiating; special hymns were sung, and a moving eulogy and sermon given. At the end of the service the organist (H. Emery) played the 'Dead March' from 'Saul'. The mourners moved outside to the cemetery where it was estimated that 2,000 persons were present. At the close of the service the firing party fired three volleys over the grave and a stalwart Highlander played a few bars of 'Lochaber no more' between the volleys. Afterwards, the bugler sounded 'Last Post'. There were many beautiful floral tributes with tokens from family and relatives. Friends at Glascote Heath sent a beautiful wreath in the shape of a life buoy of white flowers with violets to represent the rope.

The crewmembers from ships belonging to the British India Steam Navigation Co. from both world wars have a very special memorial located amongst the National Memorial Arboretum in Staffordshire. The large tablet is an exquisite bronze casting emblazoned with lions, the British India Britannia & Lion badge, the house flag and enamelled panels

The last resting place of George Brain, his headstone simple yet appealing. (Courtesy John Stephenson)

with anchor and wave motifs. It names 230 people in all, 103 of the First World War and 127 of the Second, including two women who were stewardesses on the *Domala*.

The three centre panels are headed with the words 'TO MARK THE SERVICE OF THE MEMBERS, STAFF AND CREWS OF THE B.I. COMPANY IN THE COMMON CAUSE 1914–1918 THESE GAVE THEIR LIVES.' Of the 103 names listed in the centre panels, 59 of them are attributed to the loss of the Rohilla. The two outer panels cover the 1939–1945 conflict and the 127 names seem to almost wrap around the centre panels.

The whereabouts of the memorial during the past few decades and how it came to re-appear at the memorial site are a mystery. It is thought the tablet was originally in the BISNC offices at 122 Leadenhall Street, London and later at the BISNC's office at 1 Aldgate, London.

The National Memorial Arboretum is a special place honouring those who have served, and continue to serve, our nation in many different ways. The Armed Forces Memorial is a stunning piece of architecture comprising a 43m diameter stone structure with two curved walls and two straight walls with over 16,000 names of men and women of our Armed and Merchant Services who gave the ultimate sacrifice.

Covering 150 acres, with more than 200 dedicated memorials on the site the Arboretum is a living tribute, a place of life. Over 50,000 trees line the grounds, the planting of which started in 1997.

The British India Company Memorial Tablet.

For some it's a wonderful place to stroll and enjoy the trees; for others it's a peaceful and beautiful place to remember loved ones, to acknowledge personal sacrifices. It is not solely for honouring military loss as there is a large area devoted to police who have fallen while on duty, as well as other areas devoted to the Fire and Rescue and Ambulance services. National charities representing those who have died in particular circumstances, including children, are also to be found in the Arboretum grounds.

Many of the men like those from Barnoldswick, once mobilised automatically became members of the Royal Navy. Though the *Rohilla* was so close to the shore a number of government bodies classed those who succumbed as having been lost at sea.

After the First World War, it was agreed that an appropriate commemoration had to be found for those members of the Royal Navy who had no known grave, the majority of deaths having occurred at sea where no permanent memorial could be provided. An Admiralty committee recommended that the three naval ports of Chatham, Plymouth and Portsmouth should each have an identical memorial of unmistakable naval form, an obelisk, which would serve as a leading mark for shipping.

The names of the naval ratings on the *Rohilla*, including the twelve Barnoldswick men who were lost, were added to the Chatham Naval Memorial. The three memorials were

The National Memorial Arboretum.

Chatham Naval Memorial. (Copyright Danny Robinson)

extended after the Second World War to provide the additional space required for the names of those lost in that war. The Chatham memorial commemorates 8,515 sailors of the First World War and 10,098 of the Second World War.

6

THE INQUEST PROCEDURES

As the bodies washed ashore, it became clear that numerous inquests would be required. It is a sad fact that only around half of those lost would ever be recovered. As the transcripts of the inquests are detailed and lengthy, only portions have been reproduced below. Some information mentioned previously is duplicated, because to leave it out would alter the context of the inquest statements. A number of statements have since been proven to be inaccurate, although this is to be expected given the traumatic nature of the tragedy and the swiftness of the inquests.

On Saturday afternoon at the courthouse on Spring Hill, coroner George Buchanan opened the inquest on ten of the bodies recovered. The jury comprised the harbour master, four sea captains, the secretary of the Seaman's Guild, Councillor E.L. Turner, Councillor J. Ditchburn, captains C. Vasey, T. Kirby, H. Corney, C.J. Smith, H. Heselton (harbour master), Messrs G.T. Crowther, T. Taylor (local secretary of the Imperial Merchant Service Guild), A.L. Hume, W. Eglon, H. Falkingbridge, W. James W. Readman, and E. Humphrey. Councillor E.L. Turner was elected foreman of the jury; Lt Sparkes represented the Admiralty; and the Lifeboat Institution was represented by Lt Basil Hood, Inspector.

The ten unfortunate men identified on Saturday were:

Albert Edward Shute – Sick Berth Steward
John Hare – Hospital Cook
John Reid – Hospital Cook
Canon Basil Gwydir – Roman Catholic Priest
George Gover – Storekeeper
George Brain – Carpenter
James Sellars – Sick Berth Reserve
John Fogarty – Steward
George Parsons – Sick Berth Reserve
Frederick William Morgan – Master-at-arms

Before the jury had viewed the bodies, which were at the lifeboat house, the coroner told them:

As regards this appalling disaster, what I propose to do today is take evidence of identification only, and then adjourn till Monday, when the real inquiry will begin.

I hope to be able to satisfy you as to the identity of the ten poor men whose bodies you will see. Some other bodies have been recovered, but I will not open on them today, and will have you sworn with regard to them on Monday.

Proceeding, the coroner asked the jury what time would be most suitable to assemble on Monday, and suggested seven o'clock. This met with general approval and before the jury left to view the bodies, the coroner told them they would find that each was numbered, the numbers corresponding with the list of names that had been supplied to him. Upon returning to the courthouse, evidence of identification was taken. Reid and Fogarty, both of whom belonged to Glasgow, were identified by George Smith, 2nd steward on the ill-fated *Rohilla*, and the remaining eight by John Thomas Knight, master-at-arms.

The first witness was John Thomas Knight, who, in reply to the coroner, said he was a pensioned master-at-arms in the Royal Navy, and had been called up for service during the war.

The coroner: Have you been on-board this unhappy vessel since she left the Firth of
    Forth?
JTK: Yes, sir.
Coroner: You were on duty?
JTK: Yes, sir.
Coroner: When did you leave the Firth?
JTK: About 4 o'clock on Thursday afternoon.
Coroner: I won't enquire of you what happened as regarded the vessel except as to the
    end of her cruise. About what time was it when you struck the rock here?
JTK: About 4 o'clock on the morning of Friday.
Coroner: Then I suppose she was immovable fixed on the rocks?
JTK: She was bumping about on the rocks in the sea.
Coroner: And ultimately became a wreck?
JTK: Yes, sir.
Coroner: How did you escape?
JTK: When she bumped the rocks, sir, I ran out of my cabin, and up the saloon ladder,
    and knocked out of it by a big sea, onto the starboard side.
Coroner: You were knocked over?
JTK: Yes, sir.
Coroner: Forced overboard?
JTK: I was knocked off the top of the saloon staircase onto the promenade deck. I was
    not washed off the ship.
Coroner: Then how did you come to leave the vessel?
JTK: I left in the lifeboat about half-past ten on Friday morning.
Coroner: You were brought ashore by the Whitby lifeboat?
JTK: Yes, sir.

Coroner: Was that the first time the lifeboat went out, or the second?

JTK: The first, sir.

Coroner: The women came in that one?

JTK: Yes, sir; five.

Coroner: Have you seen the bodies of these poor men now lying in the Lifeboat House?

JTK: Yes, sir; ten bodies.

Coroner: You have seen the numbers on them, and the names?

JTK: Yes, sir.

Coroner: Do you think you can speak really for all of them except the numbers 3 and 8 [Reid and Fogarty]?

JTK: Yes, sir.

Asked their ages, John Thomas Knight replied, 'Shute would be about thirty-five, Hare about sixty, Canon Gwydir about forty-five', and he added that the canon had only joined the ship about a fortnight previously; 'Gover would be about thirty-six, Brain about twenty-two, Sellars nineteen, Parson twenty-one, and Morgan forty-eight'. He knew the address of one: Morgan, who lived at 222 East India Dock Road, London.

Coroner: Are there any of these who have been brought ashore later that you can identify?

JTK: Yes, sir.

The coroner's inquiry was then adjourned and resumed on Monday morning, the additional list of dead including:

Sidney Morris – Sick Berth Steward
Edward Rose – Carpenter
Colin Gibson – Steward
Henry Barter – Sick Berth Attendant
William Perrin – Electrical Engineer
James Stewart – Fireman
Phillip William Moore – 3rd Officer
Laurence Nicholson – Quartermaster
John Brown – 3rd Engineer
Andrew Mccullum – Steward
John Murphy – Greaser
David Nisbett – Able Seaman
John Smith – Fireman
John Fogarty – Steward

Once again the first witness was John Thomas Knight, who gave evidence of identification for two of the fifteen additional bodies placed in the old drill shed, which had been numbered from 11 to 25. They included No. 11, Sidney Morris, and No. 15, Alfred Page. Morris was about 25 and Page about 30. Knight did not know where they lived – the Admiralty had all the addresses. He did not see them washed off the boat.

William Dick, a greaser on board the *Rohilla*, identified James Stewart, a fireman of Leith, aged 60; and Murphy, a greaser from Dundee, aged 40. George Smith also identified Nos 12, 16, 18, 19, 20 and 21: Rose lived at Netley, Southampton, and was about 40; Perrin lived at Southampton and was about 36; R.C. Moore was about 21, Smith did not know where he lived; L. Nicholson was about 50, and lived somewhere in the north of Scotland; Brown lived at Oakcroft, Netley Abbey, Southampton, and was about 31; McCullum lived at Glasgow, and was about 33. Since Saturday, John Fogarty's brother had identified him, not as No. 8 (as identified by a witness on Saturday). He believed No. 8 was Archibald Reid a ship's steward from Glasgow, who he believed to be about 30. Peter Campbell Cairns, secretary of the Glasgow branch of the Cooks and Stewards Union, identified John Fogarty too, as well as Colin Gibson, both of Glasgow. Gibson was about 40, and had lived at Primrose Street; Fogarty was about 32. John W. Thompson, superintendent of the Barnoldswick Ambulance Division, identified Henry James Barter, of 41 Skipton Road, Barnoldswick, about 28 years old.

Having obtained permission to address a few words to the coroner and jury, John Thompson said:

> We still have eleven of our members unaccounted for, and out of that number eight or nine were married and had families, and it was their wish to endeavour to get the bodies home when they have been recovered. I have made some enquiries, and I find that the Admiralty are quite prepared to provide coffins, but nothing further, and I think that they should go a little further and see that the bodies get to the towns they belong to. I ask you to use your influence in that direction.

The coroner said, 'When the time comes, it shall be considered; more than that we cannot say at present.'

Sergeant Hudson said that on Sunday seaman Thomas Murray, one of the survivors, had identified Nisbett. Murray was too ill to attend. The witness thought the deceased was about 50. The coroner stated that the captain and first officer were too unwell to attend, and asked the jury if, after adjourning until two o'clock, they should proceed with the remaining witnesses, or adjourn the enquiry. It was decided to proceed at two o'clock.

Upon resumption of the enquiry, Dr Littler-Jones said he was a surgeon in the Royal Naval Volunteer Reserve and a survivor of the *Rohilla*. He had been in his berth when the vessel struck. It had been heavy weather since leaving the Firth of Forth. He went to his cabin about 7.45 p.m., at dinnertime, and was on deck again about 10.30 p.m. The weather had become worse, and the ship was rolling a great deal. He did not see any of the officers. All was proceeding on board as usual. He had been on board since 4 August. Captain Neilson had been master all the time, and good discipline had been maintained. Speaking as a layman, he thought the master had managed his ship in a seamanlike way. He never slept during the night, on account of the weather. A few minutes before four o'clock on Friday morning, there was a sudden crash.

He turned on the light, which almost immediately went out, and he knew something was wrong. He put his coat and trousers on, and went on deck. It was impossible in the darkness to see where the ship was, but she was fixed. He did not see the captain then, but heard him giving directions, perfectly calmly, and they were being carried out. Everything was being done quietly and in an orderly fashion; perfect discipline and order were maintained on the ship during the time he was aboard. The captain seemed concerned about the men on the poop, and gave orders that they were all to come forward along with anyone else aft. Although the men could not pass the after part, the orders were certainly given to the men on the poop to get forward, as the seas were breaking over the well deck. The witness had taken part in the boat drill at two o'clock on the afternoon they left Queensferry, when every man was assigned to his station, and was inspected by the first officer and the fleet surgeon. The lifeboat came out to them some hours after daylight. He knew Whitby was a rocky beach. The four nursing sisters and stewardess, all the women on board, were lowered into the Whitby lifeboat by order of the captain. The captain's orders were 'women first, medical officers and sick berth staff, crew, officers, and lastly himself'.

The lifeboat reached the shore after drifting towards Whitby, and the survivors were landed. The lifeboat was then pulled along the beach towards Saltwick Nab, before starting on its second voyage to the wreck. The sea was very heavy, and the wind was blowing very hard. The spray from the waves rose as high as the top of the *Rohilla*'s funnel. It did not take long for the lifeboatmen to reach the vessel. They were helped a bit by the tide, that was Littler-Jones' impression, or by an eddy or the set of the tide. One of the medical officers who was ill was lowered into the lifeboat when it reached the ship a second time, Littler-Jones was ordered to take a place. He was the last to be lowered, and there were perhaps seventeen or eighteen survivors taken off. Littler-Jones helped to carry the sick medical officer ashore.

He could not tell whether the tide had risen. The lifeboat behaved well. The sea was very rough and all was broken water with long, heavy breakers coming in. The sea was running high. The lifeboat crew did their duty, and seemed to know what they were about. Littler-Jones got out into about 4ft of water when the lifeboat reached land. He asked people on the beach to help drag the lifeboat towards the Nab again and said he would look after the people who had come ashore. He was strong enough to do his bit in looking after the survivors. Eventually he reached Whitby, with Mr Tindale helping him along, taking him to his home.

Before the Whitby lifeboat reached the *Rohilla*, one of the steamer's lifeboats, No. 1 boat, the one to which the Littler-Jones was assigned, had been launched by the captain's orders, but Littler-Jones did not go in her. The lifeboat was in perfect working order and was complete in every detail with food, water, condensed milk, etc. Her crew comprised six of the able seamen, the 2nd officer, Gwynn, and the boatswain's mate; eight altogether. She was successfully launched for the purpose of taking a line to the shore. Despite the crew's efforts, the boat drifted towards Whitby, and a heavy sea turned her round with her stern to the shore, and the line parted about that time, before the boat reached the beach. The ship's boat landed about the same place as the Whitby lifeboat. As far as he could tell, the ship's lifeboat landed her crew in safety. He reckoned that dawn was about 6.30 a.m. as they could see the cliffs a little before that, and he thought the ship's boat landed about 7.30 a.m.

One of the men on the poop got ashore. There was an abundance of lifebelts, and a number of ordinary and collapsible lifeboats. He believed there were 2,500 lifebelts on-board, all in order. There was no difficulty in everybody getting a lifebelt, and he thought everyone knew where they were. When men were pulled onto the deck they were supplied with lifebelts if they had not already obtained one. Littler-Jones and others were on the boat-deck. Before he left the vessel, she had broken in two across the well-deck, and the after-part was swinging, so that the poop and the well-deck were quite separate. It was supposed that the engine shaft held them together. All the ship's boats had been swept away before Littler-Jones left, or were completely disabled, and the sea was breaking over the main deck, though he did not think it was breaking over the chartroom.

Those who were forward were able to take shelter in the officers' cabins on the boat-deck. Was any food available? There was none, he said. 'I saw none and the officers' cabins don't carry food, and there was only a small quantity of drinking-water.' He knew Shute. He saw some go overboard but he never saw anyone lost. He saw Canon Gwydir picked up. Some of the dead whose bodies had been picked up were on the poop. Page looked exceedingly ill. He could not, by direct evidence, say how any of the crew came to their death. Before completing his evidence, Littler-Jones said he desired to thank the people of Whitby for all they had done, high and low, rich and poor, on behalf of himself and those too ill to speak for themselves. He added that the reason the ship's lifeboat did not return to the ship was because some or all of the oars were broken.

The coroner thanked Dr Littler-Jones for his evidence and for his kind words about the people of Whitby. Littler-Jones added that he had heard one of the men say that if ever he were wrecked again, he hoped it would be at Whitby. The coroner replied, 'We hope that he will not be wrecked any more.'

Captain John Milburn, ship owner, Lloyd's agent at Whitby, and a member of the local committee of the Lifeboat Institution, said the local secretary was ill. There were three lifeboats under the Whitby Committee: two at Whitby and one at Upgang, a mile away. He first heard of the wreck at seven o'clock on Friday morning. He went down to the harbour and the lifeboat crew were there under Coxswain Langlands. He saw the sea, that it was no use launching the lifeboat, so it was taken underneath the Spa Ladder. He saw the wreck. The sea was very heavy, and the wind very strong from the east, with heavy rain squalls. He saw the lifeboat launched. The crew had great difficulty getting off, owing to the heavy sea and strong northerly current. The tide was about half-flood. The lifeboat reached the vessel, and he saw the women taken off, and the lifeboat returned. The lifeboat drifted about half a mile before she was beached. The boat was hauled along the beach and launched again, near where she was launched before. The same crew went out, and they were fit for work. She was launched successfully and, despite rougher seas, reached the vessel again, which had settled down and started to break up. The sea was getting heavier under the lee of the vessel, and it was more difficult to reach her. However, it was done, and the lifeboat reached the shore again, though he could not say whether it was damaged. She was hauled up nearer the cliff as the tide was rising rapidly. The coxswain said it was 'not prudent' to go off again owing to the state of the wind, sea and tide, and Milburn agreed with him.

That would be about 10.30 a.m., and Milburn returned to Whitby with the coxswain where they consulted about launching the big boat. They agreed that the conditions meant that it would be quite impossible to reach the *Rohilla*, as the sea was too rough and the wind too high. Milburn then asked about the Upgang boat, which he thought might be used later in lieu of the lifeboat they had left below the cliff, which they knew would be stove in. They went at once for the Upgang boat, which was brought by road to Saltwick and launched down the steep cliff to the south of the Nab. The boat could not be used then owing to the high seas, and she could not get round the Nab. When the tide was suitable it was dark and launching was out of the question. He wired for a motorboat to South Gare and one started, but had to put back to Redcar, damaged by the storm. On Saturday morning, Milburn went to Saltwick and had a look at the situation. The crew launched the lifeboat between 7 a.m. and 8 a.m., when it was possible to drag her round the Nab, but was unable to reach the wreck, and drifted away towards Whitby. In shallow water, the boat made headway to the wreck but, when she reached heavy seas, she was driven back by the strong ebb tide. Milburn then telephoned Redcar, and was informed that a motor lifeboat had left for Whitby from Tynemouth at 4.30 p.m. The motor lifeboat arrived at about one o'clock on Sunday morning and went to the wreck, and the result was entirely successful. The crew of the motor boat took with them Richard Eglon, 2nd coxswain of the Whitby No. 1 lifeboat. The wind had moderated, and the sea a little too.

On account of the strong tide, he did not think it would be possible to get the men off the wreck without a motor lifeboat. The Runswick men had offered their services and a tug was arranged to tow the Runswick lifeboat to the wreck. A tug stood by the wreck all Friday night and on Saturday, until it was clear she could not do any good. Milburn also arranged for a tug to tow the Whitby lifeboat, but she failed to reach the wreck. All this time, or during most of it, until the last survivors were rescued, rockets were fired to endeavour to establish communications with the wreck, but for one reason or another they all failed. Plenty of lines were successfully fired over the wreck, but they landed in places where those on the wreck could not get hold of them. A searchlight was sent which was of great service on Saturday night. Milburn believed the survivors on the wreck were signalled that the motorboat was on the way. Replying to Lt Hall, he said he did not think the Whitby lifeboat could have carried more survivors than she did. The foreman said it was most fortunate that they had such a capable man as Captain Milburn to take charge of affairs, and he had done everything that could be done. Replying to the foreman, Captain Milburn said that if a motor boat had been stationed at Whitby he thought that she could have reached the wreck using oil on the water and taken the survivors on Friday. However, the coast was very dangerous, and there were no tugs at Whitby.

Thomas Langlands, coxswain of No. 1 Whitby lifeboat, said he first heard of the wreck at about 4.45 a.m. on Friday. The crew assembled, but the wind and sea were tremendously strong, and it would have been impossible to use the bigger lifeboat as she would have been blown to leeward and onto Whitby beach. The smaller lifeboat was later hauled under the Spa Ladder and along the Scar to Saltwick. 'That would not be an easy job,' said the coroner. 'It was a tussle,' was the reply. When they got to Saltwick, the wreck had broken in two. A very heavy sea was running, and it was difficult to reach the wreck, but they managed. When the lifeboat got alongside, tons of water poured over the wreck and nearly washed them out of the lifeboat. Those on the wreck lowered them a small line, and they then gave them their cable. There were fourteen in the lifeboat crew, and they took off seventeen, the women first. They drifted on the passage back. After landing those who were saved, they hauled the lifeboat to windward and launched her again, but it was harder reaching the ship the second time. The tide had risen considerably and the current and sea were stronger and heavier. They reached the wreck after much effort, and took off eighteen. They had no difficulty in taking off the crew, the problem was avoiding wreckage. They landed near the previous landing place, and took the boat to windward again, but owing to the lack of helpers, they could not have launched again if they wanted to, the launchers having retreated from the rising tide. It would have been very unsafe to launch again then; indeed, Langlands thought it was impossible. There was no landing place. If they had made a third journey they would have had to land on the stones and climb up the cliff ladder. The Upgang lifeboat was dragged by road to Saltwick and launched down the cliff. The Whitby lifeboat was wrecked on the rocks at the foot of the cliff. It was not possible to launch the Upgang lifeboat as there was no landing place, and although it was launched later, on Saturday morning, it did not reach the wreck. Langlands' crew and launchers had done all they could. It would have been quite different if they had had a motor lifeboat, as it would have needed only two men: one to steer and one to manage the engines.

Lt W. Sparks, RN, thanked Coxswain Langlands on behalf of the Admiralty and the survivors for all he and his crew had done, the trouble they had taken, and the risk they had run. Coxswain Langlands returned his thanks and, replying to Lt Basil Hall, Inspector of Lifeboats, said he had been a lifeboatman for nearly forty years and had never experienced a harder job. For twenty-five years he had served with the Upgang boat, and was transferred to Whitby as a coxswain on the retirement of the late Henry Freeman.

Richard Eglon, 2nd coxswain of the Whitby lifeboat, said it was not fit to launch a third time. If they had rescued anyone, they would have had to escape up the cliff ladder. He piloted the motor lifeboat on Saturday morning. The men went to his house at 1.30 a.m.

He went with them at about half-past six, as soon as it was light. There was a rough sea, and a 'canny bit' of wind, but not as bad as the day before. The lifeboat behaved very well and was kept to leeward of the wreck, with her head close up to it. A lot of oil, 4 gallons, was put overboard and it did good for a time. They put her nose to the bridge of the ship and took off the men. It was possible to keep the lifeboat there by going half-speed ahead. There was no rope fast. The captain was the last man to leave the ship. A very heavy sea struck the lifeboat as she ran under the stern of the vessel, and he thought she would never recover, but she righted herself and landed all fifty survivors. If a motor lifeboat had been at Whitby, no one would have drowned.

Charles Sutherland Davy, chief officer of the coastguard station at Whitby, and for the time being in charge of the rocket apparatus provided by the Board of Trade, said he first attempted to use the rocket. He was called by the watchman at 4.15 a.m., and was told the ship had stranded. Eglon told him to fire one to assemble the brigade and two to warn the lifeboat authorities. He also sent a message to the lifeboat coxswain, and went to prepare the apparatus. Once sufficient men were assembled, they went to the wreck across the fields. It was very dark and they arrived abreast of the Nab on the clifftop at about 4.45 a.m. They had no horses to drag the wagon across the fields. They could only see the wreck by the signals. Eglon fired distress signals before those from the ship. His first rocket was fired between 5 a.m. and 5.30 a.m. Three rockets with good direction all fell short. He saw he was doing no good, and daylight was approaching, so he thought it best to fire from the Nab end. He took the whip and line-box down the cliff to Saltwick Nab and fired twelve rockets from there. Only the dry lines got across the wreck. Eglon was fifty hours on the job without relief. The first night and part of the next day he was on the Nab. He did all that he could. He used all his own rockets and those from Robin Hood's Bay, Staithes and other stations. The first day he wired for two dozen, and the next day for sixty more.

Coroner: It has been said the rockets were old. Is that so?

Witness: No; they were in proper order. It was the wind, shale, wet, etc. The wreck was four hundred or five hundred yards off. Four or five rockets fell on the ship, but the crew could not reach them. A man on the wreck reached one on Friday afternoon but could not use it. Nothing more could be done with the rocket apparatus.

Foreman: Could you have fired from the beach instead of the Nab at 6.30 a.m. on Friday morning?

Witness: No; you could not work there owing to the wet.

Albert James Jefferies, coastguard on duty at the time of the disaster, said he sighted the ship at 3.40 a.m. bearing north-north-west. She was then outside the rock. Because of the war, the bell on the buoy was muffled and the lights were not used. It was a very bad night, the sea running heavily, the wind blowing between force seven and nine. The vessel's course was not what it should have been and she was steering for the shore.

He used the Morse lamp and tried to warn her and, when he thought she could hear, used the foghorn. There was no reply from the boat, which struck rocks near Saltwick Nab between 4.10 a.m. and 4.15 a.m. Before the vessel struck, he sent a messenger to the chief petty officer and, once she had, he went and informed the chief officer, who told him to fire the rocket signal and warn the Whitby lifeboat. He could not see any light in Whitby that night. There was no light in his station. He saw the masthead light of the *Rohilla* first, and afterwards the starboard light. He thought his flash signals could be seen aboard but he would not say they could hear the foghorn. The Rocket Brigade men assembled quickly.

Jefferies informed his officer, but the order was not given to fire explosive signals prior to the vessel striking. As she was a hospital ship, she would have proper signal service, and relied on the Morse signal. The coroner said that they could not say anything definite about the captain (who was ill), but the first officer would, it was thought, be able to attend on Wednesday or Thursday. It was decided to adjourn the enquiry until Thursday morning, at eleven o'clock.

On Wednesday morning, the jury were again called together at the courthouse to hear evidence of identification relating to the body of James McKenzie, bedroom steward, which had been washed up and recovered on the beach on Monday. Evidence was given by George Smith, 2nd steward on the *Rohilla*, who said the deceased was about 43 years of age, and had lived in Glasgow. He also said the man who was taken to Dr Burton's house on Saturday, and who died the same day, was John Smith, a fireman from Leith. He did not see him come ashore, but he believed he had tried to swim, and reached the shore alive, but died afterwards from exhaustion. With regard to other men, he said he believed Shute died amidships, not on the poop of the vessel, from shock. The coroner told Smith that he had been very helpful.

Sergeant Richardson said he was one of the officers in charge of the arrangements made for the reception of the bodies when they were brought ashore. John Smith came ashore alive on Saturday, but another eleven were dead when they reached the shore. Richardson helped to get Smith ashore, noting that he was completely exhausted. Smith was taken to Dr Burton's, and died on Saturday. On Tuesday night, Sergeant Richardson was present when two brothers of John Fogarty (deceased) viewed the bodies, at one time, it was believed that John Smith (No. 25) was Fogarty, but the younger brother at once identified No. 8 as his brother. All the survivors on board the ship were rescued on Sunday morning. The unidentified body now numbered 25 came ashore opposite the wreck. It was that of a man about 30 to 35 years of age, dark, clean shaven, dark-brown hair, about 5ft 9in, thin build, long dark eyelashes, blue eyes, set of top false teeth, 36in chest. On Monday afternoon Richardson said that body No. 13, supposed to be that of Colin Gibson, was seen by Gibson's brothers, who could not identify him. No. 13 was now unidentified. It was the body of a man aged about 38, 5ft 5in, stout, full face, light brown hair, slight moustache, broad forehead, false teeth in the upper jaw. The foreman expressed the hope that the publication of the above particulars would lead to identifications.

At the resumption of the inquiry on Thursday, Captain Neilson, master of the *Rohilla*, told his story and a decidedly interesting one it was. W. Seaton Gray, Whitby, was present on behalf of the Admiralty, along with E.D. McKinnon, KC (instructed by Messrs Walton and London), the owners, and Captain Keighley-Peach the coastguard. Mr Gray said that the Admiralty felt the deepest sympathy for the families of those who had lost their lives, and expressed the great admiration for the heroic rescue work. He tendered the Admiralty's thanks to all who had taken part in the greatest rescue work in the annals of Whitby.

Mr MacKinnon said the owners desired him to express their profound sorrow at the calamity and their great grief for the dependents of those who were lost. It would be their duty, and a pleasing one, to see that everyone was provided for. It was an occasion which brought out the finest aspects of their common humanity and his clients desired him to express their sincere admiration and gratitude for all that had been done after the wreck. Mr Gray was one of those to whom they owed a debt of gratitude, and the most warm-hearted hospitality was shown the survivors in the town. There were all sorts of people to whom they owed their thanks and Captain Milburn, Lloyd's agent, and his brother had rendered invaluable assistance. He was told that Lord Inchcliffe, the chairman of the company had said that he felt sure he could say of all, not only the captain, but the crew and the brave and warm-hearted people of Whitby, that they had 'played the game' in accordance with the finest traditions of the British Navy and British people. (This was received with calls of 'Hear, hear'.)

Captain Neilson said the ship was engaged by the Admiralty as a hospital ship, and the number on board was 229 all told on 29 October, when they left the Firth of Forth. They had fine weather for the time of year, and the ship was staunch and sound, and well fitted. They were bound for Belgium to receive the wounded. Off St Abb's Head the weather became worse, and the sea rose during the night. The ship rolled very badly. Neilson set the ship's course. They passed the Longstones at a distance of 7 miles, as he judged from his dead reckoning. They altered the course at 10.05 p.m. to keep clear of minefields. The course was again altered at 1.50 a.m., to S 19 E., and he believed that this would bring him to 7 miles off Whitby and 4 miles off Flamborough Head. This course was kept until the disaster. He did not see any shore lights or any indication of land after they set the last course.

They passed ships going both ways, which was an indication that they were on the right course. Neilson was on deck the whole of that time, and saw that the course was kept. The chief officer, Mr Bond, was on duty from midnight to 4 a.m., when he was relieved by Mr Winstanley, senior second officer, and Mr Graham, 4th officer, assisted. At 3.40 a.m. on Friday (the time the coastguards were stated to have first seen the vessel), he believed the ship was 7 miles east-north-east of Whitby. Allowances had been made, he thought, for the effect of the wind and sea. Neilson ordered his chief officer to take a cast of the lead at 3.45 a.m. He took soundings at midnight, which showed that the vessel was keeping the course. Soundings were not taken again until about 4 a.m., for reasons which would be given later. The result reported to him was 24 fathoms, which indicated that they were nearer the shore than he expected. At that time, Neilson and the chief officer were talking on the bridge, and the chief officer said that the after boats were adrift owing to the rolling of the ship. Neilson said: 'Alright Bond, I propose turning her off the land as the weather is getting worse.' Before the result of the soundings was brought to him, the ship struck, and witness said, 'Mine, by God'. He ordered the engines full speed astern, and then full speed ahead, giving the helmsman the order hard a port. The helm was put so, and the engines went full speed ahead to put the ship into land as it was, he knew, wounded fatally.

The ship went on, as far as he could judge, for a good seven or eight minutes, and finally took to the beach with a grating sound, when he stopped her and waited for daylight to see where they were. About 3.25 a.m. they passed a ship on their starboard beam, and the chief officer saw her lights. After 4 a.m., the second officer came on the bridge and reported to Neilson, 'Someone Morseing, Sir,' and Neilson asked him to find out who it was – he thought it was a ship. They had seen no shore lights; indeed, Neilson did not know he was near the shore, and thought it was a ship's signal. He knew this coast fairly well and quite sufficient for his purpose. He knew where the High Lights were, and he knew there were no lights because of the war. If the High Lights had been burning, he would have known where he was at once, long before the disaster. If the ordinary street lamps had been burning in Whitby he would have seen the town, he thought. In any case, he thought he was at least 6 miles off shore. He knew the Skinningrove furnaces, but did not see them. It was a very dirty night, and he accounted this for the absence of lights; that or they had been reduced by design. When the ship struck, he thus thought at first that they had struck a mine. He was aware there were minefields, and the courses he set were governed by their positions. The last vessel he passed was going north at about 3.30 a.m. He still felt perfectly certain that he struck a mine outside the rock – he certainly struck something, and the sound suggested a mine. After the shock, he knew the vessel was badly damaged. However, she answered her helm fairly well before grounding.

The only choice was to run for the shore. Neilson knew that in doing so he would strike the rock and he began to give orders to save the lives of those aboard. He knew Whitby was under his lee, but that was all. It would have been suicide to put his ship off to sea and all hands would have drowned. The first shock lifted the ship up, throwing men off their feet. She was struck abaft the midship section. Her draft of water was about 24ft at the stern, and there was very little difference fore and aft. The second shock, when she took the beach was entirely different from the first and there was a distinct grating noise, lasting longer. At the time when they stranded the vessel was going 8 to 9 knots; while they started from the Firth of Forth at 12.5 knots. They would travel about a mile after the first shock in deep water but not where they expected. With a chart explained to the jury, the captain said he had been justified in assuming, after his soundings, that he had not struck a rock at the first shock, and that he was in plenty of water. If the coastguard statement was correct as to his position when he (the coastguard) saw the ship, his vessel had struck in Whitby Harbour. McKinnon said:

At 3.40 a.m., his position was eleven miles NE of Whitby, the wind gradually hauled round to ESE after he set the last course ... When the vessel struck the rock, it would be about 4.10 a.m., and [the captain] ordered "All hands on deck", and told an officer to bring the five ladies up; four nursing sisters and a stewardess. Boat crews were ordered to fall in under officers and to make ready for lowering, but on no account to lower without orders from him. The orders were obeyed, and they stood by under those conditions until daylight. The vessel was being breached fore and aft by heavy seas.

He was afraid she would soon show signs of breaking up. When daylight came, he realised the dangerous position his ship was now lying in, and fully expected her to break up. Neilson then ordered all the men clinging to the after section of the ship to go forward to amidships, as he knew this was comparatively safe. Some came, and some did not or could not, because the sea was breaking over the after well-deck. Neilson then called for a lifeboat crew and ordered her ashore with a line, with Gwyn, his second officer, in charge.

They got onshore with considerable difficulty, but the line they took with them was carried away. During the night, lights were thrown up from the shore, where their position was evidently known, and the coastguard signalled that the lifeboat was coming. In the meantime the Rocket Brigade kept firing rockets, and though several straddled parts of his ship, those aboard could not reach them, because of the heavy sea. They did succeed in reaching one line, but after a while it was carried away, cut, Neilson believed, by the jagged rock. The rocket men continued to fire. They were simply splendid, Neilson thought, and, considering the conditions, he felt that they were owed a deep debt of gratitude.

Coroner: Supposing you had a rocket apparatus on-board ship, could you have established communication with the shore?

Neilson: Easily. There was nothing to prevent a ship's rocket hitting the shore somewhere.

Coroner: Would it be a good thing if ships such as yours carried rockets for such a purpose?

Neilson: Yes, sir.

Coroner: Everything was done that could be done?

Neilson: Yes, sir.

Proceeding, Neilson said the lifeboat was hauled along the beach, and launched about 9.30 a.m. The boat managed to reach the ship. Her after part was still standing, but she had broken her back and was separated by the waves. The lifeboat took off five ladies, and three sailors, 'cowards' as he called them, jumped into the boat. He hoped those three men – 'he would not mention names' – would read what he thought of them. Altogether, the lifeboat took off seventeen or eighteen people and reached the shore safely. It was splendidly done.

The lifeboat returned for another load. The sea was then running much higher and the wind blowing hard, making it difficult for the lifeboat. It was quite impossible for the lifeboat to run alongside the after part of the ship, because of the sea. As the lifeboat took on board doctors and sick berth stewards etc., there was no confusion, and the lifeboat again reached the shore safely. At the time, he felt terribly disappointed that the boat did not return a third time, but on weighing up the situation he came to the conclusion that they could not have done it safely, owing to the sea running higher, and wind rising. He saw a lifeboat launched down a cliff, but she did not come to the ship that day. Next on Saturday morning, the Upgang lifeboat made several attempts to reach the ship, and finally got up comparatively close, when the eddy caused by the heavy sea between the after part amidships section caught her, and swirled her down to leeward. That happened every time she tried, and she failed to reach the ship, the crew being worn out. The Scarborough lifeboat was lying off on Friday night, in tow of a trawler, but was quite unable to render help.

The sea and wind got worse that night, and it always seemed so at high water. On Saturday, due to the apparent absence of help and the seriousness of the situation, the captain gave certain directions and advised those who could swim to make the attempt to reach shore. While they all had life belts, all the ship's boats had been washed away. A great number of men made the attempt to swim ashore, and he directed them as well as he could by watching the current. A number succeeded in reaching the shore alive, but some drowned. The after part of the ship broke away on Friday afternoon, at about high water, and all the men there were washed off. Neilson did not believe any were saved. On Saturday afternoon he was signalled from the shore: 'Advise you make rafts.' Neilson replied, 'No gear to make rafts with.' He was signalled from the shore that a motor lifeboat was on the way to take them all off. Witness signalled back: 'Ship breaking rapidly; look out for swimmers; no time to lose.' He called all hands on deck and told them he did not believe his ship could survive the night, and advised every officer and man to make some sort of raft with doors, shutters, any debris, and said that he thought they all ought to leave because if she went to pieces at high water, they would stand no chance.

The men agreed and set to work making rafts out of anything they could; this kept them busy too. Under Neilson's directions, the men left the ship in batches, hanging onto the rafts and many succeeded in swimming to shore. In the meantime, the tide rose and Neilson suggested all hands remaining hang on together, lying close for warmth, and take their chance. There were exactly fifty men left, and they were all huddled together in the captain's cabin, the officers' cabin and the chart room. They had no food or fire, and only a thimbleful of water (found on Saturday afternoon). There was not a dry spot on the ship, and they were thoroughly drenched from half-tide to half-tide. Neilson wished to speak of the splendid behaviour of the men who found and passed round only a mouthful each of water. On Sunday morning, they were rescued by the Tynemouth lifeboat. The wind and sea had calmed somewhat, but rowing lifeboats would have no chance of reaching them. The motor lifeboat used oil on the sea about 7.30 a.m. In reading over the depositions, the coroner was quite overcome at that part about the crew being without food and water for so long. Upon resuming after an adjournment for lunch, Captain Neilson added that it was reported to him soon after the ship struck the mine that the engine-room was flooded.

Duncan C. Graham, 4th officer, said that on Friday morning, 30 October, he was on duty on the *Rohilla* and, at 3.45 a.m., he was sent aft to take soundings, which he took at four o'clock, and found 24 fathoms of water. He went directly to the bridge to report. At the first shock, the effect on the ship was such as to make him think she had struck a mine. He confirmed the captain's evidence, up to about Saturday noon, which the coroner said was unnecessary, as he had heard the essential details. On Saturday morning, Graham swam ashore; he had a lifebelt on, but it was far from easy to make the shore. Mr MacKinnon stated that Graham's delay in taking soundings was due to directing endeavours to secure a boat adrift on the poop. He was knocked off his feet when the ship struck and rose. There was no bumping then.

Colin Campbell Gwyn, second officer, said he came on deck at four o'clock on Friday morning. Captain Neilson was then on the bridge and ordered him to tell the chief engineer to slow down, as he was going to head to sea. When the vessel struck, Gwyn was lifted off his feet. Upon arrival at the bridge, he asked the captain what was the matter, and he said, 'A mine.' Gwyn did not think it was wreckage; striking wreckage would not produce the lifting sensation he experienced. On the whole, he felt sure it was a mine, so far as the facts came within his knowledge. He came ashore in charge of the ship's lifeboat, about seven o'clock on Friday morning, after great difficulty. He had a line, which fouled the rocks twice and he was obliged to cut it, as the boat was in imminent danger of capsizing and he had already lost three oars. There was no other way. He saw all the lifesaving efforts made from the shore. He thought better use could have been made of the rocket apparatus if it had been taken at low tide on to the Scar, opposite the wreck, as was done on the Saturday. Two lines were got across to the ship, but they could not be reached by those on board. The lifeboat did very well with a fresh crew, and he thought it might have made a third trip, but those landed would have had to climb up the cliff ladder. He saw many men swim ashore, and when they got ashore there were excellent arrangements for taking charge of them by Dr Mitchell and the other doctors in the town. Every attention was given to those who came ashore alive and all had practically recovered, with the exception of one, John Smith, who had died at Dr Burton's.

Mr MacKinnon stated that when he was going to the engine room, he passed the 4th officer returning with the soundings-tube in his hand. At the first shock, which he thought was a mine, he fell on one knee and caught the handrail. The vessel was in deep water after the first shock, and until she struck the Scar.

The foreman stated that about four to six minutes passed between the first shock and the stranding. MacKinnon was near the entrance to the second-class saloon, making his way to the bridge. On the way he picked up a man who was washed down, went to the deck, then to the boat-deck, and then got orders to take charge of his lifeboat. All that work took him six minutes.

Bond, chief officer of the *Rohilla*, said it was his watch on deck from midnight to 4 a.m. on Friday. The vessel changed her course at 1.50 a.m., to S 19 E. That course would not have brought the vessel near Whitby if it had been maintained. The captain was on duty all the time and when he was not on deck he was in the chartroom. They saw several vessels during Bond's watch, from both inside and outside. At 3.25 a.m. one was passing inside going north. He did not see any shore lights of any kind. The first impact was about 4.10 a.m. on what had since been called a mine. Bond was on the boat-deck and was knocked off his feet, landing up against the bulkhead. Nothing happened after that until they stranded. He gave orders to the men to get on deck and ordered the bell to be sounded, but the carpenter soon afterwards reported that it could not be done. He went back to the bridge, and the vessel was then aground. Between the 'lifting shock' and the stranding, there was an interval of about seven minutes. He confirmed all the captain's evidence, and he attributed the cause of the first impact to a mine. He had never been in a ship that had struck a mine. The rush of water into the ship might also be consistent with having struck a rock or a derelict vessel. Bond swam ashore on Saturday night, on a box. He was well cared for afterwards. He did not know this coast well, but had the High Lights been lighted, it would not have been possible for the *Rohilla* to go ashore where she struck. Had the High Lights been lighted they would have seen them, and there would have been no danger. MacKinnon said the captain told him that the first thing the motor lifeboatmen were asked on Sunday morning was 'How's Bond?', and they broke into a cheer when told that he was saved, showing the esteem in which he was held. Captain Neilson said, 'Bond cannot swim not five yards and we were afraid we had lost him.'

Second Officer Winstanley said he had returned from the chart room to the bridge before the first shock was felt, and the captain was standing on the bridge, near him, when the shock came. He picked himself up, and heard the captain give the order to reverse engines and go hard a port, followed almost directly by full speed ahead. He heard the captain say, 'My God, a mine,' or words to that effect. He confirmed the captain's evidence. On Saturday at midday he swam ashore with a lifebelt on. When he got ashore he received every help and attention – no one could have done more for him. He thought the vessel was going 9.5 knots. If the course set had been maintained, the ship would not have struck on Whitby rock. Mackinnon said that just before the first shock he noticed a Morse signal and told the captain, who ordered him to send for a naval signalman to take what he said. When he saw the first flicker, it bore nearly four points forward of the beam on the starboard bow. The Morse signal went too quick for him to read. Captain Neilson said he did not agree with what Gwyn had said about firing rockets from the Scar – rocket experts knew more about such matters than they did. Proceeding, he said: 'I cannot thank the people of Whitby, high and low, rich and poor, enough for what they did for my ship's company and myself. That is all I have to say.' The coroner said, 'We are glad to hear it.' Captain Neilson replied, 'I cannot really say what I really feel.'

The coroner, in an able summing up, said the disaster was the worst that had happened in their history, but throughout the whole tragedy the men maintained to the full the high traditions of the British sailor, exhibiting tenacious courage, and wonderful endurance, proving their right to be called honest men and good sailors. Then he went on to form an opinion as to the stranding of the steamship, and whether anyone was to blame. Owing to the fragility of some of the witnesses, they had the cart before the horse, as it were, as a doctor, the Coastguard and others had previously given their evidence. The doctor referred to the turning on of the lights and said it was a few minutes to four o'clock when the first crash came, and that after a short time he switched on the light, which almost immediately went out. The doctor added that after he had gone on deck, he saw that the ship was fixed, but it was so dark that he could not see where they were. Coastguard Jefferies' evidence was important, added the coroner, who proceeded to re-read a portion in which that witness said the ship was 'being steered on such a course that was bound to bring her on the rocks.' Jefferies' conduct showed that that was his conviction; and that the vessel struck from ten to fifteen minutes past four o'clock. The stories told by the captain and the officers agreed, with the exception of a few differences of timing, but he asked the jury to consider the facts and not trouble themselves about such things under the circumstances. All the witnesses agreed to having experienced a curious lifting sensation and thought that it was caused by a mine. It might have been caused by striking a rock, but that was difficult to believe. The captain thought his ship was fatally damaged and that it was not only right, but his duty, to adopt a course in order to try and save the ship's company, and that was to run the vessel ashore. Even if they thought it was an honest mistake, the captain would still be entirely discharged from all blame. All that was done occurred under conditions quite different from those of peacetime, all navigation lights having been extinguished and shore lights darkened or extinguished. If anything, the blame lay with the conditions under which the voyage was made.

The Verdict

After a short retirement to consider their verdict, the jury returned to the courtroom and the coroner read their verdict, as follows: that, with the exception of John Smith, who died from exhaustion, all the men were drowned.

The jury desired to add their unanimous judgement that the steamship *Rohilla* undoubtedly struck something a little time before she grounded on the rock at Saltwick, and that, in the stormy weather which prevailed, in the absence of lights and all usual safeguards, and in view of the special risks of navigation in the North Sea since the war began, the master navigated the ship with all reasonable care, and was entirely free from blame for her loss. They also wished to say how very highly they appreciated the conduct of the master, officers and crew after the vessel was wrecked, and their brave endurance of extreme privation. They further recommend that, in future, passenger ships be supplied with a rocket apparatus, and strongly recommended that a motor lifeboat be provided for Whitby. In conclusion, the jury wished to assure the relatives of the men who had drowned of their very sincere sympathy.

Captain Neilson and four senior officers had given their evidence, confirming that it was their belief they had struck a mine. Coastguard Jefferies suggested that the ship had been off course and struck the rock, a notion dismissed by Captain Neilson. Despite all the evidence given by so many individuals the 7-mile error in calculations was never explained.

This concluded the first enquiry.

On Sunday morning, two more bodies were washed ashore, both greatly decomposed. One, found near the East Pier by a man named William Hawkesfield, was initially supposed to be that of able seaman Bert Cribb, but subsequent inquiries failed to establish his identity, the tattoos not corresponding with those Cribb was known to have. There was a pansy and a leaf tattooed on the left wrist, and some teeth were missing in the top jaw and the body was wearing navy trousers. The other body was found near Newholm Bridge by J. Pybus of Eastrow and identified as that of George Inglesby Ross, 57, of Chewton Road, Walthamstow, a sick berth steward.

The bodies were deposited in the drill hall on the pier to await an inquest, which was held on Monday afternoon at the court house on Spring Hill by G. Buchannan, coroner. Councillor E.L. Turner was chosen as foreman of the jury, which comprised the same gentlemen who acted at the inquest on the twenty-six bodies the previous week. Evidence of identification in the case of Ross was given by John Smith, second steward of the *Rohilla*, who said that eighty-four of the vessel's complement were drowned or died from exhaustion. He thought the two men were members of the crew, and 'that they were most likely drowned on Friday, when the ship struck'. He saw neither of them on the Saturday. He could not identify the body first thought to be that of Cribb; the other he identified as George Inglesby Ross of the sick berth reserve. The jury returned a verdict that the two men were drowned, probably on 30 October.

On Friday morning, the jury empanelled to investigate the cause of death of the first victims of the wreck were again called together to hold an inquest upon three more bodies recovered after being washed up. Once again the inquiry was conducted by coroner George Buchannan at the courthouse, and Councillor Turner was foreman of the jury. The bodies, which were unidentified, were placed in the old Coastguard Station.

The first body was that of a man about 5ft 7 or 8in in height, of medium build, and with the letters 'W.D.' tattooed on the right arm. The only clothing was part of a blue knitted jersey. This body was found on Thursday, between Whitby and Eastrow, by Thomas Coulson of Sandsend. The second body was that of a man about 50, 5ft 7in in height. On the little finger was a gold signet ring, and tattooed on the left arm were the letters C.S.D., clasped hands, two flowers and a barque. A star and butterfly were tattooed on the right forearm and a sailing ship with the name 'Emma' on the left forearm. This body was found between Whitby and Eastrow on the previous day by William Cook of Sandsend. The third body, found that (Friday) morning on the Scar by J. Holmes, of Tate Hill, was that of a young man, about 30 years of age, about 5ft 6in in height with the letters 'J.F.X.' or 'J.X.F.' indistinctly tattooed on the right forearm. The bodies were numbered 29, 30 and 31 respectively, and were much decomposed.

George Smith of 71 Derby Road, Southampton, second steward of the *Rohilla*, said he had seen the three bodies, and was unable to identify any of them. He had no doubt they formed part of the crew of the *Rohilla* and were probably drowned on 30 October. He thought the age of the first man (No. 29) might have been about 49; he had no idea of the age of the second (No. 30), but he thought the third (No. 31) was about 27. The 'W.D.' tattoo on the first body (No. 29) might suggest the identification of the man as William Dawson, a fireman, who was missing. Smith thought all the men in the engine room escaped. The jury returned a verdict that the men were drowned on 30 October.

On Saturday afternoon, Buchannan held another inquest upon three more bodies, none of which had been identified. They were in an advanced state of decomposition and quite unrecognisable. One (No. 82) was that of a young man about 20 years of age, about 5ft 5in in height, and minus a foot, and was found on the Scar by G. Leadley, of Tate Hill. Another (No. 38) was also that of young man, about 20 years of age, about 5ft in height, and was found on the sands by R. Harland of Crag. The letters 'D.P.' were tattooed on the left forearm and 'B.B.' on the right. A leather belt was around the waist. The third body (No. 34) was that of a man about 40, around 5ft 8 or 9in in height and was found at Eastrow by Richard Strackler.

George Smith said he thought the youngest body (No. 32) was that of a lad called Matthew Tarbet of Colintraive, Scotland, as he was the only 'lad' on the ship, being about 18 and of slim build, and also the teeth corresponded. No. 33 could have been the body of D. Patton, greaser, about 22 years of age, but he could only suppose so because the letters 'D.P.' were tattooed on his left arm. No. 34 had no marks by which he could be identified; he was a very big man about 42 years of age. Apart from these tentative suggestions, the bodies, which were beyond recognition, could not be identified. The jury returned the verdict that the men drowned, probably on 30 October.

On Saturday night, another body was washed up at Newholm Beck and was found by a Mr Cook of Eastrow. On Sunday four more were washed up, one in Collier's Hope, two at Saltwick, and on Monday morning another was found at Eastrow. A coroner's inquiry was held at the courthouse on Spring Hill on Monday morning, Councillor E.L. Turner again appointed foreman of the jury. The bodies, with one exception, were all naked and much decomposed. One (No. 36) was identified as William Barron, saloon pantryman, aged about 45. He was wearing a pair of navy-blue trousers and in one pocket was a silver Geneva watch; the minute hand had become detached and the hour hand suggested 9.15 a.m.

George Smith said he had seen the six bodies, numbered 35 to 40. He was only able to identify one, that of William Barron, born at Inverness and lived in Glasgow. It was impossible to identify the others. They bore no marks, and their condition was such that they were quite unrecognisable. Smith had no doubt the men formed part of the crew of the *Rohilla* and drowned on 30 October. The body numbered 35 was that of a man about 40 years of age. No. 36 was about 30; No. 38 about 50; and Nos 39 and 40 both about 35. The jury returned a verdict that the men drowned on 30 October.

On Monday afternoon Buchannan held another inquest, this time at the Pyman Institute, Sandsend. This inquest was called for the body of a man supposed to have been drowned from the wreck of the *Rohilla*. J. Blyth was chosen as foreman of the jury. George Smith, second steward of the *Rohilla*, again gave evidence. Owing to the advanced stage of decomposition, identification of the body was impossible. The jury returned a verdict that the deceased drowned on Friday 30 October as a result of the wreck of the *Rohilla*. A further inquest was called on the Tuesday afternoon on two more bodies that had washed up near Sandsend Beck, presumably also from the *Rohilla*.

In the course of his evidence, George Smith said that to the best of his knowledge eighty-four persons were drowned when the *Rohilla* was wrecked. There was no possibility of identification. The two bodies' condition precluded recognition and they bore no marks by which they could be identified. They were too far gone to tell their age. The jury returned the verdict that the men were found drowned at Sandsend, and that they were probably drowned when the *Rohilla* was wrecked on 30 October.

On Wednesday morning at the courthouse on Spring Hill, Buchannan held another inquest upon four more bodies (numbered 41, 42, 43 and 44). One was washed up near Eastrow, one at Newholm Beck, one near the Scotch Head and the other on the Scar. All were quite unrecognisable. Giving evidence, Smith said he thought No. 43 was about 40 years of age and was the body of a fireman, because of the Union button on the clothing. Owing to its tattoos, he believed No. 44 was J. Patton, fireman, aged about 38, but he was not certain. He had no doubt all four were part of the *Rohilla*'s crew, and were drowned on 30 October. The verdict concluded that the men were drowned in the North Sea from the steamship *Rohilla* on 30 October.

Tribute to the Police

The coroner said he had been asked by the jury to say that the police deserved praise for their work. The jury had noticed that nothing much had been said about what the police had done, and thought it their duty to say that they highly esteemed their conduct, and appreciated the way in which they had discharged their duties from beginning to end.

Behind the scenes there was something of a debate as to who was legally liable for the loss of the ship. The argument hinged specifically on whether the ship was lost as a result of a Sea Risk or a War Risk. If it were proven that the *Rohilla* was lost as a result of a Sea Risk, the Admiralty would not be responsible for covering the British India Steam Navigation Company's (BISNC) assets. The latter needed the ship's loss to be defined as a result of War Risk to lay a claim against the Admiralty. Because no official inquiry was ever convened, it was impossible to determine whether negligent navigation had caused the ship's loss. The Admiralty repeated that as far as they were concerned they had no information that any mines had been laid off Whitby, although they did later acknowledge the possibility that a rogue mine may have drifted into the area.

On 9 March 1915 the BISNC wrote for clarification of the situation. Captain Neilson had returned to India on 10 February of that year and the former officers and crew of the *Rohilla* had been dispersed for some time, making the convening of a formal enquiry a logistical nightmare. On 18 March the Board of Trade Marine Department decided that after consideration of the circumstances, the passage of time and the impracticability of holding an enquiry in the near future, they would not order a formal investigation. Sworn depositions given by the officers at the time of the wreck alluding to a mine strengthened the case against the Admiralty. The matter came before the committee of the Liverpool and London War Risks Association, who, having weighed up all the evidence, determined that the *Rohilla* should be regarded as lost due to a War Risk and not by collision or negligent navigation.

On 18 May the Admiralty conceded and the BISNC was asked to provide substantial documentation in support of any claim for compensation.

7

THE REPERCUSSIONS OF THE *ROHILLA* DISASTER

Following the inquest, those involved in the tragedy were only just beginning to truly appreciate the gravity of the ordeal they had been through. The survivors, thankful for their own lives, repeatedly asked themselves why they had survived when so many others had been lost, in many cases friends and relatives.

Those directly involved down on the foreshore could not yet come to terms with the sorrow they felt for those they had helped from the water to find they were already deceased, yet took some comfort from the number whose lives were saved. Those directly responsible for the aftercare of survivors behaved in all cases admirably, often placing the lives of the survivors before their own. They gave everything they could and more to assist and could feel proud of what they had achieved for no other medical organisation could bring together so many men and women at such short notice and commit them to aiding the needy for such lengthy periods during what was without doubt Whitby's worst maritime tragedy.

The combined St John Ambulance Brigade worked tirelessly throughout the weekend and deserved all the credit they received. Sergeant Christopher Hood, the honorary secretary of the Whitby brigade, wrote to T.C. Hutchinson, manager of the Skinningrove Ambulance Brigade to thank them for the three stretcher squads and equipment they provided on the Friday. In his letter he explained that:

The members of the Whitby Division, St John Ambulance Brigade, desire me to convey to you, and through you to the members of the Skinningrove Brigade their sincere appreciation of the splendid assistance rendered by them at the wreck of the hospital ship Rohilla. Their knowledge, skill and promptitude and willingness to take risks is greatly appreciated by all, including the medical men and officials in charge. Please carry our good wishes for the future success of the Brigade, and we shall be glad at any time to assist them in any case of urgency of necessity.

He also included a copy of the report in their Occurrence Book from Surgeon T.C. Littler-Jones FRCS RNVR, expressing his gratitude to the Admiralty:

The services rendered were excellent, the long hours on duty the arduous nature of the task and the weather were all endured cheerfully and the whole turnout was in my opinion absolutely splendid. The country is proud in the way in which The Whitby Ambulance Men did their work during this terrible disaster. Personally I found everything in working order and the men assisted by the detachments from Grosmont and Carlin How stuck to their long and arduous duties.

The account of the services rendered to the *Rohilla* in the occurrence book of the Whitby division of the St John Ambulance Brigade makes for very interesting reading; it gives a valuable insight into the kind of work they undertook:

Report of cases in wrecked hospital ship 'Rohilla'

Bodies washed ashore at 6am artificial respiration under lifeboat House and on beach for 45 minutes. Dr Penn with the brigade – Unsuccessful.

Swimmer rescued and brought ashore by brigade – Sgt. C. H. Hood and Ambulance Candidate Wilfred Harrison. First Aid treatment and removed to hospital. Brigade in sole charge.

Artificial respiration on body washed ashore Sgt. C. H. Hood under the direction of Dr Mitchell ????. Unsuccessful. 40 minutes.

Treated for shock and Collapse First aid treatment. Removed to hospital. Sergeant W. R. Knaggs in charge – Recovered.

Body recovered, Dead Removed to mortuary.

Swimmers rescued by Coastguard and bought up Cliff Ladder. First aid treatment. Dr Mitchell. Removed in Motor to hospital. Nurse Phillips and Brigade Sec. C. H. Hood

S.B.S Shute, who died onboard. Body recovered and removed to mortuary. Members of brigade.

Recovered bodies. Removed to mortuary. Worked by headlight in the dark.

Eleven swimmers recovered from sea and conveyed to emergency hospital (Miss Agar's hut Saltwick)

Received general – first aid treatment and had surface wounds and bruises dressed. Sergeant W.R. Richard Knaggs in charge in Whitby side of Scar, with Dr Mitchell + Divisional Brigade – Sgt. C. H. Hood in charge at Saltwick and of Scar, with Nurses Birch and Mackenzie. Removed casualities in stretchers up side of cliff, and hence by motor to hospital and Private Houses. Recovered.

Serious case of collapse. Artificial respiration and first aid treatment Nurse Mackenzie in charge. Removed in stretcher and improvised bed on Motor Transport. Stretcher squad in attendance. Recovered after four hours treatment.

Bodies recovered and conveyed to Saltwick, afterwards removed on stretchers to mortuary – distance two miles.

Artificial respiration and first aid treatment under Dr Mitchell + Donaldson + Sgt

W.R. Knaggs in charge. Removed to hospital and recovered.

Bodies washed ashore. Artificial respiration applied, but no result. Removed to mortuary.

Two men, who came ashore on raft, two miles away almost when recovered, but collapsed. Artificial respiration by Juniors – unsuccessful. Nurse Birch in charge. Bodies removed to mortuary.

Swimmers rescued and treated conveyed to Dr Burton's house – collapsed on the way. Artificial respiration for five hours. Dr Burton + Mitchell and member of the brigade.

Swimmers recovered and treated for immersion and shock. Removed to private houses. Recovered.

Bodies recovered. Artificial respiration in three cases. Unsuccessful. Removed to mortuary. Doctors in charge. One case broken neck.

Also 50 survivors met on arrival from lifeboat. One case of dislocation and fracture of humerous. Arm strapped to body with triangular bandage. Removed by motor to hospital, and put to bed. Afterwards healed by doctors. Hon. Sgt. C. H. Hood and voluntary help. All others conveyed to private houses. Minor wounds and bruises treated all recovered.

Signed WR Knaggs, Sergeant in charge C. H. Hood, Hon. Sgt + Secretary Marine Café Whitby.

The *Rohilla*'s Captain, and the Bravery of his Men

In conversation with a *Whitby Gazette* reporter, Captain Neilson said he wished to commend several of those on board his ship for their brave conduct, with three exceptions and these he characterised as cowards, the names of whom he well knew 'did splendidly,' he said, and it was difficult to single men out for special mention. The three 'white-livered' individuals to whom he referred jumped into the first lifeboat on Friday morning, contrary to his orders.

Dr Oram and Quartermaster Scott, said Captain Neilson, did particularly gallant service. They went overboard frequently, at the risk of their lives, helping men who were in the water near the wreck. All the officers also did splendidly. Macintosh, in the captain's opinion, deserved the Victoria Cross. He performed many deeds of heroism, frequently going overboard to help men who were in great difficulty, and volunteering for the very dangerous task of reaching a rocket line that landed at the port end of the bridge. He got the rope, but it was broken. Another sailor, whom the captain could not name, secured a rocket line on Friday afternoon by climbing along a boom and below the bridge deck, being struck by heavy seas all the while, watched eagerly from the shore. The line parted, the captain said, but the man was a hero, as were a number of others on board. It may be added that the captain himself showed the finest qualities throughout his terrible trials. He said he would be very glad when he got home to Edinburgh, as he felt he needed a rest.

Survivor Accounts

Mr F. Bigwood, a member of the Royal Navy Sick Berth Reserve, was granted a few days leave of absence after his ordeal. He stated that he had joined the *Rohilla*, 'one of the most beautifully equipped hospital ships imaginable', on 2 October. It was, he recorded, 'no secret' that the vessel was bound for Antwerp:

> During the night preceding the disaster it was very stormy. Like the great majority of the crew, I was lying in my bunk when about 3.45 a.m. the vessel struck a mine. Immediately all the lights aboard went out, but everything proceeded with as much orderliness as could be expected under such tragic circumstances.

It was Bigwood's belief that the captain immediately turned the boat for shore.

> All the crew scrambled for the lifebelts which were kept under the pillows, before having to find their way up to the hatchways as best as they could in the darkness. Water was pouring in, and many poor fellows were lost before they could reach the deck. All who possibly could made their way to the pre-arranged stations in case of disaster, only to find that more than half the boats had been washed overboard, and some of those that remained were too badly damaged to be of any service.
>
> Until 9.30 a.m. I remained on the poop deck, and then I came to the conclusion that if I stayed where I was I might get killed amongst the wreckage, so a companion and myself decided to go overboard, the ship being about three quarters of a mile from the shore. At that time I had not got a lifebelt, but managed to get one from one of the wrecked boats. Unfortunately my companion was knocked over and killed before he had a chance to leave the ship.
>
> I dived overboard, but was immediately knocked about and tumbled over and over again by the force of the waves, until I thought I should never come to the surface again. I managed, however, to keep my presence of mind and on two occasions got hold of a piece of wreckage, which were afterwards washed out of my hands. Eventually, after much struggling – I cannot possibly say how long I was in the water – I managed to get nearer to the coast, and then it was that a man waded into the raging sea until the water reached his armpits, and pulled me to safety.
>
> Though not seriously injured, he received numerous bruises but it is likely the trauma would have lasted considerably longer. At the time he had only his night attire on; all his other clothing and, in fact, everything he possessed on-board was lost in the wrecking.

(*The Nottinghamshire Free Press*, Friday 6 November 1914)

In a letter to Barnoldswick dated 31 October, Private Fred Reddiough gave a simple but comprehensive account of his personal experience, and of the manner in which he made good his escape. It paints a truly harrowing picture:

We were sailing down the East Coast bound for Dunkirk in France, on Thursday night. It was one of the roughest nights we have had since we have been away. The wind was blowing the ship everywhere it wanted. We could not get to sleep. At about 4 o'clock the following morning the ship shook from stern to stern. We all 'nipped' out of bed, and the water was pouring down the hatches in torrents. When I got out of bed I was ankle deep in water, so I slipped into my pants and grabbed a lifebelt and ran. When I got to the end of the line of bunks some bottles came dashing past, and cut one of my toes clean off, all but a bit of skin, and I was walking about like that for about four hours, so you can just think what I went through. When I got upstairs into the saloon passage it was full of water. I then went up some more steps onto the promenade deck, and then onto the boat deck. No sooner had I got onto the boat deck then I was swept off my feet about three times, the waves coming mountain high. Then I got hold of a ventilator along with some other chaps, when a wave came and swept us all off our feet right up against the rails.

Then I was in about three feet of water trying to get my wind. I got up and got behind a boat out of the way of the waves, when I saw Tony just behind me. We

Fred battled forward not knowing how bad the sea was.

went forward to get into the Marconi chap's cabin, and stayed there until daylight. The ship's doctor then came and said we had better get out of there as it was not safe. We took our chance (I was with Willie Anderson then, I had lost sight of Tony), and waited till a big wave had gone by, and then we 'nipped' forward into another cabin. Then I lost sight of Anderson, so I was on my own so far as our chaps were concerned. Well, I stayed in there for another hour and a half. There was a lifeboat coming alongside, and the Captain shouted 'Women first'. As you know, we had four Sisters and the stewards on board. Well, they got in with some more chaps, so I said to myself, 'When that boat comes back I am for it'. So I got onto the rail and waited for it to come back, and when it did come, I got hold of a rope and slid down into the lifeboat. A man pulled me in by the feet. When I looked up I saw Tony standing on the rail, so I sent the rope back, and Tony got hold of it and came down into the boat as well. I think we were the only two from Barnoldswick to get saved. I am now at the Cottage Hospital, Whitby, and have just had some relatives to see me. I am lucky to be here, I can tell you. I would not go through it again for a fortune. I think I shall be here for a while yet, and then I hope to get home on leave.

The following account was compiled by Surgeon Herbert Leith Murray, Lt-Commander, MD, RNVR, while in hospital soon after his traumatic rescue:

For ten days before the wreck I had been in bed with influenza on a milk diet and getting aspirin constantly, I had a temperature of over 101° on the night of the disaster.

Herbert Leith Murray in 1917. (Courtesy Nancy Sykes)

A terrible gale had been blowing for hours, with all the Ward room furniture broken adrift, the chairs, table and cutlery making a frightful noise from midnight until we struck about 3 a.m. and the lights went out. The jar hadn't been much more noticeable than we had been getting before from the waves. I got on deck in my pyjamas with one sea boot on, the other being lost in the darkness below.

We helped each other to put on our life – belts i.e. the officers and nurses, who alone slept in that part of the ship, and then made a rush forward to the bridge, were the boat stations were, but we were caught on the way by a very big wave. I held onto a hatch combing with one hand and to a Sister with the other. The strain very nearly made me lose hold and I 'felt something go' at my heart, making me breathless then and for months afterwards.

We got into a ship's officer's cabin, cracked in the roof, and with water pouring in at every wave. Someone broke into a locker and we got trousers for the nurses and a coat for me, we were soaking wet and hardly able to stand for the rolling of the vessel. At daybreak the ship was seen to be broken in two, with 200 people in the after end which soon disappeared and all were drowned, as they had been tied to the rails to keep them from being washed away.

The first lifeboat, which got out at 9 a.m. took off the Sisters and some officers, and three hours later a second one took off the patients, myself and some others. I was lowered down by a rope, hanging on all the time to a leading line thrown down from the ship to the boat and fell into the water (as a result of the terrific amplitude of the waves) but was hauled on board, as my wave came up and the lifeboat came down.

At the next roll of the ship I was hauled out of the boat again by the rope round me which my cold fingers could not unfasten, but fortunately I fell back in the boat, and someone set me free. The lifeboat broke her back in the landing, and I lay in bed in Whitby for a week with cardiac dilation (enlargement of the heart) but with a temperature never exceeding 99°.

Later, Leith Murray was appointed to HMHS *Garth Castle* until 1917 before transferring to HMS *Eaglet*. Following the cessation of the war he returned to his career as a gynaecologist in Liverpool.

On 25 June 1932 the *British Medical Journal* carried the following obituary:

We had to announce last week, with much regret, the death, on June 11th of Dr Herbert Leith Murray, professor of obstetrics and gynaecology in the University of Liverpool, honorary surgeon to the Hospital for Women and the Maternity Hospital, Liverpool, and honorary gynaecological surgeon to the David Lewis Northern Hospital. He was born at Aberdeen on April 21st, 1880, and was educated at the Dundee High School and the Universities of Aberdeen, St Andrews, and Paris. He graduated M.B., Ch.B. Aberd. with honours in 1901, and proceeded M.D. in 1905.

Herbert Leith Murray in 1929. (Courtesy
Nancy Sykes)

For the following appreciation we are indebted to a colleague who was closely
associated with him in his hospital work.

The tragic and sudden death of Professor Leith Murray is a grievous loss to the
city and University of Liverpool as well as to a very wide circle of friends. Leith
Murray was full of energy, and had an unlimited capacity for work, whilst never
sparing himself socially. He had a very genial disposition and a genius for friendship;
consequently he was surrounded by friends, and endeared himself to the many
medical men with whom he came in contact and with his students. He had served
throughout the war as a surgeon in the Royal Navy, and was wrecked in the hospital
ship Rohilla off Whitby in 1914, when suffering from an attack of influenza. His
loyalty and constancy to all his colleagues, and his juniors in particular, especially
endeared him to those who were privileged to be closely associated with him. His
untiring use of his own knowledge and gifts, the generosity with which he placed
them at the disposal of others, and his magnetic personality were a powerful
stimulus and inspiration to all who worked with him. He had a very large practice as
a gynaecological surgeon, and his opinion was sought over a very wide area.

His professional attainments were considerable, he was an able diagnostician,
his operative methods were neat and very simple, producing excellent results. His
writings are well known among gynaecologists, the most outstanding ones being
The Immunology of Pregnancy and Degenerative Changes in Fibroids. He was a
strong advocate of conservative surgery, as his views on Myomectomy showed,

whilst his detailed observation and careful case-recording were well illustrated by a paper he read in April of this year on ectopic pregnancy. He was a foundation Fellow of the British College of Obstetricians and Gynaecologists, a member of its council, and a strong supporter of its aims and objects. He had been a vice-president of the Liverpool Medical Institution and president of the North of England Obstetrical and Gynaecological Society.

As the author of many published papers Herbert was a successful clinician who excelled both professionally and personally, the tragedy of the Rohilla just one of the many facets to his life. He was brought to the notice of the Admiralty for valuable services in the prosecution of the War.

In response to criticism from irresponsible persons respecting the life lost, and the action of the Whitby men, the chief stoker on board SS *Rohilla* made this statement:

Being accosted at different periods by citizens resident at Whitby, and asked for an explanation as to how the Lifeboatmen acted in connexion with the rescue of those who were surviving on board the S.S. Rohilla, my statement, (and I defy contradiction) is that while aboard the above named, I was watching the heroic attempts made by the Lifeboatmen to render all possible human assistance to extract from the above all life. But owing to the exceptionally heavy weather, and rocky conditions of the inshore, I consider that human aid was impossible, and, from my point of view, it would have taken steam power to approach us, with very grave risk at that, and to the men of the Lifeboat. All honour is due to them, and to the community of Whitby at large, including the women. I cannot find words to express my gratitude to them.

Michael McCormack
Chief Stoker

Frederick Edwin Wilson (Eric) was junior Marconi operator and one of the fortunate ones to have survived the loss of the *Rohilla*, swimming ashore on the Saturday with Archibald Winstanley, the ships' senior second officer. The only surviving child of George and Elizabeth Wilson, he was born in Brixton, London on 16 January 1894 and educated at St Marylebone Higher School. Eric continued to serve in the Mercantile Marine, joining his next ship on 13 December 1914 and avoiding any further disaster until he came ashore in 1917. His diary records that he was becoming increasingly 'fed up' with life at sea, so when the call came for trained radio operators to man the shore wireless stations on the British coast, Eric was an eager volunteer. He joined the SWS (Shore Wireless Service) and rated as a petty officer RN.

On 5 May 1918 he married Dorothy, and they had three children, Joan in 1919, William in 1921 and Maurice in 1923. He came ashore from his last ship, the SS *Sunningdale*, on

11 October 1921 and resigned from the Marconi Company on 15 April 1922. Thereafter he made a career in engineering, working for many years at S.G. Brown, a prestigious company specialising in scientific instruments, particularly the gyroscope. After retirement he lived in Ealing with Dorothy, enjoying boating and fishing. He died of lung cancer aged 70 on 3 November 1964.

Need for a motor lifeboat – To the editor of the Whitby Gazette.

Sir – Perhaps the greatest lesson to be learnt from the Rohilla disaster is the need for a thoroughly efficient lifeboat service. I do not desire to cast any reflection whatever upon the magnificent work that is continually being rendered by our lifeboat crews on the coasts of the United Kingdom. Those who are in touch with happenings on the coast know full well the heroism that is such a splendid feature of our lifeboat service, but there are times when all human effort is unavailing, many hundreds of horrified spectators who from the high cliffs to the south of Whitby had to stand helplessly by while the heavy seas slowly battered the Rohilla to pieces and placed many precious lives in deadly peril, the futility of all the ordinary means of rescue was heartrending in the extreme. There is of general agreement that a motor-lifeboat might have prevailed where a row boat was helpless in the stormy seas, and, had one been available at the outset, there is no doubt that practically the whole of the ship's company would have been saved. The provision of an up to date motorboat for Whitby is an immediate necessity, but the cost of such a boat, estimated at about £3,000, is a considerable sum to be raised locally. I therefore write these lines to you, Sir in the hope that the appeal will attract a wide publicity that the people of Whitby may be assured of some help in their effort to obtain a petrol-driven boat, which alone can be thoroughly efficient on such a dangerous part of the coast. The boat would of course be taken over by the National Lifeboat Institution. Subscriptions will be gratefully received by the Whitby branches of Messrs Barclay & Company, The Yorkshire Penny Bank, the National Provincial Bank of England, the London Joint Stock Bank, the National Lifeboat Institution (London), the Whitby Gazette Office, or by Lloyds Agent (Whitby). I remain,

Yours Faithfully
John Milburn, Lloyds Agent.
Whitby, November 3rd, 1914.

P.S. The British India Steam Navigation Company, Limited (through Captain Isdale) wire that they agreed to subscribe £250 towards the fund.

Witness Accounts

W.L. Vining gave the following eyewitness account:

When I reached the top of the cliff in the early morning, the bridge of the Rohilla was the only portion of the ship appearing above the angry waves. Thirty-five members of the crew, including the nurses, were rescued during two trips by the smaller of the Whitby lifeboats during Thursday. The crew of the Upgang Lifeboat, having been warned of the impossibility of reaching the wreck from the seaward side, decided upon a daring launch. They hauled their boat overland from two miles the other side of Whitby, through the town, up the steep incline to the summit of the cliff 200ft above the sea, and then with the aid of hundreds of helpers and stout ropes, lowered her onto the beach below; an unparalleled feat. Her crew descended the cliff by means of a rope ladder and, after great difficulty, launched her. The shipwrecked crew eagerly watched this operation, and during the next half hour witnessed a terrible fight to cover the short distance to the wreck.

A huge wave carried the little lifeboat far away, and the crew were so exhausted that a further attempt was out of the question, this last failure seemed to have driven the unfortunate men to desperation, for a hand signal was received from Capt. Neilson, 'prepare for to help swimmers' and two men climbed the rail and dived into the boiling sea. The first two men, after a terrible struggle, which seemed to last for hours, reached the foot of the cliffs, but one of them only lived for a few minutes after landing. Their success encouraged many others and altogether some sixty members of the crew and medical staff, decided to make one last fight for life. Fifty remained on board. All eyes were fixed on the men in the sea fighting the battle of their lives. Men formed themselves into chains and dashed into the boiling surf directly a swimmer came within reach. George Peart whenever he saw a head appear went in and swam to the man and brought him to safety on his back.

When the *Rohilla* foundered Arthur Naylor Shepherd ought to have been celebrating his fifteenth birthday. Instead he found himself on coastwatch duty in Whitby as a patrol leader of the St Paul's 8th Scout Troop from Middlesbrough. It was not unusual for the Scouts to turn out with the Coastguards and they were soon hard at work in the dark early hours of the morning, their first task to make a fire and make some coffee, which would prove a priceless asset over the coming days and nights. With only short intervals for rest, they spent the following three days and nights in storm force conditions, most of the time wet through, trying to rescue drowning men and recover bodies along with the rest of the men on the shoreline.

The most dangerous part of the work in which Patrol Leader Shepherd took part was going with messages to the wireless station within the Coastguard lookout and bringing back supplies of rockets from the Coastguard station. In doing this, he had to make his

Arthur Shepherd aged just 16.
(Courtesy Andrew McCall)

way along the face of the cliff by a very narrow and slippery rock ledge that overhung the sea and was buffeted by high winds. It was no easy task, one he had to do alone and in the dark, where a false step or slip meant certain death. But he did it, and he did it several times.

This was not Arthur's only display of bravery for in December Whitby was attacked by the Imperial German Navy in a bombardment that included Scarborough and most of all Hartlepool. It was wrongly assumed that Whitby was armed for defence. The Scouts had just returned to their quarters from night coast-watching duty when the assault began. Realising at once that the Coastguard station had been hit, Arthur instinctively ran back to see if the Scouts' services were needed. One brave King's Scout Miller was injured and lost his leg, and the rest were described by the Coastguard Officer as so cool 'that the Germans might have been firing at them with peashooters for all they cared'. The Admiralty was most impressed with the Scouts' work, though at that time there was no award that could be presented to them.

John 'Jack' Travers Cornwell was born on 8 January 1900 and became a keen boy scout, his Scoutmaster remembered that:

Nothing was too hard for him ... he would attempt any task ... After passing his Tenderfoot he worked for his Second Class which he eventually won, and kept the pot boiling by passing his Missioner's Badge. This is as far as he got, as at the outbreak of war the officers of his troop enlisted and the Troop was dissolved.

When he was 15, Jack, as he preferred being called, walked into a local recruiting office and enlisted in the Royal Navy. After his six months basic training he undertook further training as a Sight Setter, a responsible position on a warship and one that, in the past, was the post of an experienced rating. On 27 July 1915 he passed out as Boy Seaman, First Class, J.T. Cornwell J/42563. His first posting was at Rosyth on HMS *Chester* a new light cruiser on its maiden voyage to be part of 3rd Cruiser Squadron, by 31 May, *Chester* was on station ahead of the fleet in the North Sea. Shortly afterwards the *Chester* was involved in the beginning of the Battle of Jutland, a battle that would ultimately change the face of naval warfare.

With the ship at 'action stations', Jack's job was to stand by his gun and take orders relayed through his headphones from the Gunnery Officer on the bridge. By means of a calibrated brass wheel, he was responsible for setting the gun's sights, so the gun could be brought to bear. The promptness and precision with which he carried out his orders would decide whether the shells being fired would hit their target or be undershot, or overshot, either of which could prove fatal to his vessel

Four enemy cruisers suddenly appeared concentrating their fire on the *Chester*, in no time at all she was hit by seventeen large-calibre shells, leaving just one gun operational. Jack's forward gun was one of the first to be knocked out before it could even be brought into action. He was surrounded by a scene of utter destruction; he had received a mortal wound yet stood by his weapon, even though it could not possibly have been fired. As first aid parties made their rounds they found him still beside his gun.

The ship limped back to the Humber to be met by boats which took off the wounded, Jack survived long enough to make it to the hospital where he was attended by Admiralty Surgeon, Dr C.S. Stephenson, who found the young man to be magnificently brave when told that nothing could be done for him. Jack Cornwell died of his wounds on 2 June 1916 aged just 16 years and 6 months, his last words were a message for his mother. Grimsby and District Hospital has since been demolished and replaced by the Diana, Princess of Wales Hospital, which has a 'Jack Cornwell' ward.

Jack Travers Cornwell was buried in Manor Park with full naval honours on 29 July 1916. The funeral route was lined by boy scouts and attended by tremendous crowds including hundreds of members of the armed forces, particularly sailors. The cortège left West Ham Town Hall led by mounted police. There followed a Naval band, a firing party and gun carriage bearing the coffin, draped with the Union Flag and surmounted by Jack's naval cap, together with many floral tributes including one from Admiral Sir David Beatty, who had recommended Jack for the Victoria Cross. The day of the funeral had dawned with clear blue skies and temperatures rose into the eighties. Baden-Powell described the scene

A majestic memorial to John Jack Cornwell. (Copyright Iain MacFarlaine)

in a special commemorative edition of *The Scout* published 19 August 1916. He noted that several volunteers were overcome by the heat, 'but not a Scout or Wolf Cub fell out of rank.'

The Mayor of East Ham, Mr Martin Banks, Sir John Bethel, the Member of Parliament for the area and Dr Macnamara, MP, representing the Admiralty, followed the coffin on foot, as did the Bishop of Barking, local clergy, members of the committee formed for raising money for Jack's memorial and other dignitaries. The memorial marking the final resting place for Jack Cornwell is nothing but wonderfully superb.

The tall white marble is topped with a cross and has a rope and anchor signifying his naval deeds, the memorial reads:

In Memoriam

First Class Boy JOHN TRAVERS
CORNWELL, V.C.
Born 8th January 1900
Died of wounds received at
The Battle of Jutland
2nd June 1916

This Stone was erected
by Scholars and ex-Scholars
of Schools in East Ham
'It is not wealth or ancestry
but honourable conduct and a noble
disposition that makes men great' D. M.

The St Nicholas Boys' School Band from East Ham led eighty boys from Jack's own school, Walton Road, in the procession. There then followed local military units including six boy sailors from Jack's ship, HMS *Chester*, the 2nd Cadet Battalion of the Essex Regiment and local Boy Scout Troops including the 2nd Ilford, Jack's old Troop.

On 14 September the Scout Association's Headquarters Gazette announced the introduction of the 'Cornwell Badge', and listed the criteria for the award. The recipient had to be a First Class Scout and have passed the Missioner's Badge and two other proficiency badges from a prescribed list. The Cornwell Scout Badge was to be a badge that would only be awarded to proficient and worthy Scouts who had also been brave or courageous.

As the holder of the First Class, Missioner's, and Coastwatching Badges and having got character reports from his Scoutmaster, Schoolmaster and employer which were excellent, the query left to answer was the question of whether Arthur had acted in a brave or courageous manner. There was undoubtedly never going to be an issue with this given Patrol Leader Shepherd's actions at Whitby during the loss of the *Rohilla* during the German bombardment.

In recognition of his bravery Patrol Leader Arthur Shepherd did indeed qualify for the award and became the very first recipient of the Cornwell Scout Badge which is only awarded to those who show devotion to duty, courage and endurance.

Baden-Powell made the first presentation of the Cornwell Award to Arthur Shepherd in front of an audience of 4,000 including Boys Brigade and Church Lads Brigade boys as well Scouts in Middlesbrough on 1 November 1916. He spoke on Jack Cornwell as well as the heroism of Arthur Shepherd. The large audience were, reportedly, mesmerised by the founder and followed his every word with rapt attention. Mr Shepherd took it as a great privilege to be presented the award by Baden-Powell, the chief scout of the Boy Scouts Association.

I enquired within the Scouts head office as to how many times the award had been presented since its inception, but was told that to get an accurate figure would require an extensive and very time consuming search of scouting records. It would seem that no 'Cornwell Register' exists, the closest figure given is that roughly 200-300 Cornwell Badges have been awarded to Scouts and Cubs.

In 1917 Arthur was apprenticed to the engineering trade, but this was cut short when he was enlisted into the Army as part of the National Service scheme. He was attached to 5th Kings Own Yorkshire Light Infantry, at Embken, Germany in barracks that were far removed from what he had expected.

He seemed to travel quite extensively whilst in the Army, in May 1920 he had a tour of India and then in January 1921 he had a tour of Mesopotamia (Iraq), although it was something of a short tour as his discharge papers list him as having been Discharged from Army due to 'Termination of Engagement,' on 31 March 1921.

On his return to civilian life Arthur returned to his scouting, a passion he clearly had a lot of time for.

The Scout movement kept him pretty occupied, his photograph albums confirm how active he was, seemingly always happy to go off to some camp or another.

Arthur was married in July 1936 to Dorothy Varley at the St James The Apostle Parish church, Selby. His family suffered greatly, however, and in the years thereafter it seemed cursed. On 19 March 1941 his brother Joseph died during German air raid on the Ford plant at Dagenham, Essex. Just over a year later his brother in law Hector Pinkham died during German air raids, whilst he was fighting a fire at Turners paint depot, on Linthorpe Road, which belonged to Walton, Arthur's brother. Arthur's mother Emily died from head injuries sustained in a pedestrian collision with a truck on 22 January 1945. On 19 January 1956 Arthur's father, also called Arthur died at Arthur's (Jnr) home at 2 Constance Street, North Ormesby.

In 1962 Arthur retired from the ICI plant on Teesside and moved to Overton, Lancashire with wife Dorothy, for retirement and 'sea air'. His scouting days were still not over with, in his early sixties, he became the Chairman of the 1st Overton (St Helen's)

Arthur Shepherd kitted out in his National Service Army uniform. (Courtesy Andrew McCall)

3rd Wolf Cub Pack St Pauls, Middlesbrough 1924. Arthur Shepherd sits to the right of the vicar with his hands on his knees. (Courtesy Andrew McCall)

Group for a number of years until he and his wife moved to Bare in Morecambe where they had a bungalow. After his wife passed away he spent some time on his own but never alone, he was such a charismatic gentleman. He clearly enjoyed company as on 11 July 1974, aged 75, he married Edna Elizabeth Cleasby at the West End United Reformed church, Sefton Road, Heysham Lancashire.

He still enjoyed travelling and on the 'scout circuit' he was still something of a celebrity, it seemed that the media still clamoured to know about the Cornwell Scout Badge. He gave a detailed interview to the *Lancaster Guardian* in July 1983 titled 'Arthur relives his brave act,' this was followed by another interview in the same year for the *Lancaster Evening Gazette* in October entitled 'The Rocket Boy', in reference to his bravery fetching additional rockets for the Rocket Brigade when the *Rohilla* foundered.

In 1986, Arthur was back over the east coast at a school in Guisborough where he was dutifully manning his post at the History of Scouting tent and was once again the person everyone wanted to meet. His nephew, a scout himself, must have felt proud to have had such an important figure present, it is in these photographs that I came to recognise Freda Ford.

In 1992, his second wife passed away, leaving Arthur with no relatives living close by and he moved back over to Middlesbrough staying with his niece Judith for a while before taking up residence in a care home in Linthorpe.

Arthur in a Linthorpe care home in 1992
enjoying a light-hearted moment. (Courtesy
Andrew McCall)

The scouting movement in Middlesbrough received quite a boost in 1993 with the opening of the Scout HQ in Middlesbrough, it was entirely appropriate that Arthur be invited and it was undoubtedly a welcome treat for everyone attending to be in the presence of someone who earned a unique award for devotion to duty, courage and endurance in the face of such overwhelming circumstances especially at such a young age! Lord Guisborough was called upon to officially open the unit, but given the occasion and those present I feel sure Arthur would have been busy sharing tales of his time as a scout.

He was a little quieter in 1994 although there are still a number of cuttings of his endeavours, some of which prompted his invitation as the guest of honour for the Scouts Gang Show. One would have thought that at the age of 95 he would have sought a more peaceful lifestyle. At the Little Theatre in Middlesbrough he entertained the audience with a gripping tale of the weekend the Rohilla was lost.

Arthur passed away on 29 January 1995 at the grand age of 96. It has to be said that Arthur Shepherd lived a long and productive life and never forgot his experiences of when the hospital ship was lost, having read his cuttings in detail and whatever I could find and seeing his photographs, I have a lot of admiration for him, above all one statement he made really stands out and is something I think epitomises the tragedy of the *Rohilla*: 'It was the first and only shipwreck I have seen and I don't want to see another'

Arthur in the middle, outside
the new scout headquarters
in Middlesbrough, with
Peter Hewling DC and Field
Commissioner Ron Schulze.
(Courtesy Andrew McCall)

The lady I recognised in Arthur's photographs, Mrs Freda Ford went on to write about
Arthur in numerous publications and although there is probably no badge for it she
deserves recognition for keeping alive the memory of the very first recipient of The
Cornwell Scout Badge. Whilst other scouts have followed in Arthur's footsteps he has the
distinction of truly being the first recipient of the Cornwell Scout Badge.

On 13 June 2013, the *Evening Gazette* in Middlesbrough had a story with the headline
'National Fame For Middlesbrough Scouting Hero Arthur Shepherd'. The feature surrounded
an original piece of Scouting history that was being handed to the Scout Association national
archive. It described how the first ever Cornwell Badge, described as the Scouts' equivalent of
the Victoria Cross, was presented to a Middlesbrough man, Arthur Shepherd in 1916. After
Arthur passed away, the magnificent award remained with his family, first with his niece,
Judith, and then great-nephew Andrew.

County training administrator Freda Ford said: 'The Cornwell Scout Badge was collected
from the makers by Baden-Powell himself and brought to Middlesbrough to be presented to
Arthur.' She said: 'Middlesbrough has always been proud of this boy's achievements. I had

The original Cornwell badge is handed over to the Scout Association. Proud Moment: Back row from Michelle McCall-Smith, Andrew McCall Smith, Freda Ford and Daniel Scott-Davies. Front are Andrew's sons Oscar, and Louie.

the good fortune of meeting him when I organised a County Cub Day in Guisborough in 1986.' On that occasion Arthur gave a lively account of his role.

Andrew McCall-Smith, of Linthorpe, agreed to give the badge to the Scout Association. Handing the family treasure over at a meeting of St Barnabas 15th Scouts he said: 'It's a bit poignant.' It seemed apt that his own sons, Louie, nine, and Oscar, seven, a Cub and Beaver themselves respectively, along with his wife, Michelle, were by his side.

Accepting the badge on behalf of The Scout Association, archive and heritage manager Daniel Scott-Davies said: 'We are thrilled to receive it, especially being almost 100 years since the event itself.' The original badge will now be kept in the Scout Association's archive at its headquarters in Gilwell Park, London. A replica of his award was later made and given to Middlesbrough Scout District headquarters, in recognition of Arthur's achievements. I was overjoyed when Arthur's great-nephew presented me with a high-quality replica of the award, featuring Arthur andd Baden-Powell, something I will treasure.

Martha E. Mackenzie MBE, JP, daughter of Captain William Jefferson of Whitby, recalled the tragic loss of the *Rohilla* in the following article:

Having a few days 'leave' from Mulgrave Castle War Hospital, which I had the honour of superintending for the late Marquis of Normanby, I was visiting my parents on the outskirts of Whitby on 30 October 1914 when in the early hours of the morning we were wakened by the mournful sound of the foghorn and the intermittent cry of a ship's siren. There was no more sleep for us, as dawn was breaking we dressed, had breakfast and hurried into town to hear the sad news of the hospital ship Rohilla ashore near the Saltwick Nab. We were told that the Whitby lifeboat had been out, brought in a number of survivors, and had returned on a second errand of mercy which, alas, was not to be successful as she was 'holed' on the return voyage and made useless. She had however, managed to land more people, including some injured, two of whom I was able to help into a cab and accompany to the George Hospital, which, by now, was full to overflowing.

The fury of the storm prevented further attempts at rescue other than by rocket, which was also useless. The storm increased in ferocity as the tide rose, and nothing more could be done, except to join the milling crowd of searchers who kept watch on the shore for any survivors which might be washed ashore.

This task soon ended with the high tide and fading light, as our only lights where those from bicycles and a few hurricane lanterns. Next morning I went with Dr H. Raw and Dr Ross, more or less sliding down the cliffs as what were rough-cut steps had been worn down to a muddy pathway. We reached the hut, used in summer for picnickers, there we found sitting round a boiler were a number of men waiting for daylight. As dawn broke through some were getting desperate and attempting to swim or float ashore from the wreck, which by now consisted of little more than the bridge, both bow and stern having broken away and being covered by the high seas. I was just in time, as a body clothed in officer's uniform rolled up on a breaker, and on hurrying towards it found what proved to be the second engineer. He was unconscious and almost pulse-less.

With the aid of two young St John Ambulance Brigade men we turned him over and applied artificial respiration and after twenty minutes we saw signs of recovery. We carried him into the hut where the warmth and continued massage restored him sufficiently to be taken by the only conveyance available (an army stores van) to my parents' home where he was put to bed, and although threatened with pneumonia, he made an excellent recovery in about two weeks due to the care of my parents and sister. On 1 November a supreme effort was made by the motor lifeboat, all other attempts having failed to rescue the forty-five or more men still on board.

In a letter, she says her father suggested using oil on the water and that Mr R. Spaven offered to give as many gallons as required.

P. Cairns, secretary of the National Union of Ships Stewards & Cooks and of the Glasgow Fireman's Union, told the *Whitby Gazette* that 'the surviving members of the Union desired special thanks be conveyed to the women of Whitby for their heroic work on the Scar. Everything possible was done by them to make the survivors comfortable and we feel under a deep sense of gratitude to them for their kindly sympathy.'

When questioned by a newspaper reporter a rescuer gave the following account:

A quarter of an hour after hearing the first signal gun on Friday morning, namely at 4.30 a.m., I was in the street on my way to the seafront. The morning was pitch dark and rain was falling and a gale blowing. I was joined by a friend and, together, by the occasional flashing of my electric hand lamp, we found our way down Khyber Pass to the Battery front, where we observed the constant discharge of signal rockets sent up from a vessel in distress on the Scar, to the south of the harbour entrance. We judged the position of the vessel as being off 'Yellow Sand Bight', north of Saltwick Nab. Judging by the large number of signals sent up, we estimated that the vessel was a large one, possibly a liner, but we had to remain in ignorance until day dawned. In the meantime, between five and six o'clock, we followed a small company of men down the slipway onto the sands.

One of the men carried a torch, and by its light we came across a large quantity of wreckage and this, including portions of five collapsible lifeboats, confirmed our conjecture that the ship on the rocks was a large one. On the beach immediately opposite to the West Cliff Spa were the bodies of two men, one quite nude. These were immediately taken under the care of some ambulance men, including Mr Knaggs, who immediately applied themselves in an effort to restore animation. A thoughtful gentleman who had rushed off for a doctor met Dr Pern in Skinner Street, but on his arrival we learnt the sad intelligence that life was extinct in both cases. Leaving my friend, I made my way from the sands, up the Pier, and across the bridge on to the East Pier, from which through a telescope I got my first view of the ship on the rocks, in the position I have previously indicated. One of the ship's lifeboats was at the water's edge, under the cliff and not far from the Spa Ladder.

After each tide the shoreline would be strewn with all manner of debris from the wreck, broken woodwork and cases of medical instruments, masses of bandages and dressings and medical supplies etc. There seemed to be an abundance of lifebelts, and it was possible that early in the storm the boxes that contained these valuable, almost priceless, instruments at such a time, were washed away from their lashings. Tragically among all this litter, were the bodies of people from the ship, to be recovered later when the sea abated and the tide ebbed, it was a pitiful sight brought home by the sight of portions of five collapsible lifeboats, which never had the chance to be used in anger.

At a time when people's daily lives up and down the coast were a struggle, a shipwreck could prove to be a valuable boost. The *Rohilla* was sailing down the coast with 234 crew and medical staff on board and the capacity to care for up to 250 causalities, she could only do so with her stores well stocked. Those same stores now lay strewn up and down the coast. Nobody could forget the sad scenes that had led to this bounty, but mothers had children to feed at a time when the war was beginning to take a grip and food was limited.

As soon as the ship hit the rocks the ironwork twisted, and the shattered wooden decking was washed overboard. On the shore the men carried home what they could manage, making trip after trip because as a raw material the wood had a multitude of uses.

Any rough damaged timber could be burned, providing added warmth at a time of year when it was cold enough even without winter storms, but it also provided opportunities as a source of income. Craftsmen were able to make good use of the timber, creating some exquisite pieces of furniture including free-standing corner cabinets, smaller wall-mounted cabinets and chairs, all of which are sought after today.

Skilled wood workers could also turn wood collected from the shoreline into a *Rohilla* artefact of some description, whose sale provided a welcome boost to families' income. Candlesticks seem to have been one of the most popular things to make as they often come up for sale on the internet. They are generally around the same size but differ in design and quantity. I have two pairs with different designs and know the lifeboat museum has some similar in size. Some years ago I acquired a wooden hat/coat rack made from wood washed ashore from the wreck. It was in a pretty poor state and required some attention – thankfully Whitby has a small core of wonderful traditional cabinetmakers. With it looking as good as when first made, I chose one of the most iconic photographs of the *Rohilla* to fill the centre space and I am very pleased with it.

I have come across other smaller wooden objects which are only valuable for what they represent, and have seen bowls and boxes made to a high standard, but there are so many similar boxes from the same period that they don't command much of a price. The miniature life rings come up for sale from time to time and in good condition can sometimes fetch in the region of around £60.

An ornate wall-mounted cabinet, one of my favourite *Rohilla*-related items.

A small chair engraved with the letters of the ship BISNC. (Copyright Whitby Museum)

Two sets of wooden candlesticks made from wood from the *Rohilla*.

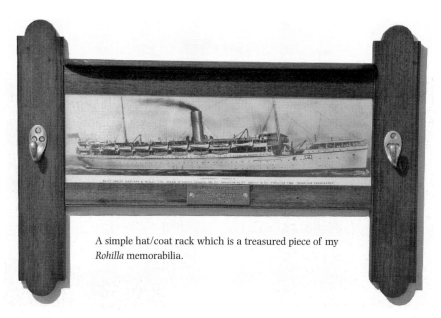

A simple hat/coat rack which is a treasured piece of my *Rohilla* memorabilia.

In 2001, however, I saw a small diorama half model of the *Rohilla* in a fetching triangular case. Also inside were two pieces of metal purported to be from the German bombardment of Whitby in December 1914. It was for sale on an internet auction website and I followed the sale with interest as the lifeboat museum has similar dioramas. I have seen less than a handful of these 12ft-long collectable items in almost three decades, making it a rare piece

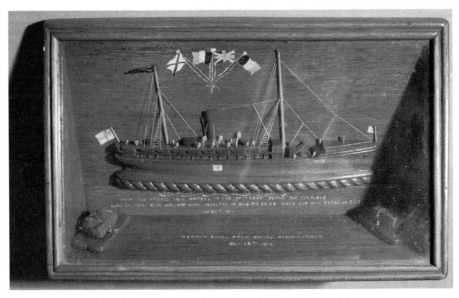

A diorama half model of the *Rohilla* with a short description of the vessel's fate.

and I therefore expected it to fetch a high price, so it didn't come as much of a surprise to see it reach just over £500.

The following letter of appreciation has been received by J.G.H. Wallis, of Custom House Hotel:

'The Anchorage', Runswick Bay – Nov, 10th, 1914

Dear Mr Willis, – The young men of Runswick desire me to convey to you their warmest and sincerest thanks for your kind and generous attention in supplying them with hot baths, hot coffee, and also for placing comfortable room for them to undress in after battling with the elements in rescuing a few of the crew of the ill-fated Rohilla. Your most kindly actions will always be indelibly engraved on the minds of the young men whom you so hospitably entertained. If ever it should be our privilege to reciprocate your great kindness, we should only be too pleased to do so.

Believe me,

Yours sincerely,

T. Patton.

J.W. Foster received the following letters from the Royal National Lifeboat Institution (RNLI) for whose local committee he was honorary secretary, relating to the services rendered at Whitby on the occasion of the wreck of the *Rohilla*. The first and second letters refer to the services of the Whitby and Upgang lifeboat, whilst the third relates to the efforts made to save life by 'personal exertion' from the shore.

Dear Sir

At a meeting of the Committee of Management, held here on the 12th instant, I laid before them the full reports of the services of the Whitby Lifeboats, as also those of the Upgang, Tynemouth, Scarborough, Robin Hood's Bay, and Teesmouth boats, in connection with the disastrous wreck of the Government Hospital Ship Rohilla, which stranded on 'Whitby Rock' during the night of 30 October in a whole ESE gale and a very heavy sea. It is needless for me to recapitulate here the full story of the action of the Whitby lifeboats under the direction of Coxswain Thomas Langlands. Suffice to say that the conduct of all concerned has characteristics of those qualities of fearless courage, splendid seamanship, endurance and humanity, which the nation associates with the Lifeboat service, and that the Whitby men have added a glorious page to the annals of heroism which form so honourable a record of their deeds. I have given on an accompanying sheet, a full statement of the rewards conferred by the Committee of Management for services rendered in connection with this week, services which were responsible for saving eighty-five lives by means of lifeboats and some fifty lives by means of gallant efforts made at great risk in some cases, from the shore.

In writing to the representative of the Whitby Branch, however, I desire on behalf of the Committee of Management to express their high appreciation of the splendid conduct of Coxswain Thomas Langlands, who in the course of arduous operations which resulted in saving so many lives, showed not only conspicuous courage and fine seamanship, but also rarer qualities of foresight, skillful organisation and dauntless perseverance which have proved his fitness as coxswain and leader of a group of gallant men. The Committee of Management have awarded to him the Gold Medal of the Institution, the highest honour that it is in their power to confer. It has been also a pleasure to award the Silver Medal of the Institution to Second Coxswain Richard Eglon, and £2 extra to each member of the crew of the Whitby No. 2 lifeboat and a pair of binocular glasses and a special letter of thanks to Captain John Milburn. The Committee have further marked their appreciation of the excellent services of Lt Basil Hall RN by awarding him the Silver Medal of the Institution. Lt Hall, as you are aware, practically took charge of the operations when he arrived at Whitby, arranged to take out a supply of oil to diminish the effect of the heavy sea breaking over the vessel, and went out in the Tynemouth motorboat, showing great judgement and gallantry in the operations connected with the final rescue of the fifty survivors. I enclose cheques representing the various momentary rewards and shall be glad of the men's receipts on the accompanying forms in due course. The medals and honorary rewards have been ordered, and I will communicate with you respecting their presentation.

George F. Shee, Secretary
Mr John W. Foster, Whitby

Dear Sir

At a meeting of the Committee of Management held here on the 12th instant, I laid before them a full report of the services of the Upgang lifeboat in connection with the attempted service to the Government Hospital Ship Rohilla. The bringing of this boat a long distance over the fields to the top of the cliff, with the aid of a large number of helpers, into Saltwick Bay was an extraordinarily fine one, and reflects great credit on the coxswain and all concerned. It is unfortunate that the conditions made it impossible for the boat to be launched on the Friday, but a gallant attempt was made to reach the wreck at dawn on Saturday, the coxswain and crew working against wind and tide until they were quite exhausted. The Committee of Management have decided to mark their appreciation of the excellent services of the coxswain and crew by awarding the thanks of the Institution engrossed on vellum, to Coxswain Pounder Robinson and to Second Coxswain T. Kelly; further an additional £1 to each of the crew, whose conduct was entirely in consonance with the fine traditions of Upgang, and of all this part of the coast, whose rocky nature and bracing climate seems well fitted to breed a race of heroes.

George F. Shee, Secretary

Mr John W. Foster, Whitby

Dear Sir

As referred to shortly in my other letter, the Committee of Management, at their other meeting, also had under their consideration, the very splendid and gallant services performed from the shore by many persons in their endeavour to save life from the Rohilla, and more particularly those performed by George Peart and the seventeen men whose names are set out in your report of the 10th instant. The Committee are satisfied that all these men displayed conspicuous gallant constantly swimming out without any life-line attached to him, and in frequently risking his life in the heavy sea. They therefore decided to bestow on him the Silver Medal of the Institution, together with a special gratuity of £10. Further, they decided to award the other men the sum of £2 each, and I enclose a cheque herewith, representing these rewards.

George F. Shee, Secretary

Mr John W. Foster, Whitby

He concluded that, at a time when the nation has daily to deplore the loss, on the field of honour, of gallant men fighting heroically for a great cause, the Committee of Management feel sure that the country will not forget those equally brave men who are prepared, day and night, in war no less than in peace, to face another enemy, the angry elements, in defence of the lives of their fellow men in peril on the sea; and the Committee appeal to the public to generously support a charity which provides and administers the

Lifeboat Service of the United Kingdom, and is thus the means of maintaining, among our maritime population, the qualities of courage, endurance and humanity which are among the best and most cherished characteristics of our race.

In addition to the ordinary scale of pay the lifeboat crewmen received the following awards:

WHITBY

Coxswain Thomas Langlands – RNLI – Gold Medal and £5
2nd Coxswain Richard Eglon – RNLI – Silver Medal
Captain John Milburn – A set of binoculars and a special letter of thanks
Each of the crew received £3 extra

UPGANG

Brought by road and lowered down the cliff with very great difficulty
Coxswain Pounder. Robinson – Thanks inscribed on vellum and £5
2nd Coxswain Thomas Kelly – RNLI – Thanks Inscribed on Vellum
Each of the crew received £3 extra

TYNEMOUTH

Captain H.E. Burton – RNLI – Gold Medal
Coxswain Robert Smith – RNLI – Gold Medal and £5
2nd Coxswain James Brownlee – RNLI – Silver Medal and £10
Permanent Motor Mechanic Thomas Cummins received a gratuity of £3
Lt Basil Hall, RN – Silver Medal of the Institution and £10.
Each of the crew received £3 extra

SCARBOROUGH

The lifeboat was towed from Scarborough by the trawler *Morning Star*, and, despite repeated attempts to get alongside the vessel during the day and night, was unable to render any assistance, both boats standing by overnight
The Coxswain received £5
Each of the crew received £3 extra

TEESMOUTH

Permanent Motor Mechanic a gratuity of £1
Each of the crew received £3 extra
Mr C.D. Bacon, Hon. Secretary received a distinctive set of binoculars, and special letter of thanks
River Tees Commissioners Tug, a special letters of thanks, and an unknown reward to the crew

HARTLEPOOL
Coxswain of the No. 2 boat   £2
Each of the crew received £3 extra.

The Hansell family, like many in Whitby, are devoted lifeboat volunteers and generation after generation have gone into the Institution. After the *Rohilla* disaster many of the lifeboatmen received a Bible from a minister who was on the *Rohilla*. It is a soft leather backed book with gold cover and the pages are all edged in gold. There is an inscription 'to John Hansell', and I think it says 'from the Rohilla'. The Bible has been passed down through generations and it is quite possible that there are very few left in Whitby.

The Master and Crew of the steam trawler Mayfly £10
The trawler owners received a special letter of thanks

Some of those on board the trawler received the following:
R.H. Whittleton, Master   £5
Captain Cappleman   £3
Captain King   £3
James Hastings   £3

In April 1915, the RNLI expressed its great appreciation of the services of the trawler *Morning Star* for its aid to the Scarborough lifeboat and a presentation of a pair of binoculars was made to skipper William Smalley. A grant of £10 was also awarded to be divided amongst the master and crew: 2nd hand T. Eves, 3rd hand F. Leadley, deck hand A. Johnstone, deck hand N. Cowling, engineer R. Anderson, engineer W. Ramm, fireman J. Wake and cook J. Bullamore. The awards were presented by C.C. Graham, the Mayor of Scarborough. W. Ramm said that 'the men were only sorry the Lifeboat could not get near some of those on the Rohilla. If such occasion arose again, the trawlermen would do what they could to help.' The owners of the trawler received a special letter of thanks and £5 compensation for two warps broken during the tow.

In March 1915, having read a report in the newspaper about the crew of the *Mayfly* being presented with a gratuity for services rendered to the *Rohilla* and the impending awards to the Scarborough lifeboat crew, Henry Sheader, the master of the Scarborough trawler *Bulldog* wrote to the Admiralty. It was his wish to ask their Lordships if his crew might also be considered worthy of being honoured with recognition for services rendered in the same incident, and outlined his case. While they did not offer any real assistance, the men of the *Bulldog* spent many long hours on the boat in poor weather.

In June, the Admiralty concluded their investigations and wrote to the captain of HM *Coastguard*, Harwich informing them that the sum of £2 would be paid to the skipper and £1 to each crewmember in recognition of their services on this occasion. The following month the district captain of HM Coastguard wrote to the Admiralty informing them that of those on the *Bulldog* at the time of the *Rohilla*'s loss, J. Barker and R. Appleby were missing from the trawler *Condor* and J.W. Duck was reported killed on the steam trawler *Aries*, thus requesting the authorities make the payments to the men's widows.

The Robin Hood's Bay Rocket Brigade later expressed great thanks to the many who supported them in their forty-eight hour vigil: Matthew Stevenson and his wife of Saltwick, W.A. and T.K. Smith of Robin Hood's Bay, and many others whose names are unknown, who helped supply food and comfort. Had it not been for their forethought, the brigade may have fared badly, attending as they did at a moment's notice, without provision and, in many cases, adequate clothing.

Whitby Police received £10 from the RNLI and £25 from the owners of the *Rohilla*. Captain Neilson was also awarded the Bronze Medal of the RSPCA for rescuing the ship's cat. Charles Davie, Coastguard Chief Officer, CPO Charles Hale and those serving at the War Signal Station, Whitby were also specially mentioned for recognition.

Sergeant Hood, honorary secretary of the Whitby Ambulance Brigade, recorded in the Occurrence Book that 'Whitby St John Ambulance Brigade, who did splendid work, have officially received nothing, which was no doubt disheartening given how extensive their work was especially as the branch was essentially a fledging unit.'

Upon leaving Whitby to return to HMS *George*, Captain Raikes was required to write a full report for the Admiralty. In the latter part of the said report he acknowledged some of those he considered worthy of mention.

Where everyone concerned behaved with so much eagerness to assist, it was difficult to single out any particular lifeboat or individual for special recognition. He declared the inhabitants of Whitby most persevering and in some cases most gallant in their efforts to assist the men who reached the shore. He noted that the residents rendered every possible assistance both in billeting the survivors and providing cars, and many local medical professionals were particularly public spirited in their services to the survivors.

Captain Goodrich and his detachment of the Devon Motor Cyclist Corps stationed at Whitby rendered the greatest possible assistance in every way, and I submit that the excellent services of this officer, and the commanding officer of the boy scouts organisation of Whitby may be brought to the notice of their Lordships, with a view to their receiving commendation.

Lt-Commander Philip W.C. Sharpe rendered invaluable assistance in tracing survivors who were scattered all over the town, so that many relations and friends were spared considerable anxiety. The Secretary of the Shipwrecked Mariners Society was most successful in his efforts to billet and clothe the survivors. Surgeon Thos. C.L. Jones RNVR, one of the survivors, also rendered valuable assistance in many ways.

The district captain of HM Coastguard, Harwich submitted to the Admiral Commanding Coast Guard and Reserves Admiralty, the following recognition in November 1914:

I would bring to your notice the good service rendered, on the occasion of the stranding of the S.S. Rohilla off Whitby, by Able Seaman Alex Corpse, R.N.R. of H.M.S. 'Queen' who, at the time was on leave after an operation for appendicitis. Lieutenant Commander P.W.C. Sharpe of H.M.S. 'St George' reported to me that Corpse rendered great assistance in getting the men who swam ashore out of the surf, continually going out with the aid of the life lines.

An urgent appeal was launched in support of the RNLI and in a letter issued by the Duke of Northumberland, President of the Institution, attention was directed to the fact that while the war was being confronted the 'conditions prevailing along our coastline such as the extinction of lights and the presence of floating minefields that greatly increase danger to shipping and added fresh risks to the hazardous work of lifeboatmen.'

The Scene Filmed

Pathé Frères, the cinematograph producing company, rushed a party of photographers and operators to Whitby upon learning of the tragedy. The footage, which can be viewed on the Pathé website, begins seaward looking at the wreck and then turns shoreward showing the anxious but helpless crowd of spectators, who, regardless of the elements, have assembled to see the last of the ill-starred ship. Rescuers are seen at work, rushing boldly into the surf with long lifelines, sometimes swept off their feet by the powerful waters. The last scene shows rescuers carrying a lifeless body from the shore.

There is another piece of footage, which can be found on the BFI Screenonline website, an online film encyclopaedia featuring hundreds of hours of film and television clips from the vast collections of the BFI National Archive. The footage is short, lasting a little over a minute, but nonetheless it is a snapshot in time and truly gives one the chance to experience the tragedy. A view of the wreck shows the bridge, the only remaining part of the ship, the top of the derrick just in front snapped and the razor-sharp jagged edges of the fore section, which the lifeboats had to avoid during rescue attempts. The film then cuts to the shattered remains of the No. 2 lifeboat, the breach seemingly running the length of the hull having made two trips to the wreck. There is a glimpse of the shoreline littered with wreckage of all kinds; wood can be seen piled high where the force of the sea had thrown it at high water. Men and women can be seen gathering what they could.

In October 1916 the British government set up a committee to produce a commemorative memorial plaque in bronze to be given to the relatives of the men and women whose deaths were attributable to the Great War. It was agreed that an open competition be set up in August 1917 for a suitable design for a plaque that would record the name of a fallen British or Dominion Forces serviceman or woman. The shortlisted entries would be offered prizes of up to £500.

On 13 August 1917, *The Times* published strict rules as to what must be included within the design of the plaque, which could be square, circular or rectangular but whose dimensions were set at 18in square with a diameter of 4.5in, if circular; if rectangular, then no larger than 5in x 3.6in. The design had to incorporate a symbolic figure and bear an inscription agreed by the committee which read 'He/She died for Freedom and Honour.' Each design should also include space for the name, initials and military unit of the deceased. More than 800 entries were received from within the United Kingdom, and across the British Empire. In October 1917 it was announced that the committee had also decided to issue a commemorative scroll to next of kin to accompany the bronze plaque. The text caused the committee some trouble. Dr Montague Rhodes James, Provost of King's College Cambridge was approached to make some changes to the wording put forward by the committee. King George V then asked for a small change to the draft so that he could be included in the wording. The final text was printed in a calligraphic script on paper bearing the Royal Arms, followed by hand-written text giving the name of the serviceman/woman, his/her rank and regiment.

The winner of the competition was Edward Carter Preston from Liverpool, whose design, 'Pyramus', depicts Britannia holding a trident and myrtle wreath with a lion standing at her feet and dolphins playing on either side. The inscription runs round the edge and below Britannia's hand is a space for the name of the deceased. The artist's initials, E.C.P., appear by the lion's fore paws. The plaques were put into production in December 1918 and over 1 million were made.

The plaques were dispatched separately from the scrolls in a stiff card wrapping enclosed within white envelopes bearing the royal arms. Both plaque and scroll were accompanied by a letter from King George V that bore a facsimile signature and read as follows:

I Join With My Grateful People In Sending You This Memorial Of A Brave Life Given For Others In The Great War.

From 1919 onwards some 1,150,000 scrolls were issued to commemorate those who had fallen and were sent out in cardboard tubes bearing the royal crest.

William Anderson's will, which he had hidden in a drawer in his father's house, was subsequently the subject of a court action. It was declared invalid on the grounds that at the time he made it, he was serving at HMS *Pembroke*, was not a ship but a barracks, meaning that he was not entitled to make a 'Sailor's Will'. His fiancée, Edith Downes, for whose benefit William had made the will, received nothing.

In 2008, I received a letter sent on by my publisher from a gentleman named Jude James, a historical consultant alerting me to the existence of a flag which once belonged to the *Rohilla* and now has pride of place in St Andrew's church, Tiptoe. Mr James had written a column for a newspaper in which he explained that the flag hangs to commemorate the loss of the *Rohilla*, he goes on to tell how it was presented to the

G v R I

HE whom this scroll commemorates
was numbered among those who,
at the call of King and Country, left all
that was dear to them, endured hardness,
faced danger, and finally passed out of
the sight of men by the path of duty
and self-sacrifice, giving up their own
lives that others might live in freedom.
Let those who come after see to it
that his name be not forgotten.

Car. Crew George Brain
H. M. Hospital S. Rohilla

The scroll sent to George Brain's next of kin. (Courtesy of John Stephenson)

The Tom Petty Commemorative Plaque.
(Courtesy Edna Chadwick)

church in December 1914 by the second officer of the ship, Charles William Fairfax Morgan, who had swum ashore.

Beneath the flag is a descriptive panel created by the renowned Milford architect William Ravenscroft: 'The flag of the "Rohilla" mined off Whitby Oct 30 1914 while serving as H.M. HOSPITAL SHIP. One of the few things saved: this Flag was given to the Church by C. W. Fairfax Morgan, R.N.R., 2nd Officer who swam ashore when the Ship was wrecked.'

The flag is unique among *Rohilla* paraphernalia, unlike anything I have come across before, and I would very much like to see it for myself, but it is too far away. The lifeboat museum curator has suggested that he already has a couple of *Rohilla* flags, but in the many years I have been involved with the sea and all it encompasses I have never seen any flags displayed.

The ship's wheel was taken to Barnoldswick, where it remained with the descendants of John Thomas Pickles. When he passed away, the wheel was moved around amongst relatives until they all agreed to donate it to the lifeboat museum. Shortly afterwards a Middlesbrough newspaper featured a story about a gentleman who had read about the donation in the *Evening Gazette* and claimed to also have a ship's wheel from the *Rohilla* which bore all the same identification marks, such as builder, etc.

The museum also has a steam whistle and ship's bell, the latter of which was rung at the end of a fundraising row. It has been mentioned that to mark the 2014 centenary there might be a short demonstration of the steam whistle, though great care must be taken given that it has probably already passed its centenary.

In collecting memorabilia myself I have been quite fortunate indeed, over the years a number of families have given me items because they are assured it is going to someone

The ship's flag, which once flew from the stern of the *Rohilla*. (Copyright Jude James)

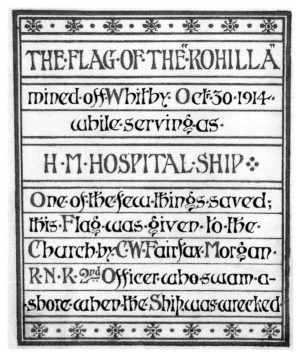

A woven panel detailing the flag's history. (Copyright Jude James)

The *Rohilla*'s wheel, bell and steam whistle.

who would appreciate it; the items are unique and are now precious to me. I also follow quite a few auction houses and have my details registered with them just in case something comes up. A couple of years ago I secured a silver purse from an online auction website, which is engraved with: 'To Miss E. Phillips from A. Winstanley'. It really caught my attention as I knew Archibald Winstanley had survived the loss of the hospital ship and Nurse E. Phillips, was a founding member of the Whitby Division of the St John Ambulance Brigade, it is therefore highly likely that Archibald may have been treated by Nurse Phillips and this was his way of showing his gratitude.

One of my latest acquisitions is an impressive ornamental eggcup, a unique object. It is a delicate little thing and has the twin flags common amongst the BISNC fleet and bears the title of HMT *Rohilla*. I have gathered all manner of silverware related to the *Rohilla* over the years, but the egg cup, being so different, stands out quite nicely. Having an assortment of *Rohilla* kitchen/tableware, I have often thought about setting up our dining table with it. It would be quite picturesque, but as there is no danger of it actually being used, my wife isn't so keen.

I came across an enamel badge for another BISNC ship, yet it was only when one was gifted to me that I thought about what others might exist. Since then I have come across other

A delicate silver purse engraved 'To Miss E. Phillips from A. Winstanley'.

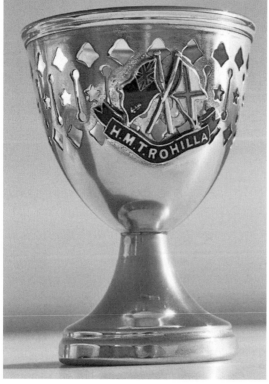

A delightful egg cup displaying the twin flags often used by the BI fleet and bearing the title of HMT *Rohilla*.

badges for the *Rohilla*. Because of their rarity they do come at some cost, one in particular on an internet auction went beyond what I was willing to pay. I still have three, which I am quite proud of and given the right occasion I might just be tempted to wear one or all of them.

Three enamel badges, which appear to be from *Rohilla*'s duties as a troopship.

8

ANNIVERSARIES AND COMMEMORATIONS

As we move towards the centenary of the loss of the *Rohilla* there is no denying that it is Whitby's worst maritime disaster and is still recorded as one of the worst services amongst the annals of the RNLI. Even with the passage of time, the tragedy that befell the *Rohilla* at Saltwick Nab in October 1914 is still felt in Whitby. At key anniversaries of the disaster large events have been held to remember those tragic scenes, not only to commemorate those who lost their lives, but to celebrate those who survived.

The Whitby division of the St John Ambulance Brigade maintained its acquaintance with the Barnoldswick division after their shared experience of such a devastating tragedy. Following the loss of the *Rohilla* and the lives of twelve Barnoldswick St John Ambulance Brigade men, the final Sunday in October was routinely set aside and referred to as 'Rohilla Sunday', a tradition that lasted for fifty years. The St John Ambulance Brigade would lead a parade through the town to the Cenotaph in Letcliffe Park, where a wreath was laid in memory of the lost twelve, followed by a united church service. There was talk of a memorial at the time of the disaster and a fund was started, but other tragedies overtook events and the names of *Rohilla*'s fatalities were finally included in the list of over 250 young lives who were lost in the 'War to end all Wars', a list augmented with many more names in a second global conflict just over two decades later.

ROHILLA DISASTER RECALLED
Memorial Service for Barnoldswick Ambulance Men
Impressive Scene at the Cemetery

One of the saddest features of the loss of the hospital ship was the impact of the deaths of the twelve members of the Barnoldswick division of the St John Ambulance Brigade. The loss of twelve men in one incident hit the small town hard. They were skilled civilian ambulance men who had volunteered for service with the Royal Naval Sick Berth Reserve. In all the party numbered fifteen, but William Eastwood, Private Anthony Waterworth and Private Fred Reddiough survived the disaster, being amongst those rescued. The men who drowned were: Corporal Milton Birtwistle, Corporal William Daly, Sergeant Arthur Petty, and privates Thomas Petty, Thomas Horsfield, Walter Horsfield, Albert Elsworth, John Pickles, Harry Hodkinson, Frank Dunkley, Henry Barter and William Anderson.

Relatives of the fallen men have at different times visited Whitby, but in the spring of 1926 Frank Widdup, president of the Barnoldswick division of the St John Ambulance Brigade made arrangements for a large group to visit. The intention was to hold a service at the *Rohilla* memorial in Whitby cemetery, where some of the Barnoldswick men were laid to rest. Superintendent Knaggs of the Whitby St John Ambulance Brigade and his officers gladly agreed to take part in the ceremony, and arrangements were made to greet their counterparts. Unfortunately, Dr Raw, the chairman of the urban district council, who was also divisional surgeon of the Whitby division, was unable to extend the welcome. Councillor W.W. Milburn, vice-chairman of the urban district council took great pride in being able to welcome such an honoured party in his place. The Rev. P.J.S. Russell was asked to give the address at the cemetery service as the Rector of Whitby (the Rev. C.R. Hone, MA, RD) was also absent that day.

About fifty members of the Barnoldswick ambulance nursing divisions and friends made the 103-mile journey by charabanc, and reached Whitby about midday. Frank Widdup accompanied the party, and Assistant-Commissioner Wilson (Middlesbrough) also accepted an invitation to be present. The excursionists enjoyed the run, especially over the moors, and showed their interest in Whitby immediately on arrival. They had the advantage of beautiful weather, and could not but contrast the brilliant sunshine and the placid sea with the terrible conditions experienced when the *Rohilla* came to grief. The headquarters for the day was Hood's Marine Cafe, which had willingly thrown open its doors during the tragedy to serve as a base for the rescuers. The visitors were treated to a hot lunch, after which a short time was given over to speeches of welcome.

Councillor W. W. Milburn said that, in the absence of Dr Raw, chairman of the Whitby urban district council, he had been asked to welcome the Barnoldswick Ambulance Division to Whitby, on behalf of the Council and the inhabitants generally, and he extended them a very hearty welcome indeed. They regretted the circumstances that led to the visit, but he thought the people of Barnoldswick would realise that they had the full sympathy of the inhabitants of Whitby, who remembered only too well the loss of the *Rohilla* and the sacrifice of many brave lives. They admired the fortitude of those who died, and the heroism of the rescuers. He desired, on behalf of the inhabitants of Whitby, to assure them that their loved ones were not and never would be forgotten by the people of Whitby.

Superintendent Knaggs said he could say truthfully that 'he had lived for the day to meet the friends and relatives of the men of the Barnoldswick division for nearly twelve years.' He said, 'They in Whitby were, somewhat isolated insofar as St John Ambulance work was concerned, and they seldom came in contact with members of other divisions; and consequently there was great enthusiasm amongst, the Whitby division for the service they were to hold that afternoon.' He explained how, in conjunction with Dr Mitchell and Ambulance Officer Hood, the Whitby division had come to be formed: although they had been connected with the St John Ambulance Association for some years, there was no local division. Three or four of them met in that room and decided in 1914 to form the Whitby Ambulance Division, but they had no proper stretchers or equipment, and had to make do. It seemed inconceivable that in the space of six or seven weeks they were called upon to render first aid in the biggest disaster that had ever occurred on this coast; and they would agree that very few divisions had been called upon to do the same kind of work.

There were about thirty trained to administer first aid, but little did they expect the demand to be of such magnitude. The men responded with great enthusiasm and from the early morning of Friday until the Sunday the work never flagged and they were on duty day and night. Dozens of cases had to be carried up to 2 miles in terribly stormy conditions, yet they were able to save lives; it was a very great pleasure to be able to do the work of the Order of St John. On behalf of the Whitby Division Superintendent Knaggs gave a hearty welcome to his brothers and sisters from Barnoldswick; they were working with one end and aim – to serve their heavenly Father. They were very grateful for the visitors' kind words regarding the Whitby division and their visit, which he hoped would be a great success.

Lady Mitchell said it gave her great pleasure to welcome the Barnoldswick ambulance and nursing divisions: the Whitby divisions would be proud to accompany them to the last resting place of the members of Barnoldswick division who lost their lives when the hospital ship *Rohilla* met her doom near Whitby. It was well that they should do this, to remind the young people of the great sacrifices that were made in the days of the Great War. Many of those present would forever remember the dreadful tragedy of those three days, now nearly twelve years ago, when they saw the most heart-rending scene anyone could witness. The brave ship torn asunder, with what remained of her gallant crew huddled together on the middle portion, washed by the high seas and buffeted by cruel wind and sleet, with no food for three days and nights, and though they were able to see them quite distinctly from the shore they were powerless to render assistance. Though a constant vigil was kept and anxious eyes watched and willing hands were waiting to receive and tend the pool souls, as they were either washed overboard or jumped into the seething waves in sheer desperation. Then Whitby folk looked back on the last, sad scene when the dead were laid to rest. The visitors had come from Barnoldswick to pay homage to their memory, and to stand beside them for a short while; and their thoughts would go

Members of the Whitby and Barnoldswick nursing divisions.

back to those dear ones who gave their lives that they all might live, and to whom they were ever grateful. She was very pleased to be there that day, and more than glad to be introduced to the survivors of the disaster. It was very pleasing to think they were here again under happier circumstances, and she was very glad to see them all.

Ambulance Officer Christopher Hood then read the account of the wreck of the *Rohilla* as recorded in the Occurrence Book of the Ambulance Division, including the message of congratulations from Surgeon T.C. Littler-Jones to the Ambulance workers for their efforts. The account was listened to with much interest. Frank Widdup, as president of the Barnoldswick Ambulance Association, said his first duty was to apologise for the party's non-appearance on 29 May. They had made preliminary arrangements to make a visit but as a result of a railway strike they had had to postpone it. It was subsequently decided to make the journey by road hence their arrival that day. In reply to the Vice-Chairman of the urban district council, he could assure them it gave him great pleasure to acknowledge the sincere welcome that had been extended to them on what was to them an auspicious occasion. That day they recalled the sad disaster that befell twelve respected members of the Barnoldswick Ambulance Division at the end of October 1914. The inhabitants of Barnoldswick would ever be grateful for the many kindnesses and valued assistance rendered by the townspeople of Whitby in endeavouring to relieve suffering. Barnoldswick St John Ambulance Brigade had wished to visit Whitby on many occasions; several members had been in the town in previous years to pay tribute to their departed comrades and had said how kindly they were treated. Mr Widdup hoped that the visit of the Barnoldswick divisions would, with the kind co-operation of the Whitby divisions, become an annual event. He offered hearty thanks to Superintendent Knaggs on behalf of the Barnoldswick Ambulance Divisions for the very kind welcome that had been accorded them. The Whitby Ambulance Division was fortunate in having such a worthy and capable officer as Superintendent Knaggs at its head, and the prosperity of the division was thereby assured. The fascinating and wretched account of the wreck of the *Rohilla* could not have been given by an abler person than Mr Hood. In listening to it, their minds were carried back to that terrible and awe-inspiring scene when the men of the Barnoldswick division went to their deaths bravely for king and country, as did members of St John Ambulance Divisions throughout the land.

Following the lunch the members of the Barnoldswick ambulance and nursing divisions, the Whitby Ambulance and Nursing Division, the lifeboat crew and ex-Ambulance men paraded outside the Seaman's Institute, and marched in procession by way of Bridge Street to the cemetery. They hoped and trusted that their former members, who lost their lives near Whitby's shore, would ever be remembered, and their resting place tended and revered for all time. They need not have worried as the last earthly resting place of those who lost their lives in the great wreck looked particularly neat and tidy for the occasion. Mrs Wallis (Custom House Hotel) and Miss L. Harrison had worked industriously cleaning up the grave and flowers given by Councillor H.A.S. Gover gave it a very nice appearance.

Large crowds lined the route, and a number of people followed the procession to pay tribute to those who lost their lives in the *Rohilla*. At the cemetery gates the company was met by it the Rev. P.J.S. Russell (representing the Rector of Whitby Rev. C.R. Hone MA, RD), Rev. T. Harrison Burnett (Wesleyan minister and president of the Whitby Free Church Council) and I. Haslop, who was charge of the Seamen's Institute at Whitby, and had been closely associated with the rescue work. The hymn 'Rock of ages, cleft for me' was started, and the procession slowly wended its way to the monument erected to the memory of those who lost their lives in the most disastrous wreck Whitby has experienced.

On arrival at the grave, the hymn 'O God, our help in ages past' was sung while the parade was marshalled in front of the monument. Amongst those present were Councillor W.W. Milburn (ex-chairman of the Whitby urban district council), Councillor R.W. Milburn, Councillor J.R. Tesseyman, Councillor F. Clough, V.S. Gray (clerk to the Whitby urban district council) and Dr E. Baines, whose excellent work in connection with the wreck of the *Rohilla* won widespread commendation.

The impressive service opened with prayers by the Rev. T. Harrison Burnett, following which he read a portion of Revelation 9. During the singing of the hymn 'Eternal Father, strong to save', several floral tributes were laid on the grave by representatives from Barnoldswick. The joint St John Ambulance Brigades sent a very handsome floral anchor, with the inscription 'From the Whitby, Skinningrove, and Grosmont Ambulance Brigades', and the simple words 'They died on duty.'

I. Haslop addressed those present with the words, 'Be thou faithful unto death and I will give to thee the crown of life.' He said that they 'stood there that afternoon in memory of

The joint brigades' floral anchor tribute 'They died on duty.'

their brothers who laid down their lives in the wreck of the hospital ship Rohilla. Those present who remembered that wreck and saw and watched for two days and nights, would never forget it, and would call to memory those who were drowned'.

With regard to the great work, he said that as he stood so close and yet so helpless, knowing all that could be done had been done, he saw men on the poop thrown one by one into the surging sea below. They did not fall into the water without a struggle, and when they were in the water they set out for the shore, and the people on the shore linked together in a human chain and went into the water to try and reach them. 'Let us not forget those who perished before they reached that chain and whose lives were lost.'

Nothing was left undone to save those men. They were heroes. They had left their homes at the call of duty and country to try and rescue their fellow men, risking death on the battlefield of France. They were not destined to meet their journey's end, and their deaths reminded them of the words. The work was finished ere scare begun. The noble spirit with which those men faced death could not have been surpassed on any battlefield. They stood on the ship and knew there was no chance of saving themselves or being saved. They fell, in the strength of life, into the sea and death. Death was faced with the courage of the battlefields, which they bore to the end when they fell struggling. They, for their part, had to strive to be faithful, and although they might not be successful in reaching the goal they would have to keep trying. He saw that grave uncovered, and was present when everybody was interred the whole length of the trench being used. Those men did not reach the goal for which they were aiming, but they had been faithful even unto death, unto God and their country. Their souls were now with God, while their mortal remains were resting in that trench.

When the people attending that service returned they went back to face the great battle of life, and they should strive for the goal for which God intended them. They stood there that day, and thought of the noble courage their brethren had shown, and they would return, he hoped, strengthened by the example of those who had been faithful and were now at rest. Their memory should be a great inspiration to all to 'be faithful unto death.'

At the conclusion of the address prayers were offered by the Rev. P.J.R. Russell, and after the pronouncement of the Benediction 'Last Post' was sounded by trumpeters Belchamber and Easton (RFA), following a two-minute silence, after which the buglers sounded Reveille.

The impressive ceremony then concluded, and the procession re-formed. After parading to Spital Bridge, the parade was dismissed and the Barnoldswick visitors proceeded to the cliffs to view the scene of the wreck before leaving.

50th Anniversary 1964

Impressive Services on Land and Sea at Whitby

The laying of wreaths in the sea off Saltwick Nab was a moving end to the last of three ceremonies commemorating the loss of the *Rohilla*. It was mild, sunny and hazy, the sea was calm, with only a gentle breeze – a great contrast to the stormy conditions of the weekend half a century. ago

The arrangements for the commemoration were made by a local committee of which William Wright, clerk of Whitby urban district council, was secretary and his counterpart from Barnoldswick F. Wilkinson, clerk of the Barnoldswick urban district council. The day's commemorations began at the Spa theatre, where the visitors from Barnoldswick and invited guests were entertained to lunch. The RNLI was represented by Field Marshal Sir Francis W. Festing and Denham Christie, members of the committee of the board of management; Commander L.F. Hill, North East District Inspector of Lifeboats; Lt B. Miles, Assistant District Inspector; Miss I.E. Morison, organising secretary for the North East District; Miss D.M. Walker, president of Whitby Ladies Lifeboat Guild; Eric Thomson, secretary of the Whitby branch; and members of the branch committee. Three lifeboatmen from Tynemouth, the station from which the *Henry Vernon* came to Whitby, also attended: Coxswain Robert Burton, William Stephenson and crewman John Elsdon. Also present were Joseph Taylor and his wife, of Grantham, and Jane the oldest granddaughter of the late Robert Smith, coxswain of the *Henry Vernon*. The Teesmouth lifeboat station was represented by Coxswain John Stonehouse, mechanic Colin Coates and Clive Porter. Two attendees worthy of high praise, Harry Richardson, aged 82, of Bakehouse Yard, Whitby, and his brother, John, aged 77, of Tate Hill, remain the only living members of the 1914 Whitby lifeboat crew.

John Mallinson, Superintendent of Whitby Ambulance Brigade, Dr W.G. Taylor, the divisional surgeon (who served his apprenticeship with the British India Steam Navigation Co.) attended, together with members of the ambulance and nursing divisions, representatives of the Whitby branch of the British Red Cross Society, and the Whitby branch of the British Legion and the Women's section.

The owners of the *Rohilla*, the British India Steam Navigation Co., were represented by Captain D.B. Lattin, chief marine superintendent (who lived in Sandsend and went to Miss Preston's school in Bagdale at the time of the disaster). Commodore D.R.P. Gun-Cunningham OBE (retired), Commodore J.P. Dobson (president), J.J. Storr (chairman) and T. Atkinson (secretary) represented Whitby Fishermen's and Boatmen's Society.

Among the party from Barnoldswick were Councillor W.H. Smith; Ambulance Superintendent Eric Wilkinson and Lady Superintendent D. Ayrton, and about fifteen men and women members of the ambulance and nursing divisions. Three of the fifteen members of the division who survived the *Rohilla* disaster also attended, as did Clarence Downes, vice-chairman of the Barnoldswick branch of the British Legion and Maurice T. Myers, the standard bearer, Charles Edward King, aged 85, of Burton Leonard, the oldest member of the Barnoldswick Ambulance Division of the St John Ambulance Brigade, and a detachment from the 45th Battalion Green Howards (TA).

One of the Barnoldswick ladies present had special privilege of a unique middle name, Hazel Rohilla Wilson, whose uncle William Anderson was lost in the disaster, was given the name at his request, the day before the ship was wrecked. The *Rohilla* wheel was brought from Barnoldswick by Norman Pickles, whose father, Tom Pickles, a member of the Barnoldswick Ambulance Division, was lost on the ship. Norman Pickles is also a nephew of Mr Reddiough, one of the survivors; and the ship's wheel was left to him by Amy Parrat of Whitby.

Welcoming the guests at the Spa theatre, Councillor H.B. Cummins, chairman of Whitby urban district council, accompanied by Mrs Cummins, said the thoughts of people from so many places must be occupied with the tragic events of fifty years ago. The tragedy of that dreadful weekend was burnt on the hearts and minds of a great many people, and they recalled with thankfulness the devoted efforts of many who endeavoured not only to rescue those on the *Rohilla*, but to sustain and comfort those who were rescued and those who were bereaved. The disaster provoked the type of response which made the British a great people.

It was a day filled with memories for two of the Barnoldswick Brigade survivors, Anthony Waterworth aged 77, then blind and living at Morecambe, and Fred Reddiough, aged 73. The only other Barnoldswick survivor, William Eastwood, had passed away shortly before the anniversary.

Two survivors of the *Rohilla* from Barnoldswick, Anthony Waterworth and Fred Reddiough, flanked by John Richardson (left) and Harry Richardson (right), two Whitby lifeboatmen on service at the wreck. (Copyright Whitby Literary & Philosophical Society)

People pause at the *Rohilla* grave in 1964 in one last act of remembrance. (Copyright Whitby Literary & Philosophical Society)

At the *Rohilla* grave in Whitby cemetery, local people were joined by 100 visitors from Barnoldswick, where earlier in the day the annual remembrance service had been held for the twelve members of the town's St John Ambulance Brigade who lost their lives serving in the *Rohilla* in the Sick Berth Reserve. Wreaths were laid by Councillor Cummins on behalf of Whitby urban district council, Captain Lattin for the British India Steam Navigation Co., Sir Francis Festing for the RNLI, Eric Wilkinson on behalf of Barnoldswick Ambulance Division, Councillor Smith for the Barnoldswick urban district council, Clarence Downes for the Barnoldswick British Legion. Sgt J. Mallinson and Sgt H. Kipling for the Whitby Ambulance Brigade, T. Atkinson for the Whitby Fishermen's Society, and numerous others were laid by relatives of those lost in the wreck. 'Last Post' and Reveille were sounded by G. Belchamber, and prayers were offered by Canon Arthur Perryman, the rector was Frank Winterbottom, missioner at Whitby Missions to Seamen

The wreath-laying at the cemetery was followed by a service of commemoration at St Mary's Parish church. The ensign of the RNLI and the house flag of the British India Steam Navigation Company hung from the chancel, and on the steps were three lifebelts from the *Rohilla* and the ship's wheel.

Canon Perryman opened the service with the words: 'We are met to remember and commend to God the souls of those who lost their lives in the wreck of the hospital ship *Rohilla*, and to commemorate the courage and endurance of those heroic efforts which affected the saving of many lives on that tragic occasion fifty years ago.' The lesson from the Book of Wisdom 3 and St John 15, was read by Rev. Norman Sugden, president of Whitby Free Church

Council. For part of the reading he used a Bible presented to Mr John Dryden, a member of the 1914 Whitby lifeboat crew, all of whom received a Bible for their services to the *Rohilla*.

In his address the rector said that the tragedy of half a century previously was an imperishable part of Whitby's history and, indeed, part of the heritage of many outside its boundaries. The indelible impression the tragedy had made upon the folk of Whitby and the surrounding district was shown by the fact that now, fifty years later, they met to remember those who gave their lives for their fellow men and for their country, as much as did any of those who served in the forces on land, at sea, or in the air. They remembered, too, the astonishing response that their need evoked from those trained and skilled to help their fellow men, and those who, having no special training in help and aid, yet opened their hearts and homes to make sure that those who were rescued received the care and comfort they required.

On that tragic occasion men and women attempting to aid their fellow man became victims of war and the fury of nature. They found themselves in need of help and succour, and found it here on these rocky shores, in the homes of men and women who well appreciate the hazards of those who to sea in ships. Here they found the love and compassion to help them in their great need. Here too, they found the love and sympathy for those whose lives were lost, and for those near and dear to them who came to this place in sorrow. So it is not surprising that fifty years on we still remember.

There is so much in the world that is regarded as worthy of notice, so much that men feel is important. But today we are witnessing something which is not just of transient importance. We are witnessing and thanking God for an integral part of man's love for his fellowmen. Today we commemorate a local saga of sacrifice, heroism and a practical expression of love and care for fellowmen. It is a saga which links up with the great example of Our Lord Himself, He who made the greatest of all sacrifices, He who was love and compassion, He who loved and served that man might know love and serve God, and find the strength and the power to love and serve his neighbour. During the service the hymns 'O God, Our Help in Ages Past', 'Eternal Father Strong to Save' and 'Praise to the Holiest' were sung.

Whitby lifeboat headed a fleet of fishing boats and numerous other small craft carrying people to Saltwick Nab, close to the scene of the disaster. Canon Perryman conducted a brief but powerful service from the lifeboat *Mary Ann Hepworth*. It was a memorable scene, the lifeboatmen clearly discernible on the crowded vessel by the red woollen caps of their service dress. As the boats rolled gently, 'Last Post' sounded to precede a moving two-minute silence broken only by the lapping of the water against the sides of the boats and the cries of seagulls wheeling over the east cliff.

Reveille echoed across the sea in a requiem for the eighty-nine lost in the disaster. Wreaths were committed to the water by Captain Lattin on behalf of the shipping company; Divisional Officer H. Waters and Private Bert Major, representing Whitby St John Ambulance Brigade; Commodore J.P. Dobson, president of Whitby Fishermen's and Boatmen's Society; 2nd Coxswain R. Pennock; and Eric Thompson, RNLI branch secretary, on behalf of the lifeboat crew.

A two-minute silence observed on the Whitby lifeboat *Mary Ann Hepworth*. (Copyright Whitby Literary & Philosophical Society)

Several hundred people watched the ceremony, for besides those afloat a big crowd lined the top of the east cliff. The brilliant orange glow of the setting sun was reflected by the sea silhouetting the onlookers on the clifftop, creating a wonderful scene to end the day.

The commemoration event held in 1964 was the last combined ceremony with Barnoldswick. Future anniversary proceedings were still held at key times, with new generations of descendants of the twelve men lost in the disaster coming to pay their respects. As the years passed the *Rohilla* was featured less in the *Whitby Gazette*, but from time to time, and especially around the time of the anniversary, there would often be a letter from someone affected by the tragedy – some of the correspondence appears here courtesy of the *Gazette*.

John Richardson and his brother Harry were the last links with the days of the Whitby lifeboatmen, when there was no motor lifeboat and they had only the strength of their arms and their oars to power them forward. Harry, or Lal, as he was more commonly known passed away in 1968, a year later, John the sole surviving Whitby lifeboatman of the epic *Rohilla* rescue was gone too, the last of a different generation of lifeboat volunteer. As a result of BBC radio's broadcasts of John's reminiscences, his death received more media attention, including a full column obituary in one of Yorkshire's main newspapers. It was, in a sense, the end of the rowing lifeboat's long and heroic story.

By 1919 Whitby had a motor lifeboat of its own and the old Upgang station closed. The station itself was dismantled and the material reclaimed where possible. The slipway became a focal point on the beach and the concrete base where the boathouse once stood hosted a beach shop where one could buy a host of drinks and sandwiches and hire the prerequisite deckchair. In time though the power of the sea damaged the slipway until it became a hazard and it was removed altogether. It is still possible to see the ravine where the lifeboat station once stood.

Upgang
lifeboat slipway
following
the station's
closure.

Whitby kept a pulling boat (the *Robert and Helen Robson*) longer than any other RNLI station, but she was more of a reserve lifeboat by this time. When the lifeboat was taken out of service in 1958 she had only been out eleven times in the previous eleven years.

Rohilla Survivor

1st May 1970, *Whitby Gazette*

Sir,

I am 78 and, like other old men, memories of the past return. I am a survivor of the ill-fated R.N. Hospital ship Rohilla wrecked off Whitby on 30th October, 1914. I completed twenty-two years in the Navy and was a survivor from other ships. I was a member of the R.N. sick berth staff in the Rohilla and what remains in an old man's memory is the help and consideration of the people of Whitby to the survivors of our ship. I remember being looked after at the West Cliff Hotel. It may be that I am the last surviving member of that ill-fated ship. If there should be others I would gladly arrange a reunion. I know there were St John Ambulance Brigade members, mostly from Yorkshire, who were members of the Sick Berth Reserve. I am the only one left of the regular Navy S.B. staff who served in the Rohilla.

Again I wish to thank the people of Whitby for the help they gave to me and other survivors of the Rohilla I know a monument was erected in Whitby Cemetery to the memory of those who were lost. Some of the names I remember: Parsons, Miller, Page, Morris and Ross. If anyone knows of other survivors I would be glad to hear from them.

Yours etc.

Leonard Long

(One time CSBPO, RNI)

In a letter to Betty Kellar, who was researching the loss of the *Rohilla* for her teaching dissertation in 1971, Leonard Long wrote of his painful memories. Leonard recalled how he had been forced to cling to the wreckage for over thirty hours in severe conditions and, with a number of others, attempted to swim ashore the following morning. He succeeded in reaching the shore safely and was taken to the West Cliff Hotel, where he was looked after for three days before being sent back to Chatham Naval Yard. After ten days' leave he was sailing the North Sea again, this time on HMS *Indomitable*.

Mr Long was nearly 80 years old when he wrote his letter, and recalled 'the ship being on its way to Antwerp to pick up wounded soldiers who assisted in defending the ports of Antwerp. All lighthouses and lightships were to all intents non-existent in wartime and a heavy sea was also running at the time. The crew were merchant marines and the hospital staff were RN, of which I was one.' Leonard remembered the enquiry, and how it was that the Captain did not get another command but he could not remember the full result.

Survivor Returns to Remember
7 October 1974, *Whitby Gazette*

A big sea disaster 60 years ago will be recalled this month when the sole survivor returns to Whitby for the first time. The hospital ship Rohilla foundered with the loss of 84 lives off Whitby on October 30th, 1914, on her way from Queensferry to Dunkirk to pick up wounded soldiers in the 1914–18 war.

Mr George Skinner of Solihull, Warwickshire now in his eighty's [*sic*] will be the guest of Councillor David Jenkinson, the Mayor of Scarborough at a special

Leslie Harmer, the mace bearer for the Langbaurgh Borough Council and dignateries view the wreaths inside the lifeboat museum. (Copyright Whitby Literary & Philosophical Society)

commemorative ceremony. He is to spend a week in Whitby, and hopes to meet some of the kind people 'who were so very kind to me.'

He will be the principal guest at a quayside service at Scotch Head on October the 30th, conducted by Rector of Whitby, Canon, Joe Penniston. After the service, Whitby lifeboat will take the official party to the spot where the Rohilla was wrecked to lay a wreath on the sea.

The Rohilla was pounded by heavy seas off Saltwick Nab and Whitby rowing lifeboat went to her aid, but the sea conditions made the task impossible. Another rowing boat was pulled to the top of the high cliff overlooking the stricken ship and lowered down the cliff face. But the lifeboat men could make little progress and the crew of Scarborough rowing lifeboat took over. Several of the Rohilla's crew of 229 attempted to swim ashore. Mr Skinner was one of the successful swimmers.

Rohilla Survivor Will Be Mayor's Guest
11 October 1974, *Whitby Gazette*

The Rohilla disaster is to be recalled by the visit to Whitby this month of Mr George Skinner, of Solihull, Warwickshire. Mr Skinner is thought to be the sole survivor of the ill-fated hospital ship wrecked off the port on October 30th 1914, with the loss of eighty-four lives. Mr Skinner, who now lives at 'Tanquards', St Bernard's Road, Solihull, returns to Whitby for the first time since the disaster as the guest of Councillor David Jenkinson, Mayor of Scarborough Borough.

Octogenarian Mr Skinner was a young sick berth attendant on board the 7,400 ton Rohilla when she left Queensferry in the Forth on October 29th, 1914, for the port of Dunkirk to pick up some of the First World War's early wounded. She carried a full complement of 229 crew and medical staff, as she made her way down the coast. Suddenly off Whitby, she ran into trouble and was soon stuck fast close inshore of Saltwick Nab just a mile south of Whitby. He is to spend a week at Whitby and hopes to meet some of the people 'who were so very kind to me'. Recalling that fateful day he said: 'I was the first to reach the shore after the Captain said swim for it. A lifeline of lifeboatmen came to meet me and the words I shall always remember were 'Come on son, you are OK'.

The Mayor's invitation to Mr Skinner to spend a week in Whitby resulted from a wish of Mr Skinner first published in the Whitby Gazette to re-visit the port and 'meet again many of the people, which were so very kind to me'.

Although no large scale commemoration service or remembrance has been organised the Mayor of Scarborough Borough will be joined by leading figures from surrounding boroughs. With six lifeboats involved in the rescue attempts councillors and visiting dignitaries are keen to show they share in the common grief of those lost in the disaster.

He will be the principal guest at a quayside service to be conducted at Scotch Head at 3 p.m. on 30 October, the sixtieth anniversary to the day of the disaster, by the Rector of Whitby, Canon J.C. Penniston.

Because this year also marks the 150th anniversary of the RNLI as well as the first year of partnership within the new Scarborough, the Mayor thought it fitting for representatives of all lifeboat services within the new community to be present and share their common heritage of land and service to those in peril on the sea. Invitations to attend the service have been sent to lifeboat stations at Runswick Bay and Filey as well as Scarborough itself.

After the service, to which many leading figures in the national and local sectors of the RNLI have also been invited, the Whitby lifeboat will take the official party out to sea to the spot of Saltwick Nab where the Rohilla foundered, to lay a wreath in memory of those who died. The memorial service will be attended by representatives of Barnoldswick St John Ambulance Brigade, a town from which many of the medical personnel on board had volunteered, and by representatives of the Tynemouth lifeboat station. Mr Skinner has given a moving account of a heroic act by the Very Rev. Canon Gwydir, a Roman Catholic priest who gave his life to help an injured sailor. Before the ship sailed from Queensferry said Mr Skinner, instructions were given to transfer all naval patients to local hospitals and then proceed to Dunkirk to collect soldiers wounded at Mons.

Mr Skinner said, 'We had on board a C of E Padre and an RC Father and they had cabins on the top deck, so they did not have to fight their way up three sets of crossed stairways, which were turned into waterfalls, by each heavy sea which hit us. The sick and our quarters were three decks down. I was on the stairway holding on while the next wave passed when I saw the Roman Catholic Father starting down. He called to me and said he was going down to sit with the patient, and I told him 'I did not think he would make it.' That was the last time Mr Skinner saw the Padre.

When at Whitby for the 60th anniversary of the disaster, Mr Skinner visited the mass grave in Whitby cemetery. On the memorial stone are the names of those who lost their lives. Mr Skinner said, 'It was a sad moment for me to see the names of some of my chums, but still sadder when I saw the name Father Gwydir, who I think came from Swansea.' Mr Skinner thinks that even after sixty years the heroism of Father Gwydir should be recognised in some way.

Rohilla Survivor Recalls Priest's Heroism

The Whitby Gazette followed up the report above in which George Skinner gave a moving account of the heroic actions of the very Rev. Canon Gwydir. George was the guest of the Borough Council at the sixtieth Rohilla anniversary service at Whitby, but stormy weather

prevented the service being held outdoors and it took place in the Lifeboat Museum instead. George had nothing but praise for Canon Gwydir and the actions that led to his death.

In my hunt for memorabilia related to the *Rohilla* I have been fortunate enough to secure an exquisite Chippendale corner cabinet made from wood gathered from the shore after the ship's loss.

I was most keen to acquire the unit as it had inside it some original papers and photographs relating to the tragedy. One of the papers detailed a personal recollection of the tragedy seen through the eyes of a young lady who was almost 14 when it occurred. It was written for the seventieth anniversary of the wreck.

My Memories Of The Hospital Ship 'Rohilla' Wrecked Off Whitby
On October 30th 1914.

I was nearly fourteen, attending, Cholmley School, Church Street, Whitby. It was our long weekend holiday – then called 'Teachers' Rest'. Friday, October 30th was wild and stormy; when I came downstairs my mother told me to get on with my breakfast, she was going out, there was a ship ashore and she was anxious to know if all on board were safe. I soon had my coat and scarf on after she had gone and went down on Tate Hill Pier; crowds of anxious people were in the street and on the sands.

I met my cousin, Lizzie Leadley; we went on the sand and under the Spa Ladder on the scaur. People were battling with the wind all along the scaur, but were unable to help at all. One of our lifeboats was badly holed and lying useless among the rocks. Rockets were falling short of the crippled ship.

We couldn't get back the way we had come as the tide was rising rapidly, we had to get on to the Nab at Saltwick. I remember Dr Raw giving my cousin and me a hand up, he was wearing a woolly hat. We went up the steps cut in the cliff side. The only times I had used these steps before was to get down to Mrs Agar's tea gardens in summer time. There was a stone building which Mrs Agar opened up each day and sold sweets, lemonade, etc. She would also supply a pot of tea. If we bought anything from her we were entitled to use the swings. She went up the 199 steps from the town and along the cliff through the fields each day until she was well in her eighties.

That weekend, October–November 1914, those steps were turned into a slippery slope with rescuers carrying stretchers bearing men who had been pulled from the sea; it must have been a very difficult task. The clifftop was lined with people night and day; a searchlight was played from the cliff on the stricken ship. By Saturday afternoon we could only see bridge of the Rohilla with the survivors clinging there. Many men had jumped off the wreck. Others had been washed overboard as the ship broke up. Brave local men went in the raging sea to help the men ashore. One I knew was Mr George Peart, a bricklayer by trade, a very strong swimmer. His son, George, who would be about nine at the time, told me he remembered seeing his mother bathe his father's torn and scratched back; drowning men had clung so desperately to him. Mr Peart was awarded a Silver Medal and Certificate; which his family still treasure.

All our neighbours stayed up each night keeping huge fires burning and warm blankets ready to comfort any rescued and rescuers. There was rejoicing on the Sunday morning when the Tyneside lifeboat brought the last of the survivors ashore.

Our school was on the east side of the harbour and on the following Wednesday we were lined up by the railings in our playground to watch the horse drawn drays bearing flower-covered coffins pass along the west pier road, followed by a crowd of mourners, on their way to Whitby Cemetery.

For weeks afterwards our sands were strewn with wreckage, crutches, Lysol, bales of cotton-wool, tins of food, tubs of butter and broken up wood of every description.

One day, during the following summer, a notice in Hornes shop window told us that a sister ship to the 'Rohilla' would be passing Whitby at a certain time. Some of the rescued medical staff were on board. People stood on the piers and cliffs to see her pass. It was a beautiful day, the sky and sea a vivid blue. The ship looked lovely with the sun shining on her white paint and red cross. The sight brought tears to the eyes of those who watched. She signalled 'Greetings to Whitby'.

(Recollections of D.L. Jackson on the seventieth anniversary of the wreck of the 'Rohilla', November 1984)

Sea Wreath – Laying To Mark Rohilla Date
Friday, 26 October 1984, *Whitby Gazette*

Whitby lifeboat will put to sea on Tuesday carrying wreaths to be laid on the waters above the wreck of the Rohilla, the hospital ship that foundered off Saltwick on 30 October, 70 years ago.

Tragedy, sacrifice and heroism were the elements in what was the worst shipping disaster in Whitby's history, a disaster which resulted in the loss of eighty-four lives. The 7,365 ton vessel went aground near Saltwick Nab at 4.00 a.m. with 229 people on-board. Gale-force winds were blowing from the south-east and tremendous seas were running at the time.

Of those on-board, eighty-five were taken off by lifeboats and sixty managed to swim ashore. The Whitby Gazette report of a special commemoration service held on the 60th anniversary of the wreck in 1974, commented: 'The whole drama lasted for fifty hours with countless untold incidents of heroism by the rescued and rescuers. The services rendered by the lifeboats are regarded as some of the most outstanding in lifeboat history.'

That jubilee service, held at the Lifeboat Museum, had been convened by the then Mayor of Scarborough, Councillor David Jenkinson. It was attended by representatives of local organisations, the lifeboat stations which took part in the rescue, and officials of the RNLI.

But the man for whom the service must have had most significance was Mr George Skinner of Solihull, then aged eighty-one and the only living survivor of the disaster. A sick berth attendant on the Rohilla, he was the first to arrive on shore after the Captain had said those who wanted could go overboard and 'swim for it'. 'A lifeline of lifeboatmen came to meet me and the words I shall always remember were "Come on son, you are OK"', he told a Gazette reporter on his 1974 visit to the town.

Plans for the lifeboat Mary Ann Hepworth to take a wreath to sea on the 60th anniversary had to be postponed because of stormy weather, which also forced the memorial indoors.

Visiting civic heads, apart from Councillor Jenkinson, included the Mayor of North Tyneside and the chairman of Pendle Urban District Council, who had brought two relatives of men lost from the Rohilla to the service. Many of the victims of the disaster came from the West Riding town of Barnoldswick.

The late Mr Richard Eglon, who lived at 4 Pier Road, Whitby, won the RNLI Silver Medal and Certificate for his part in the rescue. He piloted the Tynemouth lifeboat, Henry Vernon to the wreck, and the Tynemouth lifeboatmen gave him a Gold Medal as their personal appreciation of his gallantry.

The Institution's certificate awarded to Mr Eglon recorded that 'on the day of the wreck he assisted in saving thirty-five persons in the course of two trips in the No. 2 Whitby lifeboat John Fielden, which was damaged and broke up.' On 1 November, two days later, he piloted the Tynemouth motor lifeboat Henry Vernon when, under circumstances of danger and difficulty, he succeeded in saving the remaining survivors, fifty in number.

Mr Thomas Langlands, coxswain of the John Fielden, won the gold medal of the RNLI.

Rohilla Remembrance
Friday, 2 November 1984, *Whitby Gazette*

Eighty-four people who lost their lives in the wreck of the hospital ship Rohilla were remembered in Whitby on Tuesday – the 70th anniversary of the disaster.

Whitby lifeboat The White Rose of Yorkshire took a party including the Mayor of Pendle, the borough that includes the town of Barnoldswick from where many of the wreck victims came, to a point above the Rohilla's sunken remains, near Saltwick. There the Rector, Canon Joe Penniston, conducted a simple memorial service and wreaths were cast onto the water by Councillor Peggy Heaton, the Mayor of Pendle, and on behalf of the RNLI by the Whitby Station chairman, Mr Jim Hall. The sea was calm, conditions vastly different from those of 30 October 1914, when gale force winds from the southeast produced tremendous seas. Red roses provided by Whitby Town Mayor Reg Firth, who with the Mayoress Mrs Firth was also on the lifeboat, were placed on the sea alongside the wreaths.

The Mayor of Pendle was accompanied by the Mayoress, Mrs H. McClave, both representing the people of Barnoldswick. Others in the party were the lifeboat station crew, Middleton, and Mr Les Heath; lifeboat secretary curator, Mr E. Thomson; and the Harbour Master, Captain Gordon Cook. Before boarding the lifeboat Councillor Heaton and Mrs McClave were shown round the Rohilla section of the Lifeboat Museum. On their return from the sea, they visited the crew room for refreshments and were then taken by Councillor and Mrs Firth to Whitby cemetery to see the Rohilla memorial.

Exhibition will mark big disaster

In 1989, Colin Waters, director of the Whitby Archive Centre commemorated the seventy-fifth anniversary of Whitby's biggest shipping disaster, the 1914 sinking of the Rohilla with a special exhibition at its Grape Lane premises. Speaking to the Whitby Gazette in September, Mr Waters said, 'He anticipated the exhibition starting October 16, would run for several weeks, it was a tragedy with great loss of life which made front page news in its day because it happened only a matter of yards offshore.'

As the archive centre was in a new location, when the first edition of this book was due for release in 2002 I proposed staging a new exhibition with some of my *Rohilla* photographs, newspaper cuttings and selected memorabilia. It was originally intended as a four-week exhibition, but due to its popularity it was extended twice. I had been gathering material for some years before I had even started writing the book, allowing me to rotate the objects on

display. In the weeks before the exhibition I gathered whatever frames I could to hang as many photographs as possible. I prepared a PowerPoint slideshow for one end of the exhibition and at the other end was a unique underwater video of the wreck given to me by the present owner; people were sometimes fascinated to learn that individuals were allowed to purchase wrecks, and the video proved popular. It gave me great pleasure to give people the opportunity to see these items.

During the exhibition I received a telephone call from a BBC radio station

Whitby Archive Centre's *Rohilla* exhibition.

in Middlesbrough requesting an interview. I found the interviewer easy to speak to and was able to recount the tragedy from beginning to end, keeping it as short as I could, but still making sure I retained the main points of the story. At the end the interviewer told me he could always tell when someone felt genuinely close to their subject, it was a kind compliment and something I had not given a great deal of thought to before. Unfortunately, the interview aired almost live and I wasn't able to get a copy.

90th Anniversary 2004
Relatives Remember Historic Sea Drama

Early in 2004 a meeting was held in the old lifeboat station boathouse to discuss plans to mark the anniversary of the *Rohilla*'s loss ninety years on. After all that time, there was no shortage of enthusiasm for holding a service of commemoration. As in past years, the chosen venue was to be the bandstand, opposite the lifeboat museum. This is perhaps one of the most central locations and would permit as many people to be part of the service as wished. I volunteered to produce the service sheets with Rev. Terry Leathley, the Port Missioner. We worked through a few designs and proposed what we had to the group for acceptance. During the process of writing the first edition of this book, and afterwards, I continued to receive letters from family members whose loved ones had been involved in the tragedy and I used the contact details so we could start sending out invitations to the memorial service. There was no way of knowing how many people would turn up so I started a conservative print run of the service sheets.

Quite early on in writing the first edition I had established contact with Shirley Bracewell, whose mother Elsie Naylor had lost her father, Sgt Arthur Petty, a Barnoldswick St John Ambulance Brigade man. I really enjoyed talking to Elsie; despite her mature years she had such a young head on her shoulders. She was always keen to hear what I was up to and what was 'new' with my *Rohilla* endeavours. When I told her about the ninetieth anniversary, she told me straight away that I could put her name down for it. Her daughter Shirley told me later that she was really looking forward to coming over to Whitby despite the drive from Barnoldswick.

The service was planned for the end of October and there was some concern that the possibility of inclement weather might put off some of those travelling long distances; however, early indications seemed positive. Our plan was to hold the service at the bandstand, and then, subject to weather conditions, give descendants the opportunity of going out to sea on the former Whitby lifeboat *Mary Ann Hepworth* to leave wreaths at the site of the wreck. Other private charter skippers had made it clear that they would be willing to take out family members should there be too many for *Mary Ann Hepworth*. I felt that this was the next chapter in my *Rohilla* experience and was really pleased to be part of the planning process.

As we approached the weekend, I watched the weather forecasts closely, looking for any possibility of a change in conditions that might prevent anyone going to sea, but

Mrs Elsie Naylor with her daughter Shirley. (Copyright Doug Jackson)

also holding the service outdoors. On the morning of the service I looked out at a clear sky and wondered if that was just a whisper of blue on the horizon or just wishful thinking. There was so much to do at the bandstand and up above in the yacht club, which was being set up for people to get a warm drink. Before we set off for the bandstand I took the opportunity to take a few photographs at home with my wife and daughter as I knew once we got down to the bandstand it would be really busy. We had chosen a nice wreath and collected it the day before. Although I was hoping to go out on the *Mary Ann Hepworth*, I was prepared to let a *Rohilla* relative go instead as this occasion was more about them than me.

The bandstand was a hive of activity. The *Robert and Ellen Robson*, a static lifeboat exhibit was brought out of the museum and put on display. With the lifeboat out of the museum and chairs being positioned in front of the bandstand, people began to take an interest in what was going on. In what seemed like no time at all invited guests started to arrive, and

My wife Jane and I were press ganged into a photograph with our daughter Lucy before leaving for the bandstand.

my eyes were drawn to the crowd looking for a kind, gentle lady as eager to meet me as I was her. I had persuaded Paul Wilson, a friend who is a professional video producer, to film the day's activities for me. He has supported Whitby Lifeboat in the past and it was an easy decision for him to make.

Armed with a handful of service sheets, I seemed the likely person to approach and I was pleased to meet many of the people with whom up until then I had only shared letters or telephone conversations. A lady approached me and introduced herself as Shirley Bracewell, telling me her mother was seated across the other side of the bandstand. As I greeted Mrs Naylor I was humbled that she wanted me to call her 'Elsie'. She proved as pleasant in person as she was on the phone, and more than happy to agree to the taped interview we had discussed – despite her asking why anyone would want to see and hear her on film. We set her up with a small discreet wireless microphone and set the camera so it was a little distance away. After a few moments she was relaxed enough to give a most moving description of life as a child whose father was lost in such tragic circumstances.

After speaking to Elsie, I made my way over to David Mitchell, an ex-engineer with the British India, the original owners of the *Rohilla*. I had first met David when writing the book. He collects most things related to the British India, especially postcards and I was impressed to see his vast collection. He was another person I had lined up to be interviewed as he had a good background with the British India. He was very comfortable speaking in front of the camera and gave a very good history of the company.

More people were making themselves available for photographs and one group in particular caught my eye. One of the newspaper photographers had grouped together lifeboat crewmembers past and present in front of the *Robert and Ellen Robson*. I seized the opportunity, managing to squeeze in to get a photograph that I am very pleased with, just before the group broke up.

Whitby lifeboat crew past and present in front of the *Robert and Ellen Robson* in 2004.

As the Salvation Army band began setting up, people started filling the seats. There was a large turnout and soon every seat was taken, and many more people stood around both sides of the bandstand.

The day's proceedings started with a detailed account of the disaster given by Guy Hurst, a well-educated public speaker. Sadly, however, significant portions of the story were drowned out by the sound emanating from a group of high-powered motorcycles parked nearby, whose selfish riders revved their engines numerous times before leaving the area, much to everyone's disgust. It was clear from the wreaths on the floor that this was a service of remembrance and their actions were quite deplorable.

Rev. Leathley opened the service with the words 'We have come together this day to remember the souls of those who lost their lives in the wreck of the Hospital Ship *Rohilla*, and to commemorate the courage and endurance of those whose heroic efforts effected the saving of many lives on that tragic occasion ninety years ago.' The congregation then came together to sing the hymn 'Will your anchor hold in the storms of life'.

Rev. Leathley gave readings from scripture, which seemed to be received with some approval, one of the congregation remarking that no better choice could have been made.

Acts 27: 13–20, The Storm
When a gentle south wind began to blow, they saw their opportunity; so they weighed anchor and sailed along the shore of Crete. Before very long, a wind of hurricane force, called the Northeaster, swept down from the island. The ship was caught by the storm and could not head into the wind; so we gave way to it and were driven along. As we passed to the lee of a small island called Cauda, we were hardly able to make the lifeboat secure, so the men hoisted it aboard. Then they passed ropes under the ship itself to hold it together. Because they were afraid they would run aground on the sandbars of Syrtis, they lowered the sea anchor and let the ship be driven along. We took such a violent battering from the storm that the next day they began to throw the cargo overboard. On the third day, they threw the ship's tackle overboard with their own hands. When neither sun nor stars appeared for many days and the storm continued raging, we finally gave up all hope of being saved.

Acts 27: 39–44, The Shipwreck
When daylight came, they did not recognize the land, but they saw a bay with a sandy beach, where they decided to run the ship aground if they could. Cutting loose the anchors, they left them in the sea and at the same time untied the ropes that held the rudders. Then they hoisted the foresail to the wind and made for the beach. But the ship struck a sandbar and ran aground. The bow stuck fast and would not move, and the stern was broken to pieces by the pounding of the surf. The soldiers planned to kill the prisoners to prevent any of them from swimming away and escaping. But the centurion wanted to spare Paul's life and kept them from carrying out their plan. He ordered those who could swim to jump overboard first and get to land. The

rest were to get there on planks or on other pieces of the ship. In this way everyone reached land safely.

Bob Harland, a former lifeboatman, recited the pilot psalm:

> The Lord is my Pilot; I shall not drift.
> He lights me across dark waters:
> He steers me in deep channels.
> He keeps my log:
> He guides me by the star of holiness
> For his name's sake.
> Even though I sail mid the thunders and tempest of life,
> I will dread no danger for you are near me;
> Your love and your care they shelter me;
> You prepare a harbour before me in the homeland of eternity:
> You anoint the waves with oil so my ship rides calmly.
> Surely sunlight and starlight will favour me on the voyage I take:
> And I will rest in the port of my God forever.

The congregation was asked to sing the hymn without which no maritime remembrance service would be complete, 'Eternal Father, strong to save'. Members of the public were invited to join in and service sheets were quickly shared around by those who could spare them. Rev. Leathley led the congregation in further prayers, thanking God for the courage and self-sacrifice displayed by all those assisting in the rescue efforts and in securing the survivors.

Everyone then joined in with the 'Lord's Prayer', after which representatives of the families of those involved in the rescue operation and responsible for aiding the survivors were invited to board the *Mary Ann Hepworth* to go out to sea to lay a wreath. Though I had our wreath in my hand, I purposely held back to ensure direct family members were given every opportunity of going out. I was, however, fortunate that there was enough room for me on the boat.

Just then Elsie approached me with a bunch of roses and asked if I would do her

Former lifeboatman Robert Harland. (Copyright Margaret Whitworth)

Modern day lifeboatmen pay their respects to those affected by the maritime disaster. (Copyright Margaret Whitworth)

the honour of throwing these into the sea for her as she was a little old to go out herself and her daughter wouldn't leave her alone. I couldn't say no, but I was quite emotional that she chose me to do this for her in memory of her father. I turned round to see who was behind me and found a familiar face and asked her if she wouldn't mind placing our wreath in the sea; she agreed as she had seen Elsie ask me to throw her flowers.

The *Windsor Runner*, a large Trent class lifeboat from the relief fleet that was standing in for our lifeboat, moved into the channel waiting for the *Mary Ann Hepworth* to back off from the steps. I noticed one of the other day charter boats, the *Esk Belle*, come astern of us fully loaded, with my wife and daughter and Paul Wilson aboard and the inshore lifeboat sweeping about ensuring everyone's safety. Once we were all ready the *Windsor Runner* led the party out of the harbour in settled conditions. We were truly blessed to have fair weather at the end of October.

I directed Barry Sneddon, the owner of the *Mary Ann Hepworth* to a position over the stern section of the wreck. Each of the boats was a safe distance from the Nab and they had plenty of water under their keel, making it safe to cut their engines. The only sound to be heard was the gentle rolling of the water against the side of the boat. In what was a most serene and enchanting moment, everyone fell silent. Paul Wilson had had the foresight to set me up with a discreet wireless microphone and filmed from the *Esk Belle*.

A few moments later, standing at the bow of the lifeboat with the Whitby Lifeboat RNLI standard bearer by his side, Rev. Leathley broke the silence and addressed those on our boat, but spoke as though addressing the other boats too. He chose the universal sermon for remembrance services, which sympathetically reflected the loss of the *Rohilla's* eighty-nine lives:

They shall grow not old as we that are left grow old,
Age shall not weary them, nor the years condemn.
At the going down of the sun, and in the morning, we shall remember them.
We shall remember them.

Wreaths were laid upon the sea by John Cummins for Thomas Cummins the motor mechanic on the Tynemouth lifeboat and Peter Thomson on behalf of the gallant rescuers, both RNLI volunteers and civilians. David Mitchell laid his wreath in a personal tribute to the British India Steam Navigation Company crew, and Mary Studdon laid our wreath for all those who suffered through the *Rohilla*'s loss while I released the roses as a special tribute for Elsie Naylor. Rev. Leathley led those on the boat in a final prayer:

Almighty and eternal God, as we remember those who have died in order that we might live in peace, we ask that their example may inspire us, and that the Blessing of Almighty God Father, Son and Holy Spirit be with us all, and all who mourn this day. Amen

The boat was positioned so that everyone could get a glimpse of the wreaths. We then moved aside so those on the *Esk Belle* could do likewise. Once everyone was ready, the boats all started the journey back to the harbour. There was little conversation on the boat as we motored along, each of us wrapped up in thoughts of what had occurred in 1914. During the short trip back to the harbour the light began to fade as though some spiritual message of condolence was being offered.

Once back on shore people with some distance to drive were eager to set off, and a round of hurried formal farewells were exchanged, whilst those staying overnight went into the yacht club for a warm drink and a chance to share their thoughts of how the day went. All agreed

The *Mary Ann Hepworth* with the harbour in the background captured in the fading light.

it was a day to remember, a day of satisfaction that we had indeed honoured those who had succumbed and also celebrated those who had survived the trauma of the shipwreck.

Geoff Pickles, whose grandfather John Thomas Pickles did not survive the tragedy, said, 'You don't necessarily feel sad, 90 years is a long while.' 'It's just nice to be able to come here to remember it.' Certainly, those I spoke to all agreed the day had been successful, that we had achieved what we set out to do, and many left enquiring what we had in store for the centenary in 2014.

Centenary Commemorating the Loss of His Majesty's Hospital Ship *Rohilla*. Tragic Loss of Life to be Remembered over a Solemn Weekend

An informal meeting was held on 8 November 2011 to form a steering committee, the 'Rohilla Centenary Team', for the commemorations marking the centenary of the *Rohilla* tragedy. The committee's objective was to oversee, direct and contribute to the centenary activities. The team decided straightaway that the centenary should be marked with a solemn memorial to those who drowned and a balanced celebration of the lives saved.

As this second edition was being prepared, the preparation for the centenary is already well advanced and the team is planning events to run over the weekend to coincide with the anniversary of the ship's loss. The plans were expensive and we set about trying to raise funds. I created a DVD, which we sent out to local businesses seeking assistance. Our success was limited, but we were grateful for what we received. I was also able to create and manage a dedicated website for the centenary, which proved useful in helping descendants of those involved in the tragedy contact the team.

We were indebted to the local Civic Society for their willingness to assist us with the bronze plaque. They were there every step of the way from the planning applications, dealing with public bodies, but more importantly, the funding of such a high-profile item. The planning team were fully aware that this single element was going to be costly, requiring more funds than the team had. When approached, the Civic Society was more than happy to help us and it is true to say that we would have struggled without them!

Our initial plans included the following suggestions, but only time will tell how many of them make it through to become elements of the centenary and in what order they may eventually run:

Friday 31 October

At 11.00 a.m. Nathan Palmer, the RNLI's Interim Head of Engagement, will undertake the official opening of the weekend's activities at the Lifeboat Museum. A superb collection of Rohilla artefacts and memorabilia will be on display throughout the weekend.

The former lifeboat William Riley of Birmingham and Leamington, built in 1909 which served at Upgang and Whitby from 1909 to 1919 and now fully restored will be on static display at the bandstand periodically throughout the weekend.

Saturday 1 November

During the day, the lifeboat museum will be hosting the exhibition with each display case consisting of *Rohilla* memorabilia and artefacts; it is possibly the most specialised exhibition of *Rohilla* material for many years with many unique items on display for the first time.

At midday volunteers and lifeboat crew members will launch the William Riley at the marina and row it to the bandstand for a rowing demonstration. The aim is to not only present the boat being rowed, but to have the full complement of rowers and an additional seventeen people onboard, just as the John Fielden had on its first return from the wrecked ship in 1914. It will give a very good visual demonstration of how difficult it must have been to row the lifeboat carrying the *Rohilla* survivors albeit this demonstration will be in the safe confines of the harbour and not during a severe gale.

At 1.00 p.m. the all-weather lifeboat George and Mary Webb will lead a flotilla of lifeboats, vintage boats and invited vessels out of the harbour proceeding to the area of the wrecked hospital ship, where ceremonial wreaths will be laid commemorating the loss of the *Rohilla* and eighty-nine lives. It is hoped that some of the usual day-trip boats will be present to take out families and invited guests, subject to availability and weather conditions. Those not wishing to travel out on one of the vessels are invited to leave their wreaths to be laid by the lifeboat crew and will have the opportunity of being able to view the wreath laying from an area adjacent to the wreck site on the existing clifftop path. When the flotilla returns it will be welcomed back with the sound of the ringing of the Rohilla's bell.

At 3 p.m. On the West Pier a specially commissioned memorial bronze plaque, provided and funded by Whitby Civic Society, to mark the 100th anniversary of the wreck of the *Rohilla* will be unveiled by The Most Hon. Marquees of Normanby. The objective is for people to be able to briefly read about the tragedy whilst also being able to see the general location of the wreck at Saltwick Nab in the distance. The unveiling of the plaque will be one of the highlights of the weekend as it will be something that will live on long after the centenary.

A local sub aqua diving club is planning their own memorial for the centenary which will include placing a commemorative plaque down on the wreck itself. Although I can no longer dive this is definitely something I support it is a particularly emotional and a nice way of honouring the lives lost when the ship foundered.

Saturday Night

One of the biggest elements in planning the weekend activities has been to organise an evening of Music and Drama commencing at 7 p.m. at St Hilda's Church, on the West Cliff. The concert titled Spirit of Whitby – Rohilla Remembered will possibly include a celebrity guest who will tell the story of the *Rohilla* enlightening those who are not familiar with the tragic tale.

We have the support of Richard Grainger a respected musician who is working with Eskdale School and the Community College to produce a dramatic concert split into two halves, the first half dedicated to the ship and its demise, the second focusing on the rescues, and then finishing the evening off with a wartime sing along. At the beginning it was hoped we would have had the support of a folk duo from Barnoldswick who are intimately familiar with the tragedy and whom produced a special song dedicated to the loss of the *Rohilla*, however unscheduled commitments meant they had to pull out.

Sunday 2 November
11.00 a.m. A Service of Remembrance will be held at St Mary's Church (by the Abbey on the clifftop). The Service will be led by The Right Reverend the Bishop of Whitby. We have the pleasure of being able to welcome the Marske Fishermen's Choir who will be performing as the congregation enters the church and who will also sing during the solemn service as members of the lifeboat crew light a candle for each of those lost during the disaster. At the culmination of the service the Marske Fishermen's Choir will sing once more as the congregation leaves the church.

1 p.m. The Coxswain and crew of Whitby Lifeboat Station welcome special guests to join them for refreshments at the Boathouse. This is perhaps going to be my best opportunity of speaking with the families as I won't have the pressure of attending to activities throughout the weekend.

The Rohilla Centenary Team has worked long and hard selecting activities to recognise this important and solemn occasion setting in motion the steps to commemorate the centenary, we have had the support of a number of people and organisations for which we were most grateful. One of the positive outcomes is that any proceeds from the weekend will be donated to Whitby Lifeboat Station.

In compiling the above list of activities there were a number of considerations determining whether a particular element may or may not go ahead. I am sure, however, that throughout the weekend there will be ample opportunity for family members to see for themselves the terrain that made the rescue so difficult whilst also paying their respects to their loved ones and indeed everyone involved during the worst maritime disaster to have occurred off Whitby.

Aside from our own plans to mark the loss of the *Rohilla*, we know of a few other bodies who are also looking to mark the occasion. One must also bear in mind that this year marks the centenary of the Great War itself and as such there will be a lot of focus on big events from 1914. I have already given one radio interview and am fielding a number of email enquiries – it is shaping up to be a very busy year.

9

EXPLORING THE WRECK OF THE *ROHILLA*

The morning of the Wednesday after the tragedy the weather and sea had moderated enough for the Whitby lifeboat to leave the harbour and make for the wreck. Captains Isdale and John Milburn were accompanied by Lt-Commander Sharpe. It was their intention to see if there was anything that might be salvaged from what little remained of the ship. They were able to recover three safes and a few personal belongings from the fleet surgeon's cabin.

Fleet Surgeon Lomas, one of the last to leave the ship, was known to have the keys to the safes, but was still quite ill from his ordeal on the wrecked ship. The district captain obtained the keys from Dr Lomas and the safes were opened in the presence of the Chief Coastguard Officer and the ship's second writer George Curtis. Money to the value of £348 16s 9d was found along with a small silver mounted crucifix, and a few temporary receipts. The ship's ledgers and other accounts were not recovered. It was reported that the confidential books and papers were thrown overboard, enclosed in an iron box and the confidential charts washed away after the ship began to tear herself apart.

The salvagers Messrs T. Round & Co. were scheduled to commence diving operations in an effort to recover the bodies of those still missing and any stores or Admiralty property recoverable, but the weather prevented them from doing so. As soon as the weather abated the steam tug *Pioneer* and the salvage team made several trips to the wreck, but failed to locate any bodies, instead securing some of the floating debris. One of the divers, W. Horns, said, 'it was extremely difficult to make any headway owing to the great amount of twisted wreckage and the consequent danger of fouling the equipment.'

The following narrative appears courtesy of John Tindale, Ben Dean and Sid Weatherill and gives a valuable insight into the early days of private salvage work done on the wreck.

Whitby Marine Ventures
Not much has been told about the fate of the ship after her wrecking. She was cut up for scrap. Various companies worked on her, cutting down the remaining superstructure above water, and helmet divers eventually cut her down to about knee height. Her six massive Scotch boilers defeated them, as did some enormous pieces of her quadruple expansion engines and also her stern section. The divers worked in dark, turbulent water, their own stumbling movements continually clouding the water; these were the days of heavy, clumsy diving suits, metal helmets, and boots weighted with lead. Air was pumped down to their helmets from the surface via a hand-operated pump on the deck of a barge. Anything below knee height was

usually left alone, as bending down was difficult and dangerous, for if the diver's helmet was too low and air surged into the legs of his diving suit he was unbalanced and in real difficulty in a dark jungle of sharp, twisted metal. These divers and successive storms reduced Rohilla to a tangled mass on the seabed alongside the steep rock wall that ripped her apart. Her stern section had overhung a deep hole when she was stranded and broke off – eleven men clinging to the deck rails were carried down into a muddy chasm and drowned.

Eventually, during the 1920s, the salvagers could get no more and she was left alone. The storms continued to batter her and rust ate away at her ironwork, but the remaining bronze fittings, copper pipes, brass portholes and countless gunmetal valves and flanges remained intact and hidden. In the 1950s a small group, including myself, began scuba diving from Whitby. The sport was in its infancy, we had very little spare cash and so we made most of our equipment. Our only advantage over the old helmet divers was that we had no airlines or weights anchoring us to the bottom. We swam free, causing no disturbance, with a tank of compressed air on our backs, which would last thirty-five minutes if we were working – or longer if we were sitting and looking at the job. Today the amateur diver has safe, expensive diving gear, guidebooks to wreck sites and fast inflatable boats, so small armies of divers from far afield can explore our Yorkshire coast. This tale is about underwater search and salvage undertaken on a 'shoe string' in a different era.

The cold, murky waters off the Yorkshire coast soon whittled away most of the members' enthusiasms until only Sid Weatherill, Moia Porteous and the joint author, Ben Dean, remained. We knew the story of the Rohilla and obtained her location from an elderly ex-salvage man. How we found her is another story, but I will admit that the Rohilla scared me the first time I met her. Perhaps I took too much drama and tragedy down with me on that first dive, but she continued to give me the shivers throughout the many years we worked on her.

We found that the wreck belonged to a local scrap merchant named Jim 'Frisco' Weatherill; he had bought it unseen many years before but had never worked it. 'There's nowt left,' he declared, 'you're wasting your time.' We told him what we had seen and began to witness the immediate build-up of his legendary enthusiasm. Jim was a large, red-faced man with a few wisps of hair slicked across his bald head; he always dressed in clean denim overalls and highly polished black shoes.

His sudden swings of temper were noisy and alarming, only equalled by his mounting desire to have those boilers in his scrap yard. We knew that was impossible – each boiler was the size of my living room, but Jim's vision was undimmed.

When our proper jobs permitted, we set about recovering the non-ferrous metal objects for their owner. Jim's enthusiasm grew in proportion with the size of the increasing pile of copper and brass in his yard; but he still hankered after those boilers. When underwater conditions gave clear water with some light filtering down from a calm surface, we surveyed the deeper stern section in its dark, gloomy hole. It

Sid Weatherill and Ben Dean preparing to dive. (Courtesy Sid Weatherill)

had collapsed on its starboard side but was still a towering pyramid of jagged metal. The huge rudder lay in the mud astern. The port propeller shaft jutted out from the curved plates of the hull, the empty splines on the end bearing mute testimony to the courage and determination of the old divers in removing the great three-bladed propeller.

Was the starboard propeller still buried under the collapsed hull? No: our old salvage-man friend confirmed that both propellers had been landed at Whitby. 'Kids used to slide down the blades,' he said, 'but you watch out on that stern end – our divers didn't like it at all, they reckoned it moved and finally they refused to work on it. In fact, she's a bad ship. You'll pay for everything you get off her.' At the time we thought no more about his prediction. It was during some clear water working on the stern, while dismantling the steam steering engine, that we glimpsed a large rounded object buried deep under a mass of twisted girders. Over many weeks, when conditions allowed, we cut and cleared the girders to reveal more of our prize.

We thought it might be a bronze boss or fairing dropped off one of the propellers. Jim 'got on to' Harland and Wolff, the builders of Rohilla, and somehow obtained a copy of the foundry plans of the castings and build up of the propellers. Each had three blades made of manganese bronze which were seven feet (two metres) tall and weighed two and a quarter tons. The object still didn't make sense because the two propellers had been removed years ago, hadn't they?

Using explosives, we continued to cut and clear; more shape and huge bolt holes were uncovered. Jim was getting impatient, we were neglecting his cherished boilers. The mystery deepened when there appeared beside our object the obvious tip of

The diving over, we begin the return to the harbour in our boat the *Sea Urchin*. (Courtesy Sid Weatherill)

a large propeller blade. We had found other smaller blades in the wreck, possibly knocked off salvage craft, but this was obviously something a great deal larger. Again, we consulted the foundry plans and for the first time deciphered some small, barely legible, smudged notes in a corner of the plan, which read 'two spare blades'! The mystery was solved.

We told Jim and his reaction was explosive, his 'enthusiasm' took off at an alarming rate, and extravagant plans to have those two blades in his scrapyard next week flew like rockets. The boilers were never mentioned again. Even when we explained that the blades were still buried in steel, stone and mud, close under the towering and very dodgy ship section, his reply was: 'Oh, you'll soon shift that lot.' It took us all one summer. Jim fretted. Delays due to bad weather were a personal affront and we were roundly cursed for 'just messing about'. Rohilla, built as a troopship plying to India, had carried spare blades so that she could be repaired in faraway harbours. The helmet divers had recovered the two complete units and then, with good sense, left the creaking, unstable aft section to shift and groan in the dark until some winter gale caused it to collapse. The two blades and the steering engine ended up in a hard heap covered in wreckage.

One blade lay flat, the second was standing vertically and buried with just its tip showing. We had more scares and near-accidents clearing that 'easy' horizontal blade for lifting than with anything on other wrecks we subsequently worked on. Was it just coincidence or was it Rohilla that caused wires to slip, chains to snap, girders to collapse, and sudden squalls with white waves to burst upon us out of blue summer skies? Having cleared it, the problem was to lift it, in the days before the availability of lifting airbags, or stern trawlers with powerful hydraulic winches. Jim's 'quick lift' ideas were numerous and ranged from employing the local dredger, to using hand winches and wires, all impossible. Laboriously we worked out (no pocket calculators then) that we needed a tank big enough to hold four tons of water, sink it onto the blade, chain them together, blast compressed air into the tank until it lifted the blade, and if the whole floating contraption hung no more than

Recovery of the propeller blade still slung underneath the special buoyancy tank. (Courtesy Sid Weatherill)

eleven feet (three metres) below the surface, we could tow it into Whitby, up the river, under the bridge, into the dock and there a large crane could lift it ashore. Simple!

Jim thought we were mad. He swore terribly, but as usual 'got on' and produced a tank from an army water-tanker. The saga of that tank is too long to tell here; it had a demonic will of its own. It nearly killed us underwater on two occasions when it rammed and nearly sank our boat. It was just like a stubborn, dangerous mule, but like a mule it was the right beast for a tough job.

So eventually there we were towing that tank slowly into Whitby harbour in the middle of the town regatta. The crowds on the pier knew nothing of the massive propeller blade that was swung ponderously beneath that crazily surfing tank; we could have been mistaken for a slow-moving comedy act. Jim had seen us off into a misty dawn, driving his ancient Land Rover down the pier, waving and tooting his horn. Now he awaited his blade at the dock. The big crane took the strain, lifting tank and blade together. Jim leaned over to catch his first glimpse as the blade emerged after fifty-six years lost underwater, and his glasses fell off his nose into the muddy waters. His curses turned from rage to oaths of wonder as the great blade swung, gleaming in the sunlight. The last dive of the day was to recover Jim's glasses. Meanwhile the blade and tank were loaded on to his creaking, overstressed, elderly scrap lorry, which then lurched unsteadily off to his yard. The exhausted divers found energy for a little mild celebration before deep, untroubled sleep.

By noon the next day Jim was dead. His sudden death so soon after success and elation seemed grossly unfair. He was a big, noisy, modern-day Nelson at an unlikely Trafalgar. Even the weather changed dramatically for the worse. After the funeral, Jim's scrap workers took the blade to sell it to a firm across the moors from Whitby. While unloading, a crane collapsed, the blade knifed through the old lorry, skewering it to the ground. The shattered lorry was thrown in for scrap as part of the deal. The profit margin dwindled.

Eventually, the weather eased and the divers returned to collect items of Jim's gear from the salvage site. The water was reasonably clear as we dived into the wreck, but the sight we met was appalling. The trench left by the lifted blade was filled level with quivering bright green seaweed; the second blade, still half buried, stood at one end like a headstone over a new grave. Each diver reacted in the same way with a shake of the head, a hand signalling 'up' and a grateful return to the sunlight above. 'She's a bad ship. You'll pay for everything you get off her': prophetic words.

After buying the wreck from Jim's widow we formed a new salvage company called Whitby Marine Ventures Ltd, with one of the prime objectives being the recovery of the last propeller blade from the Rohilla. It was another year before we went back for the second propeller blade.

Richard Noble, Sid Weatherill and Ben Dean standing with one of the *Rohilla*'s tall propeller blades. (Courtesy Sid Weatherill)

A Diver's Tale – The Author's Experience

It was a warm sunny day in July, and shortly after lunch we set off across the flat shimmering water. The small inflatable sped across the sea and in what seemed no time at all we approached a small marker buoy floating on the surface. I was told that the buoy was attached to a line that dropped down to a secure point on the wreck of the SS Rohilla. It was my second dive of the day and I had heard much of the hospital ship and the tragic story that enveloped the sinking. I recollected a visit to the lifeboat museum some years previously and could recall the sight of artefacts that had been found by divers and raised over the years.

Below us the seabed lay just at ten metres, the echo sounder showed an outline picture of something which appeared to reach upwards to just a few metres below us. I was intrigued and listened carefully as the dive marshal told us how part of the wreckage lay directly below our boat's hull. Anticipating what lay ahead I kitted up, eagerly awaiting the direction to drop over the side into the water.

The cool water was a welcome relief from sitting on the boat in our dry exposure suits. Looking down I could make out a large darkened shape, last minute checks

Sid Weatherill with some of the smaller items recovered from the wreck. (Courtesy Sid Weatherill)

were made and my dive leader gave the signal to descend. As we left the surface and dropped down the buoy, the darkened shape seemed to expand and it became clear this was one of the large engine room boilers. For a few moments I looked in awe at the huge cylindrical metal objects that lay before us; the underwater visibility was such that it was possible to get a glimpse of how scattered the wreckage was. Dropping off the boiler down to the seabed we were greeted by a small shoal of pollack, which seemed oblivious to our presence, simply meandering on their way. A hole in one of the boilers gave a glimpse of the vast configuration of internal pipework. The plating of what appeared to be the side of the ship now lay collapsed on the seabed. Profusely covered in marine growth, the wreckage seemed to stretch to infinity.

Equipped to dive, I was ready to get into the water out of the sun.

Swimming along I just happened to notice something shiny sticking out from the bottom and went to investigate. It was a sort of figure of eight shape and heavily concreted. It was quite big but small enough to fit inside my glove where it spent the rest of the dive, taking a peek here and there trying to figure out its function.

I followed my diving buddy, trying in vain to take in all my surroundings at once. Notably missing were the many ship's portholes; the holes in the plating laying testament to the valuable commodity that portholes had become. We moved on, swimming along what was the side of the ship, until I was stopped. I was mystified as my buddy pointed down to a small crevice in the wreckage, but a short while later it became clear it was in fact a small hideaway. What appeared to be a large lobster avoided capture, despite the efforts of my buddy, and why he wanted to get close to the claws of the beast amazed me. Unable to spur the creature on, which was now well encased in its labyrinth, we moved on. We approached a small velvet swimming crab caught out in the open which appeared to pose for the camera. As we swam on we passed an area that was partially layered with tiles. Small white hexagonal tiles lay scattered around amongst the larger red tiles, it was clear this was some form of washroom.

Sitting strangely on its own in a clearing we came to what appeared to be an engine part. The massive piece of steel sat entombed in 'Deadmans Fingers', a marine organism found on most wreckage in British waters. Stretching out before us was a long cylindrical tube, although the propellers were long gone, the size of the propeller shaft gave some idea of how big they must have been. Fifty minutes had lapsed seemingly so quickly, and sadly the time had come to leave the wreck and head for the surface. It was clear that it would require a number of dives to fully appreciate a wreck the size of the Rohilla. Back on the surface we took off our equipment, and as we sat awaiting the other divers I was able to take in the surrounding area. even there on a sunny day I could just imagine how difficult things must have been when the ship came to grief in such a treacherous storm that fateful night, back in October 1914. It was easy to see why those on the stricken vessel had expected a swift rescue with the shore so close.

Small white hexagonal tiles, which were at one time quite prolific on the *Rohilla*.

Even as far back as 1986 the larger red tiles were mostly broken.

I took the shiny object and gave it a simple clean over the side of the boat and its shape soon revealed itself as a base from a condiment set. It had four symmetrical holes were a frame may have been secured with small ball caps underneath to act like legs. Sadly all I had was the very base only. Once home the object was placed into a plastic tub with a watered down coke and left overnight. The following morning I woke eager to see the results of my dive. And was quite pleased to see how well the coke had loosened the old crud, just a few well-placed knocks and it came away leaving a discoloured piece of metal. I took a gentle wire brush to it whilst working the coke onto the flat sides. In no time at all the discolouration came away leaving a shiny surface and some interesting marks on either side. On one side there was the unmistakable BISNC. Logo in the shape of what is referred to as the envelope badge, the other side was just as interesting with the silver hallmark belonging to Elkington & Co., whom I knew had supplied the British India line with a wealth of silverware.

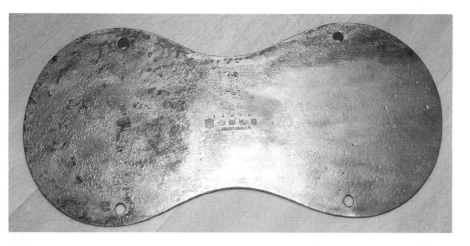

A silver condiment base, my only personal memento from the many dives I have made to the wreck.

10

RNLI COXSWAINS AND CREW

Coxswain of the Whitby Lifeboat Thomas Langlands

Thomas Langlands was born in October 1853 in Seahouses, off the Northumberland coast, and his family moved to Whitby when he was 8. Thomas had an affinity with the sea from an early age and as a fisherman was the proud owner of a traditional Whitby coble. At the age of 18 he became a member of the Whitby lifeboat crew, a role in which he excelled. He was appointed 2nd coxswain at Upgang, in 1875, and just two years later he was appointed coxswain at the very young age of 24.

Sail was still the primary power for the huge fleets of colliers, brigs, schooners and ketches that could be seen from the clifftops. The vessels, heavily laden and often badly maintained, suffered dreadful losses during bad weather. During the winter, strong gales could easily drive scores of them ashore in a single night; the fortunate ones were carried

Coxswain Thomas Langlands in front of the *John Fielden*.

The naming ceremony of the *John Fielden* in 1896.

high up the beach at the top of the tide whilst those that struck at low water suffered worse fates. Lifeboat crews were assembled ready to act at a moment's notice, before them the perilous task of trying to reach the stricken craft, and take the crew off. Sadly, however, many were swept away as waves continued to break over the decks of the ships. Vessels succumbed to the gales all too frequently, with the loss of all hands. This problem, how best to rescue men from a grounded vessel that was breaking up under the battering of heavy seas, had confronted successive generations of lifeboatmen.

The Upgang station was founded in 1865 to ensure that a lifeboat was available to go to the aid of vessels aground on Whitby beach even when it was impossible to launch from the slipway or from the harbour. In 1875, on the retirement of the Whitby coxswain, John Pickering, the lifeboat committee decided to remove responsibility for the Upgang station from the Whitby coxswain and appointed Henry Freeman coxswain of the Upgang lifeboat. In January 1877 the Whitby lifeboat was launched in the midst of a heavy gale to facilitate the rescue of the crew of the *Agenoria*, but the overpowering sea conditions proved too much for the lifeboat, which capsized with the loss of Coxswain Samuel Lacey, and two of his crew, Richard Gatenby and John Thomson. A few weeks later, Henry Freeman replaced Samuel Lacey as coxswain and Thomas Langlands was appointed Upgang lifeboat coxswain. In 1899 Henry Freeman retired and Thomas was appointed coxswain of the Whitby lifeboat *John Fielden*. The *John Fielden* (Official number 379) was built by Waterman Bros at Cremyll, near Plymouth and arrived in Whitby in November 1895.

Thomas' close friend Richard Eglon served as 2nd coxswain. With his experience of beach rescue work, it is not surprising that on his appointment he would examine the Whitby boats with their suitability for beach work in mind. The No. 1 boat *Robert and Mary Ellis* was supplied in 1881, but the crew criticised her for being too heavy when she was entered for races in the annual regatta. In 1900 the district inspector of boats recommended that she be replaced, but after some discussion the local committee expressed the opinion that there was no need for a new boat and suggested keeping her for 'service to cobles', which had been the function of the 5-year-old No. 2 boat, *John Fielden*. The committee felt that the 10-year-old Upgang boat and the *John Fielden* would be adequate to deal with emergencies on the beach and disregarded the inspector's unfavourable report on the *Robert and Mary Ellis*. His hands tied, he could do nothing, but in 1903 he persuaded the committee to sanction an improvement in the *John Fielden*'s self-righting powers by modifying her water tanks.

In 1904 the local secretary, Captain Gibson retired having been decorated for long service a few years earlier. His successor J.W. Foster was faced with two very serious problems at his first committee meeting. The road from the lifeboat house to the beach, down which

The second *Robert and Mary Ellis* is launched off the west beach on her launching carriage, during a different service. Photograph by Frank Meadow Sutcliffe, Hon. FRPS 1853–1941. (Copyright The Sutcliffe Gallery, Whitby. YO21 3BA)

the boat had to be taken for launching, was in a very poor condition. It was suggested that unless it could be repaired it would be necessary to close Whitby No. 1 Station. The slipway belonged to the Harbour Commission, which he described as an impecunious body. Eventually, with a small contribution from the harbour trustees and the urban district council, the remainder of the expenses was covered by the Institution. The other problem, the crews' dislike for the *Robert and Mary Ellis*, was considered, but no action was taken, though it is noticeable that in 1907 the committee agreed that during the winter months she should be moored in the harbour and operated from there. In effect, though not in name, she had become the No. 2 boat, used mainly for assisting the fishing fleet.

During his time as coxswain at Upgang, Thomas had rarely been called upon to assist cobles in difficulties, though the situation was very different at Whitby. The harbour bar could be very dangerous, and the entrance to the port was so narrow that in rough weather sailing vessels would anchor outside. In January 1900 three local colliers sailed for the Tyne but the following morning they had to put back in because of opposing winds. In a strong north-west wind and a heavy sea, they attempted to anchor off Sandsend, rather than risk trying to enter the port. When their anchors began to drag, the *John Fielden* was launched, but the colliers got in without assistance. An entrance which coasting craft avoided in rough weather was certainly dangerous for cobles in bad conditions.

Early one morning in February 1900 the fishing fleet put to sea in fine weather. Later in the day, watchers ashore noticed the weather beginning to deteriorate and saw that the boats had abandoned their fishing and were heading for home. The harbour bar looked dangerous and the lifeboat crew were summoned, taking what precautions they could. The *John Fielden* was launched and stood by off the harbour mouth while the Rocket Brigade prepared to put a line between the piers so that lifebuoys could be lowered to the men whose boat might overturn as she came in. Sixteen cobles were heading for the port, their sterns low in the following sea. Three came in safely, but the remainder turned away and made for Runswick Bay rather than risk the entrance to the harbour. The *John Fielden* was brought back in having stood by in atrocious conditions.

Having put to sea in good weather in May 1906, the fishing fleet were caught by a sudden gale, and headed for harbour. There was a stiff north-east wind, and the harbour bar felt the blast at its strongest. The tide was ebbing but the sea presented in a very ominous fashion. Huge rollers hurled forward onto the beach and pier ends with an additional heavy ground swell. Thomas Langland's coble the *Thankful* came in safely, but the *William and Tom*, which followed her was not so lucky. Her crew were washed overboard. Seeing the danger, Thomas turned and re-crossed the bar, and set about rescuing one man. The other two had seized a line thrown from the pier and were driven close to it by the sea. Though his own boat had lost two of her oars, Thomas went in and picked them up. He now had five men in a coble built for three, but the *Robert and Mary Ellis* under the Upgang coxswain put out from the slipway in time to take on board the men from the wrecked *William and Tom* and also three men from a third coble, the *Jane and Mary*, which was later washed ashore.

Thomas wasn't a man to second-guess everything, which worked to his favour when the men from the *William and Tom* were in dire need of assistance.

Thomas Langlands did not attempt the entrance again, but ultimately landed safely at Runswick. The incident emphasised the need for the lifeboat to stand by when the cobles were coming into the harbour during a storm force gale. Having made such gallant efforts to rescue the crew of the *William and Tom* he received the thanks of the RNLI and its Silver Medal for conspicuous bravery and excellent seamanship. The consummate lifeboat coxswain, Thomas was still a family man and enjoyed returning home to his family and the security he felt when around them. In his spare time Thomas enjoyed returning to his fishing roots, sailing out with his son Peter.

The rowing lifeboats proved their worth once more on 7 December when the Newcastle steamer *Isle of Iona* struck Upgang Rock in hazy weather, and then ran aground some 300yd south of the east pier. Between them, the two Whitby boats saved all seventeen of her crew.

In 1908 the *Robert and Mary Ellis* was condemned, and replaced by a larger boat of the same name. A new boat, the *William Riley* of Birmingham & Leamington, was supplied to the Upgang station in 1909.

The ketch *Gem of the Ocean* had left Hartlepool at 11 a.m. on 15 February 1909 in fine weather, but the weather soon deteriorated as a northerly wind arose. At 4 p.m. coastguards reported a vessel in distress: Pounder Robinson and his crew went to Upgang and brought the boat out, taking her along the beach towards Whitby to intercept the boat. The latter, having weathered Upgang Rock, made for the beach. Two of her crew were seen climbing the rigging having realised the danger. The ketch eventually struck between the Spa and the Metropole Hotel, about 200yd out, and immediately swung broadside to the beach, in danger of being submerged and broken up as the tide rose. The lifeboat was launched, and with great difficulty made her way through heavy seas to the wreck. A line was flung aboard, but the lifeboat could not get close because the ketch was pitching wildly. Eventually one of the *Gem*'s crew jumped into the lifeboat. With several broken oars the lifeboat was at times in greater danger than the men left on the wrecked ketch and they returned to the beach. Despite a broken rudder, she tried again and almost made it but was swept north of the wreck by the violent current.

Sensing the gravity of the scene unfolding before him, Thomas Langlands launched his lifeboat and made for the safety of the lee side of the wreck, managing to save the remaining member of the *Gem*'s crew. A quarter of an hour later the ship's masts snapped and the vessel began to break up. By morning there was nothing left. Both coxswains received the well deserved official 'Thanks of the Institution inscribed on vellum', which was presented to them by the Archbishop of York at a ceremony held two months later.

The next five years were comparatively uneventful, occasionally fishing vessels required assistance as they approached the harbour, and several times men were rescued from sinking cobles, but there were no more major wrecks. The new boats at Upgang and the station on Pier Road rarely had to be brought out on service: most of the work was done by the old No. 2 boat, the *John Fielden*, which was kept moored near the bridge in readiness for emergencies. In July 1910, the RNLI announced that it proposed to station a motor lifeboat at the mouth of the Tees. By 1912 Whitby fishermen were beginning to see the benefit of steam-powered craft and in time the lifeboatmen would soon find it necessary to follow their lead. By the time the pier extensions were completed it was hoped that a deeper and wider channel might make possible the use of a motor lifeboat housed somewhere within the harbour.

With the outbreak of war in August 1914, all prospect of establishing a powered lifeboat vanished. Even if the possibility had been seriously considered, what was to become known as 'The Great War' had only been in progress for three months when the *Rohilla* tragedy

Thomas Langlands and his family. (Courtesy Mrs Eleanor Prentiss)

occurred. For his service to the *Rohilla* Thomas Langlands was awarded the RNLI Gold Medal, together with an exquisite scroll for 'Preservation of Life from Shipwreck', which were presented to him by the Duke of Connaught.

In 1919, Thomas became the coxswain of Whitby's first motor lifeboat, *Margaret Harker Smith*, at the same time as the *William Riley* was brought from Upgang to Whitby as the No. 2 lifeboat with Richard Eglon as coxswain.

In September 1920 Thomas Langlands retired and Richard Eglon succeeded him as coxswain of the motor lifeboat. At the sincere request of the local committee, the Institution treated him as generously as its resources would allow, for few lifeboatmen could equal his record of service. He had joined the Whitby crew in 1871, and from 1877 to 1920 had been coxswain at Whitby and Upgang. In nearly fifty years of service he had helped save over 200 lives.

When he died in March 1922, his coffin was carried by the two serving coxswains and four of his old mates, members of his crew and representatives of the Institution. It was said that they were all so overcome they played their part with difficulty. His cortège left from his cottage, 'Langlands', on a narrow street on the west side of town, the coffin bearing the flag of the RNLI, his coxswain's hat and the Institution's wreath. Newspapers reported 'every lifeboat station from Bridlington to Hartlepool was represented and all Whitby seemed to be at the graveside.' His final resting place lies close to those of the men who had died in the wreck of the *Rohilla*. A simple service with hymns of the sea was held later at the Seaman's Mission Hall.

Thomas Langlands is perhaps not always given the credit he deserves. Most people asked about Whitby lifeboat station's famous coxswains will give another name. I am quite pleased though that even today the small house situated on the west cliff, which was once the family home, still has the name 'Langlands' on the front door. Just inside the door there is a painting of a couple, which is presumably Thomas and his wife – the figures do bear some resemblance but any artist puts part of himself into a portrait. The present occupier wasn't fully aware of the history behind the house and was pleasantly surprised when I explained its significance.

Richard Eglon, who lived at 4 Pier Road, Whitby, was presented with the RNLI Silver Medal and Certificate for his part in the *Rohilla* rescue. The certificate recorded that 'on the day of the wreck he assisted in saving thirty-five persons in the course of two trips in the Whitby lifeboat John Fielden, which was damaged and broke up.' On 1 November, two days later, he accompanied Coxswain Robert Smith and piloted the *Henry Vernon* when, under dangerous and difficult circumstances, they succeeded in saving the *Rohilla*'s fifty remaining survivors.

As an additional tribute, Richard Eglon was presented with a specially minted gold medal by the people of Tynemouth in recognition of his bravery. Although the medal was originally fitted with a gilded bar, it is now fitted with a gold necklace and remains a cherished possession of his great-granddaughter. Richard Eglon was born in 1853 and came from a family of fishermen and whalers. In 1920 he succeeded Thomas Langlands as coxswain of Whitby's first motor lifeboat, the *Margaret Harker Smith*.

The following account was given by one of Richard Eglon's children:

The storm continued throughout Friday night into Saturday, and in spite of numerous attempts, it was impossible to get a satisfactory rocket line from shore to wreck, to rescue the remaining people.

The Whitby Lifeboat was able to make two journeys to the Rohilla, and rescued some nursing staff and crew members, but with the rising tide, the gale increased, and no further trips were possible. The lifeboat, the old John Fielden was waterlogged and badly damaged and had to be abandoned by the crew, who made their escape along the cliff base. In the afternoon, it was decided to take the Upgang Lifeboat through the Whitby streets, to Saltwick, where an endeavour would be made to launch it down the steep cliffs, to affect a further rescue.

My father was second coxswain of this boat at the time, and he made a hurried visit home to tell my mother what was happening, and that she had not to worry. I remember standing amongst a crowd of people at the top of Bridge Street watching the hauling of the lifeboat, as it went clanking past on its special large caterpillar type wheels. On arrival at Saltwick, the boat was taken down the cliff, but such was the fury of the storm, that a launch into the sea could not be made. Years

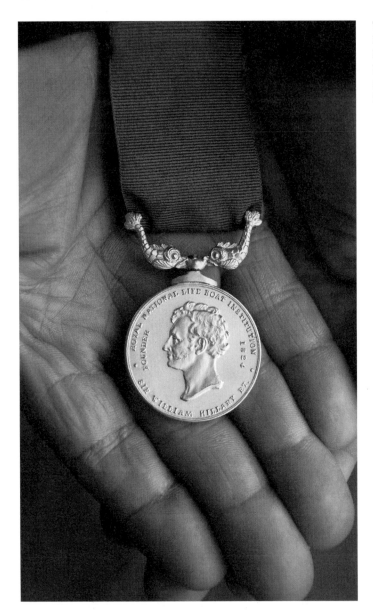

The RNLI Gold Medal, the highest honour awarded by the Institution. (Copyright RNLI/ Nigel Millard)

afterwards, I remember my father telling me that if they had been able to get the boat down to the shore, none of the crew would have survived. The intervention of an R.N.L.I. Inspector brought the attempt to an end.

I was just under 8 yrs of age at the time, and it was midterm break at school. I along with some of my pals, went up Henrietta St, and made the hazardous journey down the Spa Ladder, onto the east pier, where we could see what was left of the unfortunate Rohilla having been battered by the heavy seas. All around lay debris from the wreck, broken woodwork and masses of bandages and dressings and medical supplies etc. Tragically among all this litter, were the bodies of people from the ship, later to be recovered when the sea abated and the tide ebbed. On Saturday afternoon some attempts had been made by some of the crew on the wreck, to get ashore on rafts. Although a raft was found, there were no survivors.

Mr Peart took a leading role in the rescue work on the rocks at Saltwick in what could only be described as turbulent conditions. He was presented with a certificate on which was recorded:

At a meeting of the committee of the management of the Royal National Lifeboat Institution for the preservation of life from shipwreck, held at their offices, London, on 12 November, 1914, the following minute was ordered to be recorded on the books of the Society that the silver medal of the Royal National Lifeboat Institution be presented

A fine reproduction of the large scroll that accompanied the RNLI Gold Medal. (Copyright John Littlewood)

A painting of Thomas and his wife, which still hangs in the former Langlands family home today.

to George Peart, in recognition of his intrepid behaviour and indomitable efforts on 30 and 31 October, 1914, in saving life from the Government Hospital Ship Rohilla, which was wrecked in a whole ESE gale and a very heavy sea at Saltwick Nab, Whitby.

By his very gallant exertions he was instrumental in saving a very large number of those who were endeavouring to get ashore, and on several occasions he swam out into the breaking sea without the assistance of either a life belt or a line attached to him.

For his conspicuous bravery in going into the sea and helping save many of those who were washed, or jumped overboard from the wreck, he was also presented with £10. A native of Whitby, he followed in his father's footsteps as a coble fisherman for most of his working life, latterly in partnership with his brothers Dave and Ron on the *Sea Harvest*. He still found time to work as a member of the lifeboat launching team for twenty-one years and was head launcher from 1959 to 1974, when he retired on the arrival of the new steel lifeboat, which had its own floating berth. During the Second World War he served for six years aboard a minesweeper, known as a keen supporter of Whitby Town FC he very rarely missed a match. His silver medal and certificate today still evoke the same pride as the day they were presented to him.

Coxswain of the Tynemouth Lifeboat Robert Smith

Born the son of a fisherman on 12 July, 1849, he lived at Garden Square, Cullercoats, just a short distance from the sea that was to play such an important part in his life. As a child he attended an old Quaker school, where the main subject was spelling, and where the fee was a penny per week. He liked to help his father, and when he was still quite young it was not unusual for Robert to be seen walking up the coast to Hartley, where he would collect limpets for baiting his father's nets. He was, in fact, only 12 when he joined one of James Robinson's fishing boats.

It was the wreck of the steam ship *Stanley* on the Black Midden Rocks at Tynemouth in November 1864 that decided Robert Smith's future. Those who could turned out to see the tragedy unfold. The ship had twenty-six crew and around thirty-six choirgirls on their way from Aberdeen to London to sing in the Albert Hall for Christmas. Those on the shore could only watch helplessly as efforts were made to rescue those on the ship. The conditions were too severe for any lifeboat to survive, but the rocket apparatus successfully brought in most of the crew. Only two of the girls survived the ships loss however.

Robert could not get their cries for help out of his head and although only 15 at the time he became determined to join the Lifeboat Service as soon as he was able to pull an oar. He was determined to learn lifesaving skills himself and the following year he joined the Life Saving Association. In 1870, aged 21, he married Jane Menzies with whom he had six sons and three daughters, though they lost three in early life.

Both sides of the gold medal presented to Richard Eglon, Whitby second coxswain.

The silver medal of the RNLI. (Copyright RNLI/Nathan Williams)

Five gallant rescuers from the epic *Rohilla* tragedy. From left to right, back row: George Peart, James Brownlee. Front row: Pounder Robinson, Coxswain Langlands, Richard Eglon

He was appointed 2nd coxswain of the Tynemouth Lifeboat in 1909. Captain Burton, very impressed, appointed him coxswain in 1910. He said later, 'I knew I had a man of the right sort.' Robert held the post throughout the treacherous war years.

In January 1913, the SS *Dunelm* went aground near Blyth in a very strong gale. A call was made for the Tynemouth lifeboat, but the sea was so rough that many of the crew felt it would be impossible to travel the 10 miles to Blyth, and chose not to go. Coxswain Smith, however, felt that it was his duty to go, setting out with a crew of only five. After an hour's struggle against mountainous seas the lifeboat managed to get alongside the *Dunelm* and rescue all of the crew. On the return journey, a huge wave struck the lifeboat and Coxswain Smith was thrown to the deck, knocking him unconscious and breaking several ribs. The 2nd coxswain took over and they returned to the safety of the Tyne.

Robert's most notable rescue was that of the final fifty survivors from the *Rohilla* in October 1914. For Coxswain Smith, however, his duty was not done until the lifeboat and its crew were safely back alongside the harbour. By the time they reached the river they were all exhausted, especially Robert Smith, whose hands were almost numb from gripping the wheel, but he was determined to complete his command of the rescue, getting his crew home. Back at home in Garden Square, Jane had not slept for two nights, and was very relieved that 'her Bob' had come back safely. Afterwards Robert often remarked that he had feared every mountainous wave that hit them during the rescue, and that it was only with God's help that they had come through without harm. A while after the *Rohilla* tragedy, a poster was created and presented to the crew of the *Henry Vernon* in recognition of the services the lifeboatmen undertook at Whitby. It bore the signatures of the King of Belgium and Admiral Sir John Jellicoe, Commander-in-Chief of the Home Fleet.

Robert was a non-smoker and a teetaller. He belonged to the Primitive Methodist Church and was a member of the famous fishermen's choir for fifty years. During that time he missed only three Christmas carol services. Two of his most treasured possessions were a Bible and hymn book presented to him by the Mayor of Tynemouth after the gallant rescues from the *Rohilla*. He could often be heard singing his favourite hymn 'The Old Rugged Cross'.

On 19 November 1916 a severe easterly gale had been blowing for twenty-four hours when the Norwegian steamer *Bessheim* hit the rocks in driving rain, hail and sleet and the lifeboat was once again called to action. Coxswain Smith successfully guided the lifeboat to

Coxswain Robert Smith.

the sinking ship, and saved 118 passengers and crew in three journeys. He was presented with a silver cup in recognition of his gallantry by the King of Norway.

Meanwhile, another drama was unfolding up the coast at Blyth. Late on the evening of the 18th, the steamer *Muristan* had come ashore in Blyth Bay. She was so embedded in the sand that huge waves smashed clean over her, so high that sometimes only her funnel and the tops of the masts could be seen from shore. It was impossible to take the pulling lifeboat out, and all the following day, while the *Bessheim's* passengers were being rescued at Tynemouth, the Rocket Brigade at Blyth repeatedly fired lines, but without success.

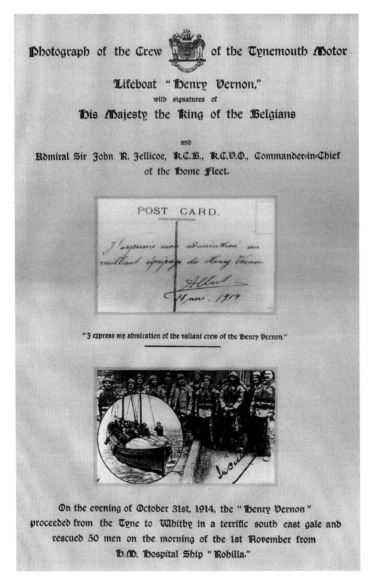

The poster created for the crew of the *Henry Vernon*.

When the *Henry Vernon* set out the sea was running so high it took incredible skill to take her safely out to sea. On her arrival, huge seas were sweeping over the *Muristan*. They went in as close as they dared, but saw no signs of life and decided to return to Tynemouth. However, after half a mile, a huge wave swamped the lifeboat and the engine stopped. They could not get the engine started, so they decided to make for Blyth under sail. Robert knew there were naval vessels in the harbour, and he found someone willing to strip down and overhaul the engine during the night.

At daybreak signs of life had been seen on the *Muristan*, so Coxswain Smith took the lifeboat out and got alongside her port side where to his relief sixteen men were found huddled together in the charthouse. Once he had the survivors in the lifeboat he set course for Blyth, and then returned to Tynemouth. For their service to the *Muristan* Coxswain Smith and 2nd Coxswain Brownlee were each awarded RNLI 2nd service silver clasps and thanks on vellum and each of the crew received a silver medal.

Robert had a very full life away from the lifeboat service. He was also harbour master at Cullercoats for twenty years, and on at least eight occasions saved people from drowning with his own traditional coble. He could often be seen at the watch house gazing out across the bay, and if ever anyone was in danger, the shrill sound of his whistle would alert them immediately. He served on the Tyne Salmon Conservancy board for forty years and on the Tyne Fishery Board for nineteen. Throughout the years Robert received many calls for assistance, which were never refused. His answer was always 'Ready, aye ready'.

During the fifty years of Robert's connection with the Tynemouth Lifeboat, he was 2nd coxswain for one year, and a coxswain for ten until he retired in 1920 at the age of 71. When he retired he was still in good health, although he was sometimes troubled by a cough caused years previously as a result of struggling against fumes to rescue a man who had set his house on fire whilst smoking in bed. The honours he had received by the time of his retirement were numerous and included the following medals:

Gold Medal – 'For Heroic Conduct'
Gold Medal – 'For Duty Nobly Done'
Silver Medal – 'For Bravery'
The Tynemouth Medal (Silver)
The Tynemouth Medal (Gold) – 'For Conspicuous Lifeboat Service'
RNLI Gold Medal – 'For Conspicuous Gallantry'
RNLI Silver Medal with Second Service Clasp
Board of Trade Rocket Apparatus Long Service Medal

During its first century the RNLI awarded its gold medal for gallantry and conspicuous service in saving life from shipwreck ninety-five times. In 1924 only eight of the ninety recipients of the medal, which is seen as the Victoria Cross of the lifeboat service, were still alive. These eight were invited to attend a centenary dinner in London as guests of the RNLI. Only seven were able to attend the lavish centenary dinner:

Captain Thomas McCombie, of Kingstown, Ireland

Major Herbert Edgar Burton RE, Hon. Superintendent of the Tynemouth Motor Lifeboat

Coxswain Robert Smith, of Tynemouth

Coxswain Henry George Blogg, of Cromer

Coxswain John Howells, of Fishguard

Coxswain William George. Fleming, of Gorleston

Coxswain John Swan, of Lowestoft

Rev. John M. O'Shea, of Ardmore, Co. Waterford was too ill to attend.

In June 1924 Robert received perhaps the highest recognition of his gallantry. As part of the centenary celebrations, the eight surviving gold medallists were invited to Buckingham Palace. Robert travelled to London accompanied by his daughter Hilda, with whom he had lived since the death of his wife five years before.

The seven men were received at Buckingham Palace by King George V on the morning of 30 June. They were accompanied by Sir Godfrey Baring, Baronet (Chairman of the

Coxswain Smith and the silver cup presented to him by the King of Norway.

Robert Smith with his
daughter Hilda.

Committee of Management), the Hon. George Colville (Deputy Chairman), George F. Shee,
MA (Secretary), and Captain Howard F.J. Rowley, CBE, RN (Chief Inspector of Lifeboats).
The king decorated them with the Medal for Gallantry of the Most Excellent Order of the
British Empire, which was replaced in 1942 by the George Cross. The king expressed his
great regret that Rev. O'Shea was too ill to attend and handed his medal to Sir Godfrey
Baring. In presenting the awards to Major Burton and Coxswain Smith, their heroic deeds
were given as follows:

Major H. E. Burton, R.E., Honorary Superintendent of the Tynemouth Motor Lifeboat
1914.
     For his gallant conduct and fine seamanship in bringing the Tynemouth Motor
Life-boat forty-four miles through the night and storm, unaided by coast lights, to
Whitby and, after all other efforts had failed, rescuing on 1st November, fifty persons

from the Government Hospital Steamer Rohilla, wrecked at Whitby, on 30 October, 1914.

Awarded the Silver Medal for putting off with a reduced crew to the assistance of the S.S. Dunelm, which was wrecked close to Blyth Pier, during a whole S.E. gale with a very heavy sea, on the 11th January, 1913.

Robert Smith, Ex-Coxswain, Tynemouth Motor Lifeboat. 1914.

For his intrepid conduct and fine seamanship, in conjunction with Major Burton, when the Lifeboat under his command proceeded to Whitby and, on 1st November, 1914, saved fifty persons from the Government Hospital Steamer Rohilla, wrecked at Whitby, as stated above.

Awarded Silver Medal for putting off with Major Burton and a reduced crew to the help of the Dunelm, as stated above.

Also awarded Silver Second Service Clasp for rescuing on 21st November, 1916, sixteen of the crew of SS. Muristan, of Swansea, which was wrecked in Blyth Bay, during a strong E. gale with a very heavy sea.

After the ceremony, some of the men gave their impressions of meeting the king. Coxswain Swan of Lowestoft said:

We all liked the friendly way in which the King shook hands with us. We found the King a very nice gentleman to speak to, and very homely. I had been given a little hint before we got there by someone who knew. He said, 'Do you go to him in your ordinary way, and he will think more of yon. If you don't he will come round on you for it.' Of course, Mr Smith got most of the talk, being the oldest, and having the most medals. The King talked to him quite a time.

This was a momentous occasion for all concerned, and Robert's daughter, who was watching the scene at the reception, often recalled how in his eagerness to greet Coxswain Smith, the Prince of Wales leapt over a table in order to shake him by the hand.

There was, however, a note of sadness to the day for Coxswain Smith, as by now he was almost blind. He had hoped to recognise the king by his distinctive naval uniform, but as he was dressed less formally, he was unable to identify him. He said:

The King wanted to know all about my medals, and the presentation gold watch, and what they were given for. I told him all about them, and I told him how one was for saving the life of a bed-ridden old man from fire, and how I went in and carried him out in my arms. Then he wanted to know about this one, and I told him it was given for life-saving out of a fund started by an American gentleman. And I told him about the silver cup the King of Norway gave me and this watch given by the people of Tynemouth 'for heroic lifeboat services'.

Although the king spoke to him at length, Robert did not realise who he was. It was not until he asked a fellow lifeboatman when they would be meeting His Majesty and was told, 'You've just been talking to him Scraper' that he realised what had happened – the moment he had looked forward to for so long had gone. This was undoubtedly one of the greatest disappointments in Robert Smith's life.

On his return to Cullercoats, he was quite astounded by the reception he received. Hundreds of villagers were at the railway station to greet him, and they cheered him continuously on his walk home to Garden Square. Once there, they gathered outside his home singing 'For He's a Jolly Good Fellow' and with tears brimming in his now almost unseeing eyes, their famous lifeboat Coxswain waved to them from an upstairs window.

After becoming one of the most famous lifeboat skippers in the country, Coxswain Robert Smith died on 30 October 1927 at the age of 78. By uncanny coincidence, he died exactly thirteen years to the day after the tragedy of the *Rohilla* in whose aftermath his contribution was monumental.

For the last few weeks of his life he was totally blind, unable to look upon the sea or his beloved little red, white and blue boat. But he had still been able to hear the pounding waves of a rough sea on the shore, or their gentle murmur on a calm day. Robert had been well loved by the people of Cullercoats, and his death was a great loss to them all. No longer would they see his familiar figure in blue jersey and peaked cap walking briskly by.

RNLI gold medal holders leaving Buckingham Palace.

On the day of his funeral, the route from his home at Garden Square to the Primitive Methodist church where he had worshipped was lined with people, and the flags at the watch house and schools were flown at half-mast in respect. At the church, a memorial service was held in the presence of a large congregation that included fisherwives in their picturesque costumes. Lifeboatmen and fishermen were present in large numbers together with civic representatives from the district. The procession, led by members of the Tynemouth Volunteer Life Brigade, proceeded to St Paul's churchyard at Whitley Bay and was followed by many mourners. It was said to have been one of largest funeral processions ever seen at Cullercoats. Very little remains of Cullercoats as a reminder of the picturesque fishing village it used to be. There has long been a painting of Robert Smith hanging in the old watch house overlooking the bay he loved so much. Along the coast at Tynemouth, the Life Brigade House contains a number of photographs as well as other reminders of his brave deeds.

At Whitby, one of Coxswain Robert Smith's descendants was fortunate enough to attend the memorial service held on the sixtieth anniversary of the *Rohilla*'s loss. She was very interested to see the Lifeboat Museum with its many reminders of the past, and in particular the *Rohilla* display. It was perhaps an odd coincidence that on this occasion the lifeboat was unable to turn out to place a wreath at the scene of the wreck because of the rough seas. Sadly, today none of Robert Smith's descendants are in the Lifeboat Service. His youngest grandson, Robert, would no doubt have followed in his footsteps, but he was killed at sea whilst serving with the Merchant Navy during the Second World War. Robert Smith had been a very modest man with a dislike of publicity, and although he has been mentioned in numerous books about the Lifeboats, his name is unknown to many. Yet, as long as there are lifeboats around our coasts the name of Coxswain Smith will always be held in high regard by the men who sail in them.

As I compiled this section on his life, it became obvious that Robert Smith had left behind him a great record and a name that will be remembered with honour and appreciation. No man more gallantly or more admirably carried on the great traditions of the RNLI off the Tynemouth coastline, where men and women have shown great bravery in the work of saving lives from the sea.

Major Herbert Edgar Burton, GC, OBE

When the hospital ship foundered, Major Herbert Edgar Burton was the honorary superintendent of the Tynemouth motor lifeboat. Born in 1864, Herbert Burton was the son of a Quartermaster School instructor at Chatham School of Military Engineering. He enlisted in the Royal Engineers in 1878 aged just 14, and progressed from bugler to company sergeant major by 1888. By 1894 he was a warrant officer and was commissioned in 1902 'for good services in the field'. Major Burton had three sons and one daughter. One son was lost during the Great War when the ship he was serving on was sunk.

Coxswain Smith's haul of medals are without doubt priceless, of great historical value, and are kept in a sealed case.

The Royal Engineers stationed in Clifford's Fort were the Tyne Electrical Engineers, who had been ormed as a specialist unit in Newcastle in the early 1880s. They were responsible for defending the port with submarine mines and searchlights to protect it from any enemy invasion. As their work and numbers grew they became so proficient at the task that the Tyne Electrical Engineers became a fully fledged unit of the Royal Engineers. In the Great War the unit pioneered the use of mobile searchlights, defending ports on its native Tyneside and at Gosport from air and sea attack. They also operated searchlights at the Spanish Battery and at the shore end of the pier.

The loss of the *Rohilla* was to be one of the pivotal moments in his career, during which he and Coxswain Smith brought the Tynemouth motor lifeboat down the coast to rescue the final survivors from the wrecked ship. A few days later Captain Burton received the following telegram from the Admiralty:

O.H.M.S. Admiralty, 6.52 a.m., to Captain Burton, R.E.
Admiralty have received through the Senior Naval Officer present, account of your services in proceeding in Lifeboat to Whitby in heavy gale, and then going alongside the Rohilla. The skill and courage shown call for highest praise, and their Lordships desire me to express on behalf of Naval Medical Service their grateful thanks to you and whole Lifeboat's crew for their gallant action.-Admiralty.

To this Captain Burton replied, 'The Tynemouth Life-boat crew and I feel greatly honoured by their Lordships' expression of appreciation on the services rendered on the wreck of the Rohilla.' Coxswain Robert Smith also published the following notice in the press:

Coxswain Robert Smith desires to acknowledge the valuable assistance he received from Lieut. Basil Hall, R.N., Inspector of Life-boats, and Mr Richard Eglon, Second Coxswain of the Whitby Life-boat, in manoeuvring the boat alongside the wreck of the Rohilla at Whitby, and in helping in the rescue of the shipwrecked men.

Apart from many awards made to those directly concerned in the *Rohilla* disaster, Major Burton received the gold medal of the RNLI and a gold medal from the Henry Vernon Lifeboat Crew Fund. He also received the clasp to the gold medal of the Tynemouth Medal Trust and a silver tea and coffee service by public subscription. In 1915 he was awarded the American Gold Cross of Honour, given only once every two years by the United States to a foreign national. This was only the second occasion of such an award. Burton was equally pleased to receive the thanks of the Lords of the Admiralty and to have his services entered in the records by order of the Army Council.

As honorary superintendent of the Tynemouth motor lifeboat he resigned from active lifeboat service, confident that the *Henry Vernon* had proven the value of motor lifeboats, pleased that the local men, led by Coxswain Smith, shared his faith in this new breed of boat. The outbreak of war brought new responsibilities and Burton was instrumental in work on the Tyne defence and the training schools. His great understanding of engineering, signalling, telephony and anti-gas education made heavy demands on him. In the beginning, as the commander, he had just six instructors, but as his rate of success increased the numbers swelled to over a thousand and it is thought that around 10,000 officers and 18,000 NCOs passed through the schools. Such was his standing that he received the OBE, and the Coronation Medal as a personal gift from the king.

Burton was made a brevet major in 1917 'for services in The Great War', and was major of the Coast Battalion on his retirement in 1919. His services amounted to almost sixteen years in the ranks, nearly eight years as a warrant officer and over seventeen as an officer. But Major Burton had by no means ended his career. In 1921 he was recalled as T/Major with the Defence Force, and was called upon to serve as an adjutant to recruit and organise the 50th Divisional Engineers TA from 1922 to 1927. For his actions on 1 November 1914, leading gallant lifeboat crewmembers to rescue the final fifty souls from the wreck of the *Rohilla*, that he duly received the Empire Gallantry Medal and the following citation:

Major Burton displayed great gallantry and fine seamanship in bringing the Tynemouth motor lifeboat forty-four miles through a stormy night, unaided by coast lights, to Whitby and, after all other efforts had failed, rescued fifty people from the government hospital steamer Rohilla, which had been wrecked at Whitby two days earlier.

(*London Gazette*, 30 June 1924)

Approaching his sixtieth birthday, he still enjoyed a very active and varied lifestyle, his interests including the sea scouts and benevolent work for ex-service men. He finally settled happily amongst the community of Beadnell, in Northumberland, living the life of a fisherman. He was one of the founding members of the boating club and planned the annual regattas with great enthusiasm.

His retirement was curtailed once again in 1939 and he returned to the 50th and 23rd Divisions, his ability and keenness unimpaired. He was called upon to organise mobilisation schemes for the District Local Defence Volunteers, which later became the Home Guard. Towards the latter stages of the war, the government appealed for yachtsmen to carry out particular harbour duties. Major Burton had no hesitation in applying to work around the harbour and was accepted, but before he could begin illness intervened preventing him from doing so.

The Empire Gallantry Medal he received on 30 of June 1924 for his part in the *Rohilla* rescue was exchanged by the king for the George Cross in 1942.

Major Herbert Edgar Burton, GC, OBE, passed away on 7 December 1944, aged 80, at Beadnell, Northumberland. Today he lies in a small country churchyard not far from the sea he loved so well. He knew it in all its many moods, it provided him with his greatest moments and like every other challenge in his long eventful life, he faced it with unflinching courage.

Major Herbert
Edgar Burton.

The Order of the British Empire (OBE) was divided into military and civil divisions, Major Burton wore his medal suspended on a purple ribbon, with a red central stripe denoting his position as a military figure; the Queen's South Africa Medal with clasps 'Transvaal', 'Orange Free State' and 'Cape Colony'; the King's South Africa Medal with clasps 'South Africa 1901' and '1902'; the British War Medal; the Victory Medal (sadly missing from his group at the Royal Engineers Museum); 1911 Coronation Medal; and Army Long Service & Good Conduct Medal. He also received the RNLI Silver Medal for the rescue of survivors of the wreck SS *Dunelm* in 1913. He was mentioned twice in dispatches. Major Burton's promotion and retirement were announced in the *London Gazette* as follows:

Capt HE Burton to be T/Major 5.9.15

Capt HE Burton RE awarded Brevet Major

Capt and Bt Maj HE Burton OBE RE to be Major 4.6.19

Maj HE Burton OBE Coast Bn, RE retired on retired pay having reached the age limit 15.9.19

2nd Coxswain James 'Jim' Brownlee

Born on 27 September 1877 at the east end of North Shields, overlooking the river Tyne, Jim was the middle child of seven. His father was a labourer turned fisherman with his own coble, and Jim was happy to follow the same career for he loved being at sea. Early in life he worked for a time on the Shields Ferry, but left because it was too much like a shore job. His elder brother John Robert 'Tagger' had been a lifeboatman, but resigned with the rest of the crew in a show of no confidence in the new breed of motor-powered lifeboat in 1905.

James Brownlee, affectionately known as 'gentleman Jim'.
(Courtesy Mrs Dorothy Brownlee)

James Brownlee's
RNLI Silver Medal.
(Courtesy Mrs
Dorothy Brownlee)

They watched with great interet as the new boat was put through her paces with Lt Burton and his crew of sappers. He was ultimtaely faced with finding a crew from the local men and later reported that in James Brownlee, Thomas Cummins and John Robert Brownlee he had the right kind of men for the lifeboat. They still faced some difficulties working against the feelings of the local boatmen. They were met with jeers and ironical cheers when they went forth and were dammed by faint praise both in the press and by the public generally.

In 1914 Jim was appointed the *Henry Vernon*'s 2nd coxswain and John became bowman. With Coxswain Robert Smith at the helm and the rest of the lifeboatmen supporting them they served the Institution most admirably. In 1920, Coxswain Robert Smith retired. Jim, being 2nd coxswain, thought it likely he'd be the next coxswain, but he heard rumours to the contrary. He was a very proud man and rather than suffer the indignity of being rejected, he too resigned – only to find afterwards that he would have been promoted. He was shocked and dejected, regretting what he'd done. His wife always said that he 'stood in his own light' however. In later years he was a 'scratch' crewman and shore helper at the station and was bowman from 1940 to 1942.

Like his father, in time he bought his own fishing coble and, influenced by his experience in the motor lifeboat, saved up to buy a motor. Jim married Emily in 1902 and had six

James aged 70 in the centre, with John Robert Brownlee aged 77, right, with the Duke of Northumberland. (Courtesy Mrs Dorothy Brownlee)

daughters and one son, all of whom attributed their long lives to the fish they ate in childhood. Jim was a 'home bird', enjoying family life. As the family grew up, the small upstairs flat was always a busy place in the evenings, with teenagers and young adults playing card games around the table, or singing by the piano. There was smoking, but alcohol was not encouraged.

Jim's eldest daughter recalled that he was known as 'gentleman Jim' – probably because, rarely for that era, he preferred to be clean shaven. He always went to the barber and never shaved himself.

He had a number of boats, the last of which was *Eileen*, named after his youngest daughter and specially built at Amble. He'd had it for only two years when it was requisitioned in 1940 for the Dunkirk evacuation. At 63, he knew he was too old to consider another boat, and instead chose to spend the rest of his working life making crab pots and mending nets for others. He died in December 1958, aged 81. One of the highlights of James' lifeboat career was meeting the Duke of Northumberland in 1947 as he prepared to open the new lifeboat house, built to replace the one bombed in 1941.

Jim's medals and awards are spread around the UK among his surviving descendants. He was involved in some very courageous rescues, which resulted in an impressive collection of rewards, including the RNLI Silver Medal with 2nd Service Clasp, the Tynemouth Trust Silver Medal, the *Henry Vernon* Crew Medal (gold). He was presented with a gold medal and gold watch by the people of Blyth, a silver medal from the King of Norway and numerous certificates, one of which is in Norwegian, and a very impressive Bible from a minister in Edinburgh.

Jim's grandson-in-law Ian, a herring buyer for a leading company in North Shields in the 1970s, proudly displayed the Norwegian certificate in his office. A group of Norwegian fishermen once came into his office and were so impressed with the details of the rescue and how Ian came to have the certificate that they gave Ian their business.

James gave the following account of the *Henry Vernon*'s challenging voyage down the north-east coast in very poor weather. He paints the whole scene in the same way he lived life, taking it in his stride, meeting the encounter with all that he could bring to bear. He used to keep a small notebook, a sort of diary if you will. On the rescue of the last men from the *Rohilla* he simply wrote 'saved fifty lives'.

A Motor Lifeboatman's Story

An interesting account of the eventful trip was recorded by James Brownlee, 2nd coxswain of the *Henry Vernon*. He said that the motor ran magnificently, and the boat made the journey from the Tyne to Whitby, a distance of about 44 miles, without a stop and without the slightest trouble with the engine. The journey was accomplished in eight-and-three-quarter hours, a very satisfactory record, considering that, though the gale was moderating, the sea was still very heavy. They experienced the worst of the gale off Hartlepool, where the seas were mountainous, but the boat got through without mishap. On arriving at Whitby, at about one o'clock in the morning, they found that it was impossible to carry out the rescue owing to the darkness and to the fact that the heavy seas and the ebb tide were causing a violent current through the narrow channel between the rocks and the *Rohilla*.

Captain Burton used an electric lamp to signal in Morse code to the survivors that help was at hand, and the boat was taken into Whitby, where the mast was unshipped and all superfluous gear taken out to make more room in the boat for the people on board the *Rohilla*. The lifeboatmen were provided with much-needed refreshments, and after an hour or two of rest they proceeded to the wreck. The current was still very strong, and it was with very great difficulty that the lifeboat manoeuvred alongside the wreck. The *Rohilla* had broken into three parts. The fore part and the stern had fallen away and become submerged, but the midship part was still standing upright, probably kept steady by the weight of the engines and boilers.

The survivors were clustered about the bridge and the spectacle was most heartrending. Many of the men had very little clothing, having evidently rushed from their beds when the ship struck, and been unable to get back to their cabins to procure more clothing. They had been exposed to the cold and the spray all day long and were numb, but, weak as they were, they showed great courage and coolness. Some of them lowered themselves by ropes from the wreck, and sprang into the lifeboat as it was carried up against the ship by the sea; others watched for an opportunity to jump on-board. He recalled that one man fell overboard and he pulled him into the boat. A number of the survivors 'had secured empty tins, and had tied them to their necks in order to keep themselves afloat in the event of their being washed overboard.

All fifty people and the cat were rescued in one trip lasting two hours. After they had been landed at Whitby, the motorboat set out on the return journey to the Tyne, which was uneventful.

Thomas Cummins and the Motor Lifeboats

Thomas was born on 19 February 1875 in North Shields and worked for most of his life as a fisherman and labourer. He started his working life as an apprentice carpenter but on his father's death he left for the more lucrative life of a fisherman. In 1898, aged 23 he married Elizabeth Wight, a widow whose husband was lost with his fishing boat during a winter storm. He was a voluntary member of the Tynemouth lifeboat crew for many years and had joined the service at the turn of the century before the advent of the motor lifeboat.

The Tynemouth station received the RNLI's first motor lifeboat, the *J. McConnel Hussey*, for trials in 1905. Before being sent to Tynemouth the lifeboat was stationed at Newhaven. Following various trials the crew reported positive feedback for the lifeboat. It was a former

Thomas Cummins. (Courtesy
John Cummins)

38ft twelve-oared self-righting standard lifeboat, with no transporting carriage, 8ft beam,
7ft stern, 8ft wooden/steel keels, 19ft 6in bilge keels, 3ft 5in thwarts, three water tanks,
two masts, two yards, one mizzen boom, and a no. 1 rig, the overall weight 4 tons 3 cwts.
The boat was built in 1892 by W.T. Ellis No. E6 at the cost of £418 6s, which was donated
by Miss Curling of London. The lifeboat was stationed at Folkestone on 4 December 1893
until 31 March 1903. While at Folkestone it was launched four times and saved ten lives.
It was withdrawn and reappropriated for motor experiments and returned to London for
fitting out.

The 9bhp motor was designed by Fay & Brown of New York, and weighed 24 cwts with
its fittings. The boat was equipped to hold 16 gallons of fuel and used 1.5 pints per bhp per
hour at an average speed of almost 6 knots. The lifeboat had repairs to damaged planking
and aircases and was reduced to ten oars from twelve. It was placed in the relief fleet as a
trials boat known as *R2A*. The lifeboat was allocated to the Newhaven station in November

1904 and underwent numerous trials; it was only ever launched on service once. The boat was then returned to the Institution store yard and repainted by Leslie & Harbin.

Thomas was part of the lifeboat crew when the *J. McConnel Hussey* was sent to Tynemouth in May 1905 for further trials. A survey in 1906 found small defects, which were made good, and she remained at the station until June 1911. While at Tynemouth the lifeboat was launched sixteen times, saving eighteen lives. In 1911 the lifeboat was transferred to Sunderland, where she remained until July 1914, making a further six launches and saving

Thomas was recognised for his dedication to duty and presented with numerous awards, including those from the Tynemouth Medal Trust and the Henry Vernon Lifeboat Crew Fund.

another three lives. As the RNLI's first motor lifeboat, she was launched a total of twenty-three times saving twenty-one lives, a most notable record for a trial lifeboat.

When the *J. McConnel Hussey* was withdrawn from Tynemouth in April 1911, she was replaced by a new motor lifeboat, the *Henry Vernon*. Despite the good feedback from Newhaven and the experiences they had with *J. McConnel Hussey* themselves, the local fishermen, who normally formed the crew of the Tynemouth lifeboat, were still reluctant to place their trust in this new breed of motor lifeboat.

The lifeboat was instead manned by sappers of the Royal Engineers. Thomas must have recognised the potential of a powered lifeboat as he embraced the technology, learning all he could about the engineering aspect of the boat. His commitment was rewarded on 1 October 1907, when he was appointed motor mechanic for the lifeboat. Whenever they took the boat out the crew endured the jeers and taunts of the local boatmen, but as the new boat began to prove herself, some gradually lost their mistrust of the new motor technology and began to take their places aboard her.

Thomas was one of the *Henry Vernon*'s crew during the rescue of the last surviving crew members of the *Rohilla*. When not at sea he worked as a labourer in the construction industry.

Thomas received a gold watch and was no doubt impressed by the personal message. (Courtesy John Cummins)

Whilst working on one of the piers at North Shields he saw a runaway cart heading for a group of workmen. He tried to slow it down by wedging a spike into its wheels. Unfortunately, the weight and momentum of the cart was such that the spike shattered, sending splinters everywhere. Thomas was in terrible pain and he knew instantly that some of the shards had gone into his face. He was devastated to learn nothing could be done to save the vision in one eye, ultimately meaning he was no longer fit to serve as a lifeboat crewmember.

He was forced to take a different path after the accident and became widely known for his charitable acts, he enjoyed growing plants and herbs from which he made herbal remedies dispensed to the locals; he also spent many hours making wooden toys for children at a time of great austerity. His weekends were spent helping at the local Sunday school, sometimes giving the Sunday service.

Thomas died in 1927, aged just 51. His family had the satisfaction of knowing that he gave willingly of his time. Like his fellow lifeboat men, he was always there, always willing to do what it took to save lives when needed, even if it meant putting his own life at risk, no matter how rough or treacherous the storms, always ready to answer the call.

Thomas had a long and illustrious career with the RNLI and he was presented with a number of awards, including a silver medal from the Tynemouth Medal Trust, a gold medal and savings bank book from the Henry Vernon Lifeboat Crew Fund and a wonderful gold watch, which is a treasured item still kept by a member of the family. The watch is inscribed with a touching message: 'Presented To Thomas Cummins By The Inhabitants Of Tynemouth In Recognition Of Heroic Life Boat Services.'

THE *WILLIAM RILEY* OF BIRMINGHAM AND LEAMINGTON

In 2005 I received a telephone call from Peter Thomson, the curator of the lifeboat museum. He was clearly excited as he relayed a call he had received informing him of the existence of the former Upgang lifeboat *William Riley* of Birmingham and Leamington. The lifeboat had been spotted on an internet auction website in a visibly poor state by an observant lifeboat enthusiast from Northumberland. As so many years had passed since the *Rohilla* tragedy it had never occurred to me that any of the six lifeboats involved in rescue attempts might still exist. It therefore came as a pleasant surprise to learn about the *William Riley*.

The Ruby class lifeboat was built by the Thames Iron Works at Canning Town in London in 1909 at a cost of £722 9s 1d funded by a legacy from William Riley of Coventry.

The *William Riley* lifeboat in the harbour following her dedication in 1909. (Courtesy Anne Poole)

The 34ft self-righting lifeboat had an 8ft beam, with six tubes used for releasing any water washed inboard. The boat had a wooden/iron keel with two bilge keels as well as two water ballast tanks weighing in at two tons; it had neither sails nor motor and was rowed by ten oarsmen. The *William Riley* was taken into service by the RNLI on 11 June 1909 and her official number became ON 594. She was placed on trials until 18 June, arriving at the Upgang station on 27 July to relieve the previous station boat *Upgang*. The *William Riley* of Birmingham and Leamington was named on 23 August 1909 by the wife of the local MP the Hon. Mrs Gervasse.

The Upgang station closed on 13 November 1919 and the *William Riley* was transferred to the Whitby station, and stayed on there until 27 May 1931, when she was effectively decommissioned. The *William Riley* was launched on service twice at Upgang and a further thirty-one times at Whitby, saving ten lives. After being decommissioned, the *William Riley* was returned to the store yard where her early trials had been conducted and placed as the first reserve, until finally sold in November 1931 for just £35. Following her sale she was converted into a private motor cruiser, and it is believed she spent the '60s and '70s at Redstone wharf in Stourport on the River Severn. The ownership of the lifeboat was transferred to a builder in Stourport in 1982, who restored her, fitting a 2.2l BMC diesel engine.

The *William Riley* after her first conversion to a motor cruiser. (Copyright RNLI/Graham Farr)

The hull of the boat clearly shows years of abuse and serious damage. (Courtesy Tim Hicking)

In the early '90s the *William Riley* was moved to Devon and moored at Barnstaple. She changed owners again in 2001 and underwent yet another conversion, this time with the addition of a cabin and stern-mounted engine and further restoration. Nothing came of this restoration, presumably after she had somehow 'sailed herself' into a low bridge at Barnstaple, almost taking the wheelhouse completely off. Later, on a low tide the boat settled onto a mooring post putting a hole in the hull below the waterline and it was in this state that she was found after many years of neglect.

With the identification of the boat confirmed as the *William Riley*, a private deal was arranged with the seller and the auction terminated. The buyer's initial plans were to transport the boat to Newbiggin in Northumberland, where it could be restored alongside another ex-lifeboat, but after speaking with the Whitby lifeboat museum curator it was clear there was some level of enthusiasm for seeing the lifeboat return. A select number of people interested in its restoration were invited to a meeting in what was then the old lifeboat station.

At the meeting the mystery buyer was introduced as Dave Charlton from Haltwhistle in Northumberland. An avid lifeboat enthusiast, he explained that since securing the boat he and his partner had made a number of trips to it in Barnstaple and that when they saw it for the first time it was nothing more than a hulk of rotting timber. All the superstructure had been removed, along with the engine and all ironwork that could easily be detached; thereafter the damage to the hull and vandalism had taken a heavy toll. He went on to explain that they been down to try and clean out what they could but that decades of abuse would not be easy to eradicate. Photographs were handed round showing the boat in its present state and it soon became obvious that restoring it was going to be quite a demanding task and one that would come at some considerable cost.

It was agreed that any restoration would require a band of willing supporters, but that some of the work would also require a person skilled in traditional boat building. To take on a project of this magnitude was no easy decision. In light of the estimated costs it was agreed that a charitable trust be formed to oversee the restoration. If we could gain status as a registered charity it would enable us to apply in the interim for Lottery funding, giving the project a huge boost. It was agreed to call the charity the Whitby Historic Lifeboat Trust. The election of trustees was straightforward, each chosen for their own skillset. Peter Thomson was elected chairman, Tim Hicking as treasurer and David Charlton as secretary; with my obvious interest in the *Rohilla* I was only too happy to accept an invitation to become a trustee. It was clear my disability would hinder my ability to physically work on the restoration itself, so instead I offered to create and manage a trust website whilst maintaining a photographic record of the restoration progress.

The boat lay neglected on a grass bank and a substantial amount of debris had built up over the years causing damage to the hull. To all intents and purposes she looked beyond help, but, remarkably for a boat of her age, the underlying timber was in good condition, though quite a bit of surface timber required replacing. Having had an engine fitted during her conversions, a substantial amount of waste oil, lubricants, dirt and grime had accumulated in the bilge, all of which had to be manually removed and safely disposed of.

At the next meeting an unpromising progress report was given. It seemed that retrieving the boat was going to be a logistical challenge. She had been moored on the River Taw for so many years that successive high tides had pushed her so far up the grass bank that she would only float on the highest of tides. A drawing was revealed which showed that the only point at which the boat could be 'lifted' out of the water was approximately 100yd from its mooring and that to get it to this point the boat had to be floated and then dragged along and around a mixed group of old boats, submerged mooring posts and deep obstacles all the while mindful of the flow of the river and the time constraints imposed by tidal heights.

A spring tide was expected for 19 August 2005 that would provide the right height to float the boat and offer the best opportunity to retrieve her, but this was only the first hurdle. In order to prepare the boat, volunteers had cleared out what could be removed, and in doing so had revealed the size of the holes in the hull. The trust was also faced with getting the boat lifted out of the water and transported back to Whitby. A plea for assistance was made in the local paper and Geoffrey Robinson of Dawson and Robinson (Transport) Ltd, Skinningrove kindly agreed to transport the boat back to Whitby, leaving only the hire of the crane to be covered.

The recovery team set off loaded with essential equipment. Temporary patches were made in order to make the lifeboat semi-watertight and it was then a matter of waiting with baited breath for the rising tide. As the river rose the boat slowly began to float, proof that the temporary patches were holding. With no time to waste the team had to manually tow the boat to the lifting point, navigating around a scattering of boats moored precariously along the chosen route. The lifeboat was pulled alongside a small quayside and secured ready for lifting, strops were placed under the hull and positioned close to timber that had been placed width-ways as spreaders to prevent the top of the hull from collapsing inwards. The recovery team was mindful of getting the hull lifted out of the water as soon as possible while the temporary patches held.

Saved from certain destruction in Devon, news of the *William Riley* arriving back in Whitby quickly spread, and a crowd of interested onlookers gathered to witness the homecoming. With the boat back in Whitby all that was left to do was to remove it from the trailer. Thankfully, Coates Marine were only too happy to help with their travel lift.

To begin with the boat was kept in the marina car park. We still had no secure way of supporting the boat during its restoration and were really pleased when the haulage company offered us an old redundant low loader-style trailer, which proved to be more than we could have hoped for. We had secured a base for the boat in a barn nearby, which provided a roof and plenty of room to work in. The first task was the remedial work of removing all redundant structures fitted since the *William Riley*'s withdrawal from the RNLI fleet. Mike Davis and Tim

Safely loaded on the trailer, the *William Riley* is ready to return to Whitby. (Courtesy Tim Hicking)

Hicking set to removing any wood that did not belong to the lifeboat. Roy Weatherill was one of many volunteers who spent copious amounts of time laboriously removing the many brass screws used to secure the raised wooden structures. It was a difficult task to first locate the screws and dig out the wood in order to gain access to the screws themselves.

In expectation of colder weather we were offered the use of a different barn on the same site, which was much better and would be a more permanent base. Once again, Tim Hicking was more than ready for the job. I don't know whether it is because he is not very tall or because he is so keen, but even though access was difficult he was soon busy. The next barn had last seen use as a cow shed and was still sporting significant evidence of such. The first step was to give the barn a thorough cleaning from top to bottom and the stalwart Tim was on hand as ever. Even with a commercial jet washer, he found it necessary to clean the barn a number of times to get it to a state suitable for the lifeboat.

Once the trailer had been backed into the barn there was room to erect a stable working platform. Mike Davies, a builder by trade, used his connections and managed to get the trust a long-term loan of a significant quantity of scaffolding and boards. That night he and Tim Hicking met at the barn and started erecting the layers of scaffold. I was there to capture the scene and, expecting to lose the light, I took one of my Arri 1,000 Watt Focusing Flood Lights with me, which soon lit the barn making it easier to work. It was

The late Roy Weatherill and Mike Davis remove a piece of timber, revealing the original lines of the lifeboat.

quite a large area to scaffold in such a way as to provide a level working surface without compromising the safety of anyone moving around in the barn. We all agreed to meet up the following evening so that Mike and Tim could finish the scaffolding.

The new base certainly opened up the amount of work going on, but we found areas of the boat that were difficult to work on, such as the underside, and came up with a novel system of rolling the whole boat. Now able to safely access the hull, we turned our attention to the holes, work that was definitely the domain of someone professionally skilled in traditional boat building methods. We sought guidance from Michael Coates, as he has done extensive repairs to the hull of the *Mary Ann Hepworth*, another of Whitby's former lifeboats with the same double planking. He started by removing wood around the holes until he reached sound timber, and it was then that the full extent of the damage became clear and just how important it was to have a skilled craftsmen doing the work. Mike is the consummate professional and we were extremely fortunate to have his support. He knew each of us personally and was willing to help us with the overall fee. That said, his work speaks volumes and was very much worth the expense. Mike gave guidance to some of the trustees who were willing to have a go at some of the smaller holes. With his work complete, the restoration seemed to move forward quite quickly.

The next phase was quite possibly one of the most important, that of sheathing the entire hull with a polyester resin and glass mat to ensure it was watertight. The process is applied to the hull a section at a time by first liberally applying the resin, making sure the section was fully covered. The glass mat sheet was then laid over the resin and pushed down into the resin with a roller. The mat must be thoroughly soaked with resin and it is vital that the roller is used to eradicate any air bubbles, ensuring a flat and uniform surface before the resin begins to harden. The same process is repeated around the hull with a small overlap on the matting and it is then left for a week to fully harden. The resin hardened, it was sanded back to a fine finish and any imperfections treated.

Finally the moment arrived that everyone had waited for – applying the first coat of paint. The ultimate aim was to see the boat in the water, but given the derelict state she was found in, this was a huge moment. A road trailer had been purchased and the boat slowly lifted from its working base. Ever so carefully it was swung over the trailer and lowered onto the trailer rollers. For the first time in three years the boat was wheeled out into the fresh air and work commenced on clearing out the barn. Tim was as ever at the forefront, never shy about getting his hands dirty. The boat was given a wipe down before being returned to the barn and it was agreed to go back at the weekend to get the first layer of paint on. Over the course of a couple of weeks the *William Riley* was painted and then sanded with a very fine sandpaper to achieve the smoothest of finishes.

The project was not without its problems and it wasn't all plain sailing. With the exception of some finishing touches, there was little left to be done barring the last major job of fitting a new deck and thwarts to the same standards as was used in this class of lifeboat. It was going to be a demanding job, requiring the skills of someone used to traditional woodworking methods.

A glass fibre outer shell is applied to keep the boat watertight and also provide support for the century-old boat.

On 1 June 2008 the boat was officially unveiled, and despite the onslaught of non-stop rain around 100 people turned up to see the remarkable transformation of the *William Riley* of Birmingham and Leamington. The unveiling started with a speech from the new treasurer about the former lifeboat and how it was lowered down the cliff during the *Rohilla* tragedy, securing its place in Whitby's lifeboat heritage. The ex-chairman then gave a short talk congratulating those involved in the restoration project. The boat was officially unveiled by Maureen Goodwill, wife of Robert Goodwill MP, which marked the culmination of two and a half years of work.

The boat was blessed by Canon David Smith and the guests were then invited to view the *William Riley* for themselves. Afterwards the boat was transferred to the marina, where it was launched into the River Esk. Some of those who had taken part in the project were given the opportunity to be among the first to row the boat. Seeing the satisfaction on Tim Hicking's face was wonderful as he had put so much into the restoration. As a founding member of the charity and a trustee, I am pleased that I was able to play my own part in the process. I see the *William Riley* as an integral part of the *Rohilla* story.

The lifeboat did not have a very long RNLI career, with thirty-one launches, saving ten lives, but its involvement in the *Rohilla* disaster was testament to the ingenuity, dedication and gallantry of the lifeboatmen of the day. The *William Riley* is destined to be used for display purposes, both static and practical, and there was little doubt among those present that the fully restored lifeboat is expected to enjoy a healthy future raising money for the RNLI. From this aspect it is quite possibly set for a very productive career, perhaps one longer than its RNLI service.

The *William Riley* had its first major fundraising venture in 2008, recreating the journey undertaken by the *Henry Vernon* in 1914 from Tynemouth to Whitby, but unlike the *Henry Vernon* the *William Riley* had to rely on the power of its ten oarsmen. Six drinking buddies and fundraising enthusiasts from York, known as the 'Ales Angels' were looking forward to the challenge and thankful that they could call upon support from lifeboat volunteers from the stations along the route. The Angels, Graham Hughes, Steve Cook, Graham Chaddock, Syd Scott, David Foster and Steve Morrison, have undertaken various ambitious fundraising challenges in the past. The journey was too far to be completed in one go so it was broken down into key stages from Tynemouth to Sunderland, Sunderland to Hartlepool, Hartlepool to Staithes, and the penultimate stage from Staithes to Whitby with the *William Riley* escorted by RNLI lifeboats from neighbouring stations. It was quite a challenge, but former trustee Tim Hicking was looking forward to joining the Sunderland to Hartlepool stage and also the final stage from Staithes to Whitby.

Around a week before the culmination of the fundraising challenge it came to light that a bell alleged to be the *Rohilla*'s original bell had been in the possession of the late Sir John Harrowing, a local ship builder in the 1800s, who lived at Aislaby Hall. Sir John's grandson, John Colin Harrowing, now lives in the hall with his daughter, Wendy, who remembers seeing the bell when the stables were being cleaned out many years ago, but does not know how it came to be in her family's possession. She said 'I have no idea where it came from. It might have been a gift or it could have been salvaged but I never really took any notice of it.' The bell is inscribed with the details of the wreck and when the stables were converted into holiday accommodation it was put in the living room. The inscription refers to the fate of the *Rohilla* and the lives lost:

THE GREAT WAR 1914–1918

H.M. HOSPITAL SHIP

S.S. 'ROHILLA'

STRANDED AT SALTWICK, WHITBY

30, OCTOBER 1914

92 LIVES LOST

I went to see the bell for myself down at the lifeboat station and found Mike Russell the coxswain on the floor with a tin of Brasso, apparently undeterred by the amount of work the bell required when it was brought to him. It was surprising how impressive the bell was even with the amount polishing still needed. I had to hand it to Mike for his effort and how good the bell looked.

Robert Goodwill MP and his wife Maureen officially unveil the boat to a crowd of 100 people despite the rain. (Courtesy Lucy Brittain)

The Harrowing family agreed to loan the bell to the organisers of the lifeboat weekend and historic *William Riley* row and as the restored boat came into Whitby the bell was rung out. Mrs Harrowing was to be the guest of honour at the blessing of the boats on the Sunday that coincides with lifeboat weekend and the historic row to hear the bell being rung.

The bell is a complex enigma in itself though, as during the disaster it would have been a fixture of the bridge and would have presumably gone down with the ship. It might well be that the bridge was the only part of the ship above water long enough for it to have been salvaged, though early salvage records do not indicate the recovery of the ship's bell, or indeed any bells. It was therefore surprising when it appeared in the possession of the late Sir John Harrowing. It was common practice for ship owners and builders to hold a stock of blank bells as replacements, which Sir John, as a local shipbuilder, might have done himself.

A ship's main bell rarely bears anything other than the name of the ship to which it is attached, yet this bell not only bears the name of the *Rohilla* but also details of her demise. It is entirely conceivable the bell originally held just the ship's name, but the size of the text used for the name is simply too small for a main ship's bell. There is no denying that it is a large and very heavy ship's bell, but is it the original bell from the *Rohilla*? As a ship builder, Sir John Harrowing most likely had access to ship's bells or had the means to have had one inscribed with the aforementioned wording. Whatever the truth, it is still an impressive item.

On Sunday 13 July the final stage of this epic challenge was very nearly cancelled because of difficulties getting the *William Riley* out of Staithes Harbour. Once safely clear of the harbour, the rowers realised that the swell had increased making it difficult going. However, undeterred, they embarked on the final stage of the immense fundraising quest, the pinnacle of its challenge culminating in its arrival back in Whitby during the annual lifeboat weekend. As the *William Riley* neared Upgang, the location of its original lifeboat station, the rowers stopped for a final break, they were extremely pleased to see the small flotilla of boats intent on escorting them safely home. The all-weather lifeboat *George & Mary Webb* had the distinction of leading the flotilla into the harbour.

The old lifeboat was always assured a warm welcome when it arrived at Whitby, particularly after such a mammoth undertaking. It was amazing to see the crowds that had gathered along the full length of the piers. During the epic row from Tynemouth the men rowed 316,680 strokes, without doubt an impressive and exhausting figure. Shortly afterwards the *William Riley* and its band of supporters headed towards Cullercoats, where the BBC was filming an episode of the hit series *Coast*, recreating an overland launch where a lifeboat had been hauled by women to the wreck of the *Lovely Nellie*. Ropes were set up to make pulling the *William Riley* easier. Three local female rugby teams and two shire horses played their own role in the making of the episode with Neil Oliver himself trying his hand.

The *William Riley* was then returned to the Northumberland workshop who made the decking for the gunwale to be repainted and re-varnished so she would be ready in time for the Dunbar bi-centenary on 29 August. The *William Riley* and her crew with shipped oars were an important part of a parade along the high street admired by all those who had the

Still some polishing to do, but our station coxswain Michael Russell (right) looks as pleased as I do.

opportunity to inspect her. The boat then went back to the workshop for a final top coat and a filler coat added to remove the weave effect from the glass fibre matting used to make the hull watertight.

In June 2009 the *William Riley* appeared at the Bradford RNLI branch special celebratory flag day an event arranged to mark 150 years of fundraising in the city for the lifeboat charity. The Teesmouth lifeboat *Bradford* had set off for Whitby in response to the loss of the *Rohilla*, but had to turn back due to damage sustained in the difficult conditions. The *William Riley* was located in Centenary Square in the city centre, along with RNLI displays and collectors.

On 16 July the *William Riley* went to Fleetwood for a week where it was planned to be on display at the Great Eccleston Show on Saturday the 18th along with RNLI stalls. Its next appearance was part of the Fleetwood Transport Festival on the 19th, where it was an integral part of a parade manually pulled through the town in the mayoral procession. The highlight of the trip was no doubt the 150th Lifeboat Weekend, for which a whole host of events were arranged. The 29 July saw the boat at Scarborough as part of its lifeboat weekend, she went by road to Scarborough but was rowed back to Whitby by members drawn from the Scarborough Rowing Club, the Sub Aqua Club and some of the Scarborough Lifeboat crew.

The 8 August marked Whitby's swing bridge's centenary and posters throughout the town had the *William Riley* listed as being part of the celebrations. On the day, however, there was no sign of her though it was the perfect opportunity to maximise the boat's public relations presence. August continued the busy trend with a number of challenges, including another ambitious 'Ales Angels' row, this time from Fort William to Inverness on 10–12 August.

During their Scottish coast-to-coast fundraiser the Angels rowed along the 60-mile Caledonian Canal with help from volunteer RNLI crewmembers from Mallaig, Loch Ness and Kessock stations. The aim of the fundraising scheme on this occasion was to raise in excess of £5,000 for the RNLI, particularly for the more remote stations whose volunteers were supporting the Caledonian fundraiser. The Caledonian Canal is part of the Great Glen and to help the team raise money local people were invited to take up the Great Glen Ways 'Boot, Bike and Boat' challenge by running, walking or cycling the route. A group of up to fifteen cyclists from Whitby Rugby Club were to provide additional support to the rowers.

2009 was the *William Riley's* centenary and I recall that when I was a trustee one of our objectives during the restoration was to have the boat re-dedicated on the beach in the same fashion that the boat was originally dedicated. It was thought Mrs Goodwill would do the honours as the lifeboat was dedicated by the wife of the sitting MP in 1909. I learnt the trust was planning a talk to mark the boat's centenary after coming across

The rowers take a break and savour the sight of Whitby Abbey high on the clifftop before starting the final row into Whitby.

With Tom Clarke, the coxswain of the Scarborough Lifeboat at the helm, the *William Riley* leaves Scarborough bound for Whitby.

a poster of the presentation, but with such little promotion there is no wonder there was but a handful of people present. The centenary of the swing bridge and *William Riley* was the perfect opportunity to increase the boat's presence and it is quite a shame the trust let them slip by.

There was no Ale Angel fundraising row in 2010, but the *William Riley* was as busy as ever with a number of engagements. Another attempt was made at launching a 'Sponsor an Oar' scheme, this time with better results. When it was first attempted the proposed price per oar was £1,000 and was aimed at businesses whose company name would be added to an individual oar. The scheme received some interest but not enough to guarantee success. In the latest attempt, the sponsor fee was set at £100, making it more widely affordable, and this time it was supported by trust members past and present and members of the public. Sponsors were given the opportunity of having a small dedication added to the oars. Fifty per cent of the costs involved in the oars was met by the National Lottery, which enabled the trust to engage the services of boat builder Steve, who offered to obtain the wood and work on shaping them.

Vinyl letters were cut and applied to the oars for the dedications each sponsor gave. The *William Riley*'s first trip out was to Porthmadog, Wales, and the Ffestiniogs Quirks and Curiosities Gala Weekend on 30 April to 3 May, where the oars were used for the first time. The rowers' experience was used to determine how much, if any, balance adjustment is needed. The boat's next appointment was as part of the Buckie lifeboat station 150th anniversary on 20 June.

On 11 July all those who had taken up the offer of sponsoring an oar met up at the boat to see their oar complete with personal dedications; ours was 'For Elsie & all the *Rohilla* victims'.

Every year the boat can usually be counted upon to be present as a static display positioned up on the west cliff during the annual regatta. The static display allows people to get up close to the boat, and there is usually a range of display boards with photographs showing the *William Riley*'s journey to its present stage. It also allows people to speak to members of the trust if they have any questions. At the end of the three-day regatta there is always a float parade headed by the young lady crowned that year's Miss Whitby. The *William Riley* is normally found at the front of the parade with up to sixteen men pulling her along on her trailer and some additional 'brake' men on ropes at the rear to hold the boat's progress should her speed increase.

The parade's route is anything but flat and actually includes Khyber Pass, a very steep bank with a tight turn. The floats must navigate the route with pedestrians nipping here and there whilst also avoiding the market stalls either side at the most difficult part of the route where space is at a premium. In 2010 the weather was horrendous with torrential rain right when the floats set off, but undeterred the parade went ahead and the spectators surprisingly stood their ground to bear witness to those who valiantly carried on with the show.

All the participants of the Sponsor an Oar scheme stand by the oar carrying their personal dedication.

The *William Riley* is rowed through the Aberchalder swing bridge on the Caledonian Canal by the Ales Angels and a crew from Loch Ness Lifeboat Station. (Copyright RNLI)

In September 2010 the *William Riley* was involved in a challenge unlike anything she had ever done before as one of over 300 rowing vessels of every conceivable type participating in The Great River Race, London's River Marathon. The event is a spectacular boat race up the River Thames between the London Docklands and Richmond attracting crews from all over the globe and appealing to every level of competitor.

Teams from the Fishermen's club have competed in the prestigious 21-mile Great River Race every year and have won some of the top prizes, but it was the first year they had been able to take the *William Riley*, and by sheer coincidence take her close to where she was built. The Fishermen's club captain, Barry Brown, said it was the first year the Fishermen's crew had raised money for St Catherine's Hospice and they were pleased to be able to support the local cause. The ten-man crew of rowing veterans started training with the *William Riley* for the epic boat race. The training in the *William Riley* was different to other boats they have used as the crew had to familiarise themselves with the short pull technique needed. They practised for two hours at a time three times a week, in and around the harbour in the run up to leaving for London.

Despite the torrential rain the volunteers pulled the boat around the route, much to the surprise of those who had thought the parade might be cancelled. Les Brewster at the front on the left still manages half a smile. (Copyright Alan Wastell)

The rowers set off for London well in advance of 25 September, the day of the challenge, in an effort to try and get a feel for the course and try the *William Riley* on the Thames. On the day of the race the boat was taken to a designated car park where a large static crane was being used to ship the boats from their trailers and into the Thames. The nearest slipway was tidal and with so many boats to get into the water it would undoubtedly soon become gridlocked. Strops were strategically placed under the hull and the boat lifted aloft with Barry Brown still on board monitoring the lift throughout. There was quite lot of interest in the *William Riley*: people were constantly asking about its past and were amazed when shown the photographs of the boat before the restoration project began.

Fundraisers from St Catherine's, which operates a day hospice in Whitby alongside their main Scarborough centre, were delighted with the support offered and had helped out by giving the rowers vests and a flag emblazoned with the hospice's logo, commemorating twenty-five years of their vital work. Penny Campbell, fundraising co-ordinator for the hospice, said:

It is great to see people going the extra mile to support us. They are putting in a lot of time and effort, and it is not a simple task. It is just a shame for us we cannot all go down to London and cheer them on from the shore, but the pictures will be lovely to see.

Whitby Fishermen's veterans rowing team get some practice in, using the *William Riley* in Whitby Harbour. (Copyright Ceri Oakes)

At approximately 12.49 p.m. there was a large boom announcing the start for the *William Riley* and the rest of the boats in her class, which were all lined up as best they could. The organisers of the annual race allotted the RNLI Ruby Class 1908, lifeboat number 113. The high-profile race began in earnest with the striking Docklands skyline at the start, as the Thames weaved its way through central London before reaching its semi-rural Surrey conclusion. The *William Riley* made her way along the course jostling for the best position as she approached the many bridges she had to go under, many of which were packed with spectators searching for a particular boat and enjoying the spectacle, the intriguing mix of colours, the intense competition and fun. The Fishermen's veteran rowing team reached the finishing line at 4.14 p.m., having taken just under three and a half hours to navigate the 21-mile course, finishing 162 out of over 300 boats, a very respectable placing given the size and weight of boat.

The year ended with the *Scarborough News* printing a brief story about a team of forty rowers who had raised almost £5,000 for two good causes in memory of a Scarborough diver who tragically died in August 2009 in a diving accident off the coast near Hartlepool. The Friends of Colin Bell presented £2,459 to Scarborough RNLI and Help For Heroes after rowing the *William Riley* between Scarborough and Whitby. John Porter, a Scarborough RNLI press officer, said he could not thank them enough. He added, 'It's a marvellous donation and the people have worked very hard to raise such a staggering amount of money.' He added that the event was organised by members of Scarborough Sub Aqua Club and that Mr Bell's widow, Jean, was a driving force behind it. Colin Bell was an experienced diver and an active and enthusiastic member of the branch and will be sadly missed by all who knew him. He was a teacher at Yorkshire Coast College where students described him as a 'larger than life' character who will be 'massively missed'.

In July 2010 I received an email from one of the crew of the RNLI at Rye Harbour, East Sussex expressing an interest in having the *William Riley* for a fundraising row in January for the RNLI SOS Day in 2011. I was told that the *William Riley* is of a similar design to the *John William Dudley*, a lifeboat that was stationed at Rye until 1917 and replaced in 1928 by the *Mary Stamford*, which was sadly lost on service with all seventeen of her crew. The local RNLI branch wished to reproduce the 10-mile row towards Dungeness that the *Mary Stamford* took before capsizing. Although I am not actively involved in the day-to-day running of the *William Riley* I was happy to pass the enquiry onto the relevant person.

It was a pleasure to learn that 2011 began with the lifeboat crew from Rye Harbour stepping back in time on 29 January to take the historic lifeboat on an endurance row from Rye Harbour to Hastings and back as part of the annual RNLI SOS Day. The remaining voluntary crew and fundraisers at Dungeness lifeboat station were planning to take part in a sponsored twenty-four-hour bike ride beginning on Friday 28 and finishing on the Saturday. A 'Soap Our Saloons' carwash day was planned for the Saturday and people were invited take their cars to the boathouse for the crews to clean for £5 a car.

William Riley being lifted into the air from her trailer and into the Thames, in preperation for the Great River Race, London's River Marathon. (Copyright Barry Brown)

The boat's next engagement was in February in its home port of Whitby, where a service of remembrance was held to commemorate the twelve lifeboatmen who died during the great storm of 1861 in one of the region's worst lifeboat disasters. The men had been attempting to rescue sailors from a stricken collier called the *Merchant* and had put to sea for the sixth time that day. Henry Freeman was on his first lifeboat launch when the lifeboat capsized. He was the only man wearing the new cork lifejacket and was the sole survivor. He was awarded an RNLI Silver Medal for his part in the incident and went on to become one of Whitby's most well-known lifeboatmen during more than twenty years as Whitby RNLI Coxswain. To commemorate the twelve men who died, there was a short Act of Remembrance at Whitby lifeboat station. Whitby's all-weather lifeboat *George and Mary Webb* and the

William Riley were launched and descendants of some of those who died joined members of the lifeboat crew to scatter roses at the spot where the lifeboat capsized.

The *William Riley* was once again present as a static display on the west cliff during the annual regatta. Memories fresh from the previous year, we could only hope that it would not rain again. On the morning of the parade I imagine I was not the only one opening the curtains looking for fair weather to be greeted with a warm glow as the sun rose above the horizon. Batteries charged and drinks cooled we were soon ready to go. This year we were accompanied by Les Brewster's son, Jack. I was located so that I caught the floats coming along the main Pier Road, my wife Jane had the boat coming around the lifeboat museum corner and Jack was well positioned on the steps to the west cliff. In complete contrast to the year before it was a bright sunny day, which really made the difference.

Nobody could have predicted such a rosy future for the boat when we started its restoration. A diverse team of twenty men including Whitby trio Paul Headlam, Roger Turton and John Scott and a gentleman from South Korea raised more than £6,000 by rowing the *William Riley* across Ullswater, Coniston and Windermere to raise money for the Great North Air Ambulance. Organiser Paul Headlam said, 'We had great weather, made many new friends and most importantly raised a lot of money for a service that

Brixham-based Torbay lifeboat crewmembers take a break during the row to Torquay. (Copyright David Ham)

is used frequently in our area.' He paid tribute to all those who took part and supported the event.

In 2012, to mark the annual RNLI SOS Day on 28 January, the Brixham-based Torbay lifeboat crew incorporated the *William Riley* into a fundraising row to Torquay. The twenty-two-strong crew took it in turns to row the boat row via Haldon Quay to Torquay dressed like an 1880s' lifeboat crew.

The row was run in parallel with a separate challenge that saw the crew's wives and girlfriends (WAGs) pull an inshore lifeboat on its trailer by road from Brixham to Torquay via Paignton. The historic boat stayed alongside its modern counterpart for half an hour before rowing to Paignton Pier. Spokesman Colin Bower said the WAGs were collecting money en route, but the main revenue was expected to be raised via corporate sponsorship: 'We are asking local companies to sponsor individual crewmen for a minimum of £100 and for the ladies a minimum of £50. For this they will have their name displayed on the Torbay RNLI website www.torbaylifeboat.org.uk for 12 months.'

The *William Riley* was escorted by the RNLB *Alec and Christina Dykes*, a Severn class all-weather lifeboat, the inshore lifeboat and a private boat for safety and crew changes. As the *William Riley* made its way out the 2-metre swell made itself known but the boat coped most admirably. Once in the shelter of the bay the crew could ease back a little, although not as far as one of the crew, who seemed to forget the thwarts don't have backs.

All funds raised in the bay were to be spent locally so crews could be equipped with the new and improved RNLI lifejackets. Mr Bower said:

There is nothing wrong with the ones they have got now, but they are 10 years old and need to be serviced every three months. The new ones are a lot more comfortable to use and offer greater ease of movement. The new lifejackets only need to be serviced once a year. That in itself will save the RNLI money. The £10,000 fundraising target would help pay for new lifejackets for all twenty-two RNLI crew members in the Bay.

The WAGs' adventurous lifeboat challenge went equally smoothly considering they too were all dressed in the fashion of the day and had 10 miles to cover on a busy sweltering day. Unlike the boat on water, the landlocked challenge required coping with some steep hills and equally steep declines and pulling the lifeboat through some very built up parts of the town, with a steady backlog of traffic behind them.

As the ladies made their way towards Torbay's first lifeboat house and the end of their challenge eight lifeboat crewmen took up position either side of the road, a guard of honour one might say, in what could only be described as a true show of respect and admiration. One of the Brixham WAGs, Michelle Heatley, said:

These men and women who support our lifeboats are an inspiration to us all. From the early crews who hauled boats overland, to the modern crews who give the

Torbay wives and girlfriends pull the inshore lifeboat from Brixham to Torquay. (Copyright David Ham)

essential service to anyone who needs them, the Brixham crew with the help of Whitby's own piece of RNLI history keep our shores safe.

It's not often that an occasion brings together so many Superb Outstanding Special people. The SOS event is one of the charity's most important national fundraising events. Last year people cooked and sold sausages on Brixham Harbour using the acronym SOS for Sizzle Our Sausages, while the lifeboat crew took part in the Surf Off Scillies event, which raised over £4,000. Mark Criddle, RNLI coxswain at Torbay, said:

It's just incredible to think of what the volunteers went out to in an open lifeboat with just man power to get them to the casualty. Today, the lifeboat crew at Torbay are extremely lucky to have both an all-weather and inshore lifeboat and the most up to date equipment and training.

The *William Riley* was bestowed her greatest honour in 2012 when she was accepted as one of the boats to participate in the Thames Diamond Jubilee Pageant on 3 June. The demand for a place in the pageant was such that each one received three applications.

The vessels that took part included military, commercial, pleasure craft and sailing vessels. Those too tall to pass under the bridges were moored as an 'Avenue of Sail' downstream of London Bridge with smaller craft in St Katherine Docks. An enthusiastic team of rowers and volunteers, including members of Whitby Fisherman's Rowing Club, Ales Angels and local RNLI fund-raising supporters travelled down to London to support the *William Riley*.

The *Gratitude*, a former Whitby boat built in 1976 by David Wharton, one of the founding trustees of the Whitby Historic Lifeboat Trust, also took part in the pageant. When commissioned, the *Gratitude* was intended as a floating museum piece designed to preserve the tradition of Yorkshire cobles, once a common sight on the Whitby coast. The *Gratitude* was purchased in 1995 by Alan Richmond, who relocated her to Scarborough and gave her a full refit.

The *Spider T*, the last remaining Humber 'super sloop', a sail-powered cargo vessel built in 1926 that visited Whitby in August 2012, was also accepted for the pageant, whose owner Mal Nicholson said: 'I feel truly honoured that the *Spider T* has been chosen. She reflects the heritage of our region and is a testament to the ship-building skills on the Humber.'

The number of vessels presented the largest flotilla in living memory, stretching out over 12 miles, which, according to the Guinness World Records, was the largest ever boat parade.

Everyone involved in the annual SOS challenges, including the crews of the inshore and offshore lifeboats, the wives and girlfriends, support staff, friends and family, and the crew of the *William Riley*, who made the day really worthwhile. (Copyright RNLI/Nigel Millard)

It is estimated that 1 million spectators watched from the banks of the Thames. The pageant was broadcast live by the BBC and Sky News and subsequently broadcast around the world on other networks. More than 10 million tuned into the BBC's four and a half hour coverage.

Every vessel will proudly take its place in the flotilla alongside the Queen and other members of the Royal family aboard the Royal barge, *The Spirit of Chartwell*. During the televised pageant the *William Riley* could be spotted a short distance behind the royal barge in what could only be described as a coveted position, albeit only briefly. The RNLI played an important role with lifeboats patrolling the outer edges of the pageant, just in case anyone fell overboard, into the maelstrom of vessels. They also kept watch for anyone who might irresponsibly enter the water from the shore.

Shortly after returning the *William Riley* was once again called into action, this time for the Scarborough Diving Club Colin Bell Memorial Row from Scarborough to Whitby, the proceeds of which were to be divided between the RNLI and the Yorkshire Air Ambulance. The club had the use of the ex-Dutch beam trawler, *Hatherleigh*, which allowed me to be part of the proceedings to some extent. We left Scarborough at 6 a.m. expecting to arrive off Whitby around midday. The trawler is a great diving platform and is well kitted out, no expense spared. I certainly felt really comfortable, my camera bag on the table, a tripod lashed to the side and my monopod further down. I am grateful to the diving club for allowing me to be part of the event, my only regret being that I am unable to row the boat myself.

In 2013, it was not till June that the *William Riley* had her first major fundraising event – an ambitious row of 40 miles along the Norfolk Broads. It was no doubt quite a sight to see a pulling lifeboat making its way along the waterways. Crews from Great Yarmouth and Gorleston, Cromer, Sheringham and Wells joined the Ales Angels as they made their way from Worxham to Yarmouth and Yarmouth to Brundall, stopping at pubs along the route to collect donations for the RNLI – and to rest their weary limbs!

The *William Riley*, her crew looking quite calm taking in the scenery. (Copyright Ian Morris)

The challenge started on 29 June at Brundall Bay Marina with a team from Cromer lifeboat station taking the first leg, rowing 13.5 miles to the Ade Bridge Inn before the Sheringham crew took over, rowing 10.25 miles to Yarmouth Yacht Station. The Yarmouth and Gorleston crew rowed 9 miles to Reedham Ferry Bridge on Sunday 30 June before the Wells crew take over for the 10.5-mile final stretch to the Yare pub in Brundall. Between them the crews covered 43.5 miles and rowed for about ten hours more, with the support of four Norfolk lifeboat stations, the *William Riley* snaked her way along the rivers Bure and Yare at the weekend to raise funds for the RNLI.

Alan Churchman, a crewmember of Great Yarmouth and Gorleston lifeboat station, said:

It's not often you get an opportunity to row an old lifeboat like this one – it should be good fun. I've not done a lot of rowing so that'll be interesting – I'm not that good when it comes to two oars and two hands, but our station is really keen to get out in the public and help raise money for the RNLI.

Andy Woods, deputy coxswain, said that it was hard work, but they felt privileged to sit aboard the historic vessel. Contemplating the loss of the *John Fielden*, he said 'They must have gone to hell and back. There seemed very little space on the boat with 13, and they sometimes had to get 20 people on board as well as the rowers.'

In 2013 the *William Riley* had a relatively quiet year. She had her usual static displays for the annual regatta and flag weekend treating visitors to a demonstration of the boat in action in the harbour.

In September the *William Riley* was invited to be part of the celebrations in tribute to the courage of Grace Darling and her father on 7 September 1838. But Grace wasn't the only person to spot the wrecked SS *Forfarshire* that morning 175 years ago. On the Northumberland coast at Bamburgh Castle, the charity workers of the Crewe Trust spotted the wreck at daybreak and raised the alarm. What occurred next was recreated in September 2013.

Without telephones or pagers to reach the lifeboat crew at Seahouses, a Crewe Trust administrator jumped on a horse and rode to North Sunderland to alert the nearest lifeboat volunteers. It was 7 a.m. By 7.30 a.m., a crew of volunteers had gathered and were ready to launch. They included Grace Darling's 19-year-old brother, Brooks, and the well-respected Seahouses lifeboat coxswain, William Robson. Robson decided that his crew's purpose-built lifeboat would be too light for such rough seas, so the crew launched on the coxswain's own fishing boat.

The sea that had wrecked the *Forfarshire* the previous night still raged. Yet, somehow, the lifeboat crew rowed 5 miles to the site of the shipwreck. To their sorrow, they found no survivors and felt it safer to row to Longstone Lighthouse. When they arrived they were rather surprised to find Grace Darling and her father had rescued nine people from the shipwreck, who were recovering inside.

Seahouses lifeboat station played host to the *William Riley* during the celebrations to mark the 175th anniversary of Grace Darling's exploits. (Courtesy Barbara Carr)

In tribute to that gruelling row, RNLI volunteers took up the oars of *William Riley* and headed out to sea on 7 September, facing a 2m swell and 20mph winds. It was agreed that it was not safe to go all the way out to Longstone Lighthouse so the rowers took a short trip outside the harbour aboard the *William Riley*. In the meantime, Seahouses' all-weather lifeboat headed to the lighthouse, where crewmembers laid flowers in memory of Grace and all those lost in the shipwreck.

Virginia Mayes-Wright, manager of the RNLI Grace Darling museum said, 'The RNLI charity wanted to commemorate the anniversary of the rescue, not only because Grace's deed epitomises the bravery and selflessness of its volunteer lifeboat crews of today, but because Grace is an inspiration to all who learn about what she did.'

The *William Riley* continues to make an excellent platform for fundraising events and seems to have a successful future ahead of her. I am proud to be one of the founding trustees of the Whitby Historic Lifeboat Trust knowing I had my own role to play in the *William Riley*'s restoration.

THE TYNEMOUTH MOTOR LIFEBOAT
HENRY VERNON

Scenes of remarkable enthusiasm were witnessed on North Shields Fish Quay when the motor lifeboat *Henry Vernon* returned home from Whitby and the *Rohilla* at about four o'clock in the afternoon on 1 November 1914. The heroes found awaiting them a distinguished gathering including Brigadier General Baylay (commanding the Coast Defence), the Mayor of Tynemouth (Councillor Gregg), the town clerk S. Wilson, a number of the Corporation, the Tyneside Volunteer Life Brigade under the command of J.A. Catchside and J.A. Williamson the honorary secretary.

The lifeboat was escorted into the harbour by the pilot cutter, and was given a rousing reception, the steam whistles of vessels in the harbour joining in the cheering of the crowds on the quay and on the torpedo boats lying in the river. A formal reception took place in the drill grounds of the Cliffords Fort. The mayor noted that he could not think of a braver action than the taking of the motor lifeboat on such a long journey through such a tempestuous sea. Captain Burton performed a very worthy act, despite having a scratch crew. Mr Catchside said he did not know what one had to do to receive the VC, but he thought that the *Henry Vernon*'s crew deserved such an honour. Although the crew had been recognised on previous occasions, he thought that if the mayor opened a fund the public would recognise their bravery in a practical manner.

In reply, Captain Burton said that the last thing he wanted was to be put in the foreground, for more credit was due to the crew than to himself, because he was a man trained to take risks. After a reference to his old friend Robert Smith the coxswain, the captain said, 'I cannot make a speech, and if you had seen the sights we saw this morning, and seen those poor fellows on board that ship, practically without clothing and bruised from head to foot, you would not feel able to make a speech.'

They had been at sea in a severe gale for about twenty-four hours, and the crew of the lifeboat seemed remarkably fresh, but they were quite ready for the soup and refreshments generously provided for them.

The Monday after the return of the lifeboat a public meeting was convened in which a fund was inaugurated to finance a presentation to the crew of the motor lifeboat, in recognition of their services.

Congratulations An Admirable Piece of Work – The Lifeboat Institution's Message

The lifeboat institution, London, have sent a congratulatory message to Capt. Burton, expressing the institutions appreciation of the motor boats fine achievement on Sunday. The telegram reads; 'Please accept my heartiest congratulations, and tribute of admiration for the splendid work of the Tynemouth boat, under coxswain Smith and yourself. The whole crew have done an admirable piece of work which adds lustre to the record of the Tynemouth lifeboat service – Shee, Lifeboat Institution, London.' Capt. Burton, Coxswain Smith, and the whole of the crew that braved the elements to Whitby and back, are to attend the first performance of the Howard Hall, North Shields, tonight, when special pictures of the exploit of the motor lifeboat Henry Vernon, will be shown. The performance will be under the patronage of the Mayor of Tynemouth (Counc. H. Greg), the town clerk (Mr S. Wilson), and the aldermen and the councillors of the borough. The Mayor and Alderman Black are expected to address a few words of congratulation to the crew.

Cinema Enterprise

A cinematograph operator representing the Albion Cinema was on the quay when the motor lifeboat returned, and obtained footage of the boat and the enthusiastic reception, and also of the more formal proceedings inside Cliffords Fort. The memorable voyage of the motor lifeboat *Henry Vernon* to Whitby and the successful rescue the following day, were recalled at the great public meeting held in the Albion Assembly Rooms, North Shields on 21 December 1914, when a worthy tribute was given to the members of the lifeboat crew. As reported in the *Shields Gazette*:

> The presentation was promoted by the public committee of which J. Howard Catcheside and J. Williamson were the honorary secretaries. The function was organised in a manner utterly worthy of the occasion. The Mayor of Tynemouth H. Gregg presided and was supported by His Grace the Duke of Northumberland KG, General Sir Herbert Plumer KCB, General Baylay (commanding the Coast Defence), Lt-Commander Herbert J. Craig MP (Naval Volunteers), Sir Walter Runciman Bart. MP, Lt Commander Basil Hall RN (RNLI), the Right Honourable the Mayor of Newcastle (Ald. John Fitzgerald), Captain Burton (commander of the motor lifeboat), Mayor Richardson of South Shields, Ald. J.M. Rennoldson, Rev. H.J. Blount Fry, Rev. R.R. Holmes (Vicar of Tynemouth) Rev. R.D.R. Greene (Chaplain to the Forces), Major H. Oswin Bell ASC, Jas Hogg, Lt-Col. Fred Scott VD (commanding Tyne Engineers), Alfred Robinson JP, Col. Petrie, Dr Wilkinson, Ald. Isaac Black, Charles Percy, J.R. Davison, Ald. S.T. Harrison, Ald. J.R. Hogg, Commander Stapylton RN, Captain Wake RN, Major Newman, William Baird JP, J. McConnell, H. Dennison, the Mayoress of Tynemouth (Mrs Gregg), the Lady Mayoress of Newcastle (Miss Fitzgerald), Lt Strother Steward, Mrs Herbert Craig, Mrs Burton, Miss Burton, Mrs Stewart, Mrs McConnell, and the crew of the lifeboat.

The large audience included a considerable sprinkling of military men in uniform, and members of the Life Brigade. The hall was tastefully decorated for the occasion, with the words 'Very well done' in very large letters on the wall behind the platform, and a relic of the wreck, in the shape of a lifebelt from the ship *Rohilla*, was placed in front of the table on the platform.

The chief function of the evening was the presentation of the following rewards:

To Captain Burton RE
The RNLI Gold Medal
A gold medal from the Tynemouth Medal Trust
A gold medal and silver tray with silver tea service from the Henry Vernon Lifeboat Crew Fund

To Coxswain Robert Smith
The RNLI Gold Medal
A gold medal from the Tynemouth Medal Trust
A gold medal from the Henry Vernon Lifeboat Crew Fund and a savings bank book, with a sum to his credit

To 2nd Coxswain James Brownlee
The RNLI Silver Medal
A silver medal from the Tynemouth Medal Trust
A gold medal from the Henry Vernon Lifeboat Crew Fund and a savings bank book, with a sum to his credit

To John Brownlee (bowman)
A silver medal from the Tynemouth Medal Trust
A gold medal and savings bank book, with a sum to his credit from the Henry Vernon Lifeboat Crew Fund

To Colin McFadyen (motorman)
A silver medal from the Tynemouth Medal Trust
A gold medal and savings bank book, with a sum to his credit from the Henry Vernon Lifeboat Crew Fund

To Thomas Cummins
A silver medal from the Tynemouth Medal Trust
A gold medal and savings bank book, with a sum to his credit from the Henry Vernon Lifeboat Crew Fund

To David Martin, Archibald Craig, J.T. Scarth, J.S. Kay, J.S. Henry and William Storey
A parchment certificate to each man from the Tynemouth Medal Trust
A gold medal and savings bank book, with a sum to their credit from the Henry
Vernon Lifeboat Crew Fund

To Messrs Smith and Williams, who volunteered to go in the lifeboat, £2.10s each

To Lt-Commander Basil Hall RN
A gold medal from the Henry Vernon Lifeboat Crew Fund

To Richard Eglon (2nd coxswain of the Whitby Lifeboat)
A gold medal from the Henry Vernon Lifeboat Crew Fund and cheque

To J.G. Bellas (Tynemouth Volunteer Life Brigade)
A silver medal for life saving from the Tynemouth Volunteer Life Brigade

To Lt R.A. Mountain, a cigarette case

To six Tyne Electrical Engineers, pipes etc.

In addition, the crewmembers were each presented with framed pictures of the
lifeboat and crew, with the King of Belgium's congratulatory message lithographed
and Admiral Sir John Jellicoe's signature.

The solid gold medals presented to the crew by subscribers, and the solid silver tray, kettle
and tea service, were designed and supplied by goldsmiths Grant & Son of North Shields. On
the obverse side of the medals is a finely moulded scene in high relief of the *Rohilla* wreck
with the *Henry Vernon* approaching, surrounded by the inscription in raised letters, 'For
brave conduct, wreck of the Rohilla November 1st 1914' and the recipient's name. The full
arms of Tynemouth, with supporters, appear on the reverse side, also in relief, surrounded
by a laurel wreath. The silver tray, kettle and tea service were of Georgian design, with
garland and shell border, the tray bearing the same inscription and Tynemouth arms.

The Kingham Hill Tragedy

The *Tynemouth* motor lifeboat Henry Vernon had an illustrious career with the RNLI. But
with the advancement of technology and new safety features early lifeboat versions were
sold off to the general public for leisure and recreational use. In September 1959, the former
lifeboat inexplicably met her own tragic end when she was lost without trace with two crew
and five boys from Kingham Hill School. After saving so many lives as an RNLI lifeboat it was
such a cruel twist of fate for the Henry Vernon to be lost in such tragic circumstances.

The motor sailor *Rohilla* in 1958. (Courtesy Mrs Margaret Tawse)

George Tawse relaxing with one of his favourite cigars. (Courtesy Mrs Margaret Tawse)

The Henry Vernon was purchased from the RNLI by George Tawse in 1936, converted into a motor sailing yacht, and renamed Rohilla in recognition of the lives she rescued from the hospital ship in 1914.

George and his family enjoyed sailing the boat and he was a consummate captain, impeccably smart at all times and known for his love of cigars. George's nephews Andrew and Gerald first learnt to sail on the boat and often sailed with George on mini voyages along the coast.

During the Second World War, the boat was requisitioned by the Ministry of War and was believed to have been one of the boats used in the Dunkirk evacuation. After the war, the Ministry offered to return the boat but on inspection George was saddened to see how badly she had been treated and declined. He wanted her to be given to a voluntary organisation such as the sea scouts, who would benefit from her use.

In 1959 the Kingham Hill School chartered the Rohilla from Birdham Pool, Chichester for two adventurous sailing expeditions to the Channel Islands. During the cross-Channel voyages, the Rohilla would be skippered by school scoutmaster Colin Edwin Noble, a maths tutor and reputedly a fine sailor and crewed by his friend John Clewett. Colin Berwick, a boarder at the school, recalled going on the sailing trip the previous year with Matthew Rudman, David Earl and Colin Noble and having had a great time of it. He had wanted to go with them on the Rohilla and had booked a place, but gave it up when his mother could not cover the expense.

Colin Noble was born in Wiltshire on 21 August 1923 at Fisherton Delamere. His mother, Eleanor Annie Noble, was a domestic servant and his father, Lawrence Edwin

Noble, was recorded as a gardener. They lived in Maids Morton just outside Buckingham and Colin was educated at the Royal Latin School. At the outset of hostilities in 1939, Colin was a member of the Home Guard but he returned to his education at the end of the conflict. He graduated from Culham Teacher Training College, taking up his first teaching post in 1948, aged 25.

Whilst running the scouts Colin took boys camping in Cornwall and France, and he was a tutor who was held in high esteem throughout the school. As plans were being made for the

Colin Noble after his graduation from Culham Teacher Training College.

first cross-channel voyage, Colin was known to be excited about the opportunity to sail the *Rohilla*, which he said was a converted lifeboat and therefore very safe.

In September the *Rohilla* began her first crossing to Cherbourg then onto St Peter Port, Guernsey and then onto the Isle of Sark. After a short stay, the return voyage passed without any trouble back across the English Channel to Falmouth, Cornwall. A week later the *Rohilla* made a second successful voyage crossing the channel to Sark, staying for a few days. The return voyage was planned for 19 September from Sark to Boscombe in Dorset, Hampshire until 1974. Worried staff and parents contacted the coastguard when the boat failed to arrive. When all attempts to contact the *Rohilla* failed, the coastguard declared the boat overdue and initiated a full-scale search and recovery operation. On the return journey with Colin Noble and John Clewitt the five boys from the school were:

David Earle, 16 (Norwich House)
Peter Knight, 15 (Clyde House)
Robin Green, 15 (Bradford House)
Anthony Gould, 15 (Clyde House)
Matthew Rudman, 14 (Durham House)

Naval Frigate in sweep off the Devon coast

The search for the missing yacht with a schoolmaster, his friend and five boys aboard was intensified by air and sea to investigate reports of a sighting off the south coast of Devon. The frigate *Loch Inch* steamed in to begin a search of the area backed up by a combined Anglo-French search and rescue operation with the joint efforts of the RAF, the Royal Naval College Dartmouth and the French Navy, while ships were alerted to watch for any signs of the yacht. Brixham Coastguards said 'a yacht answering the Rohilla's description was sighted at 8.30 a.m., about two or three miles off Bolt Head.' Reporters were informed that aircraft involved in the search included a Shackleton from Northern Ireland and a French Neptune. The Admiralty had released a statement earlier that the frigate *Starling* was searching for wreckage which was reported south-west of Guernsey, while ships at sea were warned to watch for the yacht. At the same time, the RAF sent a high-speed launch to head off the yacht while cadets at Dartmouth, put to sea in their picket boat to join in the search.

It was sadly apparent that some unknown tragedy had befallen the boat on the second voyage, when a lifebuoy bearing the name of the *Rohilla* was picked up by the French trawler *La Belle Poule* in the English Channel, 35 miles off Start Point. The Royal Navy searched a wide area with both British and French air force planes looking for the yacht day and night while hope remained of finding anyone alive. The Admiralty then said 'it had to be accepted that through some unknown cause, the yacht had sunk'. Mr C. Cooper, warden of Kingham Hill School, confirmed, 'there was one buoy attached to the forward mast marked Rohilla.'

In a small sunlit chapel beside a rugby pitch 200 grey-suited boys bent their heads in silent prayer for the lives of five form mates and a master lost at sea. The boys and masters waited anxiously for news of their missing colleagues. Despite a large-scale,

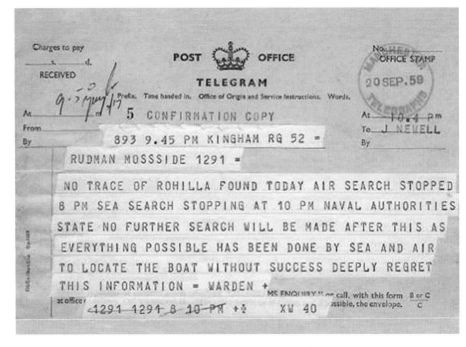

Post Office telegram advising that the searches were being called off.

non-stop search and recovery operation, hopes for the boys' safe return were all but gone. In the chapel, the Rev. Harry Wilkinson offered special prayers for relatives and friends.

Police confirmed the bodies of two of the boys from the yacht *Rohilla* had been recovered on the Cornish coast. They were later identified as Peter Knight, of Oxfordshire and Robin Green, both aged 15, the schoolhouse number tag was on his clothing. A day later, a dinghy from the yacht was found on the beach between Downderry and Crafthole, East Cornwall. The school warden said that he would be attending the inquest on the body of Robin Greene. Mr Noble's body was washed ashore at Ventnor on the Isle of Wight; sadly none of the other bodies were ever located. Peter Knight and Robin Green are buried side by side in Kingham churchyard.

The Inquests

A verdict of misadventure was recorded at an inquest at Liskeard on both boys. Dr F.D.M. Hocking, Cornwall County Pathologist, said that Robin, whose body was taken from the sea off Start Point by a Looe fishing boat, died from drowning. Dr Hocking said that the other boy, Peter Knight, whose body was washed ashore at Seaton near Looe wearing a lifejacket, had died not from drowning but from shock. Captain John Miller Cummin, senior nautical surveyor of the Ministry of Transport said the yacht left Boshom on 2 September, and that she was last sighted in a freshening wind in the Race of Alderney on 13 September. From his enquiries, he believed the vessel to have been seaworthy. There might have been a collision with another boat, which would be consistent with the medical evidence that one of the boys had died from shock.

Despite widespread air and sea searches the loss of the yacht remained a mystery. A sailor who followed the *Rohilla* out of the harbour in her own yacht declared that the boat ran into foul weather crossing the channel, but no one knows for certain what happened. Over the years it has been speculated that the *Rohilla* was run down by a much larger vessel. Perhaps the fact that both a life buoy and the dingy with the name of the *Rohilla* were found, but no other wreckage was ever washed up, lends credence to this theory.

Rohilla *Victims Plaque*

On 31 October 1959 at 3.15 p.m. a memorial service was held in the Kingham Hill School chapel, during which a plaque was unveiled in memory of Colin Noble and the five pupils who lost their lives in the *Rohilla* yacht disaster the previous September. Following the unveiling, the warden E.C. Cooper said 'Colin Noble was a devoted schoolmaster, conscientious and capable.' The brass plaque can be found in the school chapel, placed discreetly on the back wall under the gallery.

The tragedy is very much part of the school's history and each year it holds a commemorative *Rohilla* Day on the last Sunday in September.

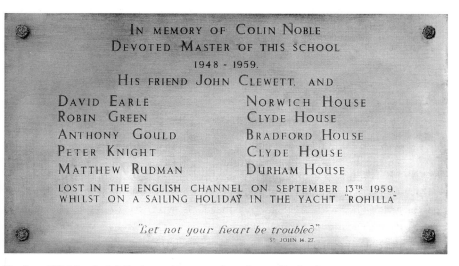

Kingham Hill School's *Rohilla* plaque. (Courtesy of Kingham Hill School)

FLEET SURGEON ERNEST COURTNEY LOMAS

In November 2011 I received an email from Paul Macnaughton, a gentleman who works in the antiques trade in southern Scotland. He explained that he specialises in industrial/ commercial clearances. He described buying the contents of a newspaper office a few years earlier in East Lothian which had amalgamated with a larger media company and finding amongst the papers and junk in the editor's office all sorts of clippings and letters from contributors and readers going back some years. After selling off the bulk of the items he had procured, he was left with the clippings and letters, which had to be sorted and were left sitting in boxes. As he was sifting through the papers, he noticed an envelope of clippings and letters which included some letters from Buckingham Palace to Fleet Surgeon Lomas thanking him for looking after Prince Albert on board the *Rohilla*. Paul was not aware of the significance of the *Rohilla* and looked to the internet for answers, after a simple search he came across my website (www.rohilla.co.uk) and found more than enough to satisfy his curiosity. It was at this point that he contacted me, believing quite rightly that I would be interested in the papers.

I replied to Paul's email at the first opportunity, explaining my background and interest in the papers relating to Prince Albert. Two weeks later I received another email from Paul in which he told me he had met a semi-retired book dealer who sounded quite interested in the papers and would do some research on them for him. The dealer thought they had a not inconsiderable commercial value, especially since the success of the film *The King's Speech* the previous year. Paul added, 'As I buy and sell for a living, it is necessary for me to try to get a reasonable price for items which pass through my hands. As soon as I can, I will let you know their likely current value.'

I have been collecting *Rohilla* memorabilia for many years, but once in a while I am pleasantly surprised by something special or extremely rare, though like most collectibles these items tend to command a higher price. Undeterred, I asked for some information on what the papers consisted of and some photographs of them.

Paul promised me a detailed breakdown of the papers but in the meantime he told me they consisted of two letters from Buckingham Palace to Fleet Surgeon Dr Ernest Courtney Lomas, thanking him for looking after Prince Albert on the *Rohilla*, another letter in Albert's hand regarding photographs of himself he had sent to surgeon Lomas, and a letter from Prince Albert's secretary asking whether the photos had been lost in the wreck. The letters also included newspaper cuttings which appear to have been collected at the time of

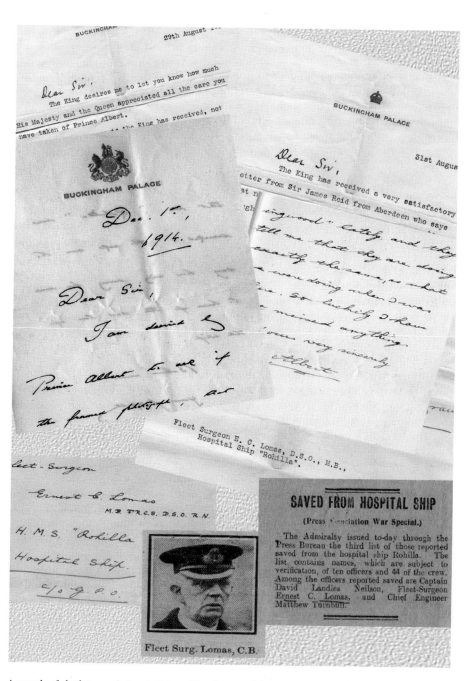

A sample of the letters relating to Prince Albert's care whilst on the *Rohilla*.

the wreck from contemporary newspapers, six in total, covering the evacuation of Prince Albert to Aberdeen on *Rohilla*, three about the wreck and survival of Dr Lomas, from the *Haddingtonshire Courier*, one of which has a small halftone photo of Dr Lomas pinned to it and one from a later paper recalling the wreck. The connection with East Lothian seems to have been Dr Lomas' family, who lived near Haddington, and who may have given the correspondence to the editor for publication and forgotten to retrieve it.

A short while afterwards I received an email from Paul with a more detailed breakdown of the papers and knew straight away that they were something quite exquisite and there would be nothing else like them. I simply couldn't let them pass me by. Paul and I shared a few emails regarding the value of the papers, for him it was a business transaction with the bonus of knowing they would be going to someone who would appreciate them, but for me it was purely about where they fit into the story of the hospital ship's tragic loss. There is no denying that they held some value given the royal connection, who they represented and the reason why they were written, but I was more captivated by the important royal/ *Rohilla* connection. It didn't take long for us to come to a mutually agreeable price for the papers. Getting them was thankfully not the hurdle I expected it would be. Given what the papers stood for I was quite concerned about them being lost in the postal system, they were irreplaceable.

The royal papers, which are possibly one of my most treasured artefacts relating to the *Rohilla*.

Paul had business coming up in Middlesbrough, which is just 30 miles north of Whitby, a town where I was born and bred. Paul proved to be a gentleman and travelled to Whitby to hand deliver the papers. It was really nice to put a face to the name and to get hold of the papers, which were everything I expected them to be.

Later that afternoon I had more time to look carefully at the papers and found them to be quite revealing. The first letter was typewritten and dated 29 August 1914 on embossed Buckingham Palace paper, to Dr Lomas from Colonel Clive Wigram, who was the Assistant Private Secretary to King George V at the time. He wrote:

The King desires me to let you know how much His Majesty and the Queen appreciated all the care you have taken of Prince Albert. From the reports the King has received, nothing more could have been done or be left undone to ensure that he received every possible attention. Prince Albert is now safe at Aberdeen in a Nursing Home and Their Majesties hope that he may be soon well enough again to join his ship. The King and Queen feel very much the great disappointment of the boy through, this inopportune illness at this time.

A second similar typewritten letter dated 31 August 1914 was sent to Dr Lomas bearing comparable sentiments, but with mention that the king had received a very satisfactory letter from *Sir James Reid, who said 'that nothing could have exceeded your kindness to/and thoughtful care of Prince Albert'. In assuring Dr Lomas of their majesties' deep appreciation of all he had done, they asked if he would be so good as to express their sincere thanks to **Miss Bennett for the care she had taken of Prince Albert.

* Sir James Reid, GCVO, KCB, VD, JP, MD, LLD, was physician in ordinary to three British monarchs.
**Miss Bennett was one of the fortunate women taken off the wreck in the first lifeboat to reach the stricken *Rohilla*.

The next paper was a letter dated 20 October in Prince Albert's hand, on palace notepaper. The letter apparently accompanied four framed photographs of the prince – one each for Dr Lomas, Captain Nielson, Dr McBean and Sister Bennett. The prince added 'I hope you will accept them as a remembrance of the short time I was in the Rohilla, where you were all so very kind to me.' Writing a fortnight after leaving the *Rohilla*, the prince spoke about his improved health and three days' shooting in Norfolk, and his hope to return shortly to the *Collingwood*. This letter has an envelope with it, which is an added bonus as envelopes of this era seldom survive. It is embossed with a red crown on the flap, is addressed in Albert's hand to Fleet Surgeon Ernest Courtney Lomas MB FRCS DSO RN, HMS *Rohilla*, Hospital ship, c/o GPO, and has a small monogram 'A' in the bottom left corner.

On 1 December 1914, Henry P. Hansell, tutor to the sons of King George V, wrote to Dr Lomas on behalf of the prince:

Dear Sir, I am desired of Prince Albert to ask if the framed photograph that His Royal Highness sent to you, was lost at the time that the Rohilla was wrecked. He asks me to say how very sorry he was to hear of the sad loss of the ship.

Thoughtfulness appears to have been one of the prince's virtues, for having written to Captain Neilson acknowledging him as a survivor of the disaster he offered to send him another signed photograph. The first gift might have been a formality, but the second showed a thoughtfulness that made it doubly treasured. I feel so privileged to have been able to secure the letters, not for any financial gain but for what they represent.

Ernest Courtney Lomas was born on 24 December 1864, son of George Lomas, of Didsbury, Lancashire. He was educated at Owens College, Manchester; he graduated MB and ChB of Victoria University in 1888, and took the MRCS in that year. After filling the

Fleet Surgeon Ernest Courtney Lomas.

posts of house surgeon to the Manchester Royal Infirmary, and of senior house surgeon to the Royal Albert Edward Infirmary, Wigan, and of resident medical officer of the Barnes Convalescent Hospital, Cheadle, he entered the Royal Navy as a surgeon on 11 February 1891. He was specially promoted to staff surgeon in 21 October 1900 for service in the South African War where he accompanied the Naval Brigade, attached to the Ladysmith Relief Column. The *London Gazette* of 19 April 1901 carried a citation that read 'Ernest Courtney Lomas, MB, Staff Surgeon RN. In recognition of services during the operations in South Africa.' The insignia were sent to the Admiralty 12 July 1901, and presented by the king on 25 July 1901. The same year saw his marriage to Eleanor Mary Ruthven, daughter of Robert Howden, of East Lothian. Dr Lomas was made fleet surgeon 21 October 1904, and became a Fellow of the Royal College of Surgeons (Edinburgh) in 1907.

On 10 June 1912 Fleet Surgeon Lomas was appointed senior medical officer to the hospital ship *Maine*. The ship went aground in thick fog and was wrecked on a small island named Eilean Straide Eun (Frank Lockwood's Island) about two miles north of the entrance to Loch Buie on the south-east coast of the Isle of Mull, but he was not on board at the time as his wife was ill. The ship suffered serious damage forward, but there were no serious casualties. On 20 June 1914 salvage attempts were abandoned as a result of the ship's age and the potential salvage bill. It was sold to a local scrap dealer in July. On 23 September 1969 what remained of the *Maine* was found in deep water broken up and spread over a wide area. It was found to be of interest to the Royal Commission on the Ancient and Historical Monuments of Scotland.

When the hospital ship *Rohilla* foundered in 1914, Dr Lomas was amongst those who sheltered on what was left of the grand ship enduring the worst the North Sea could throw at them as they awaited rescue. He suffered considerably from exposure before finally being rescued among the final fifty souls taken from the wrecked ship. Despite the traumatic experience, he stuck to his career and was appointed the senior medical officer to the hospital ship *Garth Castle* in 1915. He likely felt at home quite quickly as a number of the nursing staff from the *Rohilla* transferred to the *Garth Castle* after a short leave of absence. Those who served with him regarded it as a model and happy ship under his genial and tactful guidance.

He was awarded the CB in 1916 for his services during the war. In October he organised and opened the Royal Naval Hospital, Granton, near Edinburgh. After serving as the senior medical officer in charge of three hospital ships in succession he was placed in charge of Granton 1916–18, his first land-based position for a number of years. Lomas was presented with a wonderful trophy by the medical staff and nursing sisters as a memento of his two years as senior medical officer in charge of hospital ships in wartime. HMHS *Rohilla* and HMHS *Garth Castle* are identified at the top of the trophy and the base is engraved with signatures.

Fleet Surgeon Lomas was promoted to surgeon captain on 13 September 1918. After suffering a long and painful illness he told his friends and colleagues that he was retiring on 28 July 1919. His retirement was a severe blow to the Naval Medical Service, not only on account

A trophy celebrating
Dr Lomas' time
as senior medical
officer in charge of
hospital ships in
wartime.

of his surgical and administrative abilities, but also for the loss of an especially attractive and lovable personality to those who knew him. Although retired from active service he retained an interest in the field of medicine. In 1916 he contributed a special paper describing the equipment and working of hospital ships to the *British Medical Journal*, which was published in the special issue *British Medicine in the War 1914–17*. He had every reason to be proud to have been given his responsibility caring for Prince Albert, heir to the throne.

Surgeon Captain Lomas died on 24 February 1921. After his death, Sir Humphrey Rolleston stated that Ernest Courtney Lomas was:

Not only a most efficient organizer and, until administrative duties absorbed his time, a keen and capable surgeon, a most unselfish worker, never sparing himself, whilst looking after his subordinates in the most kindly way so that they were devoted to him. He was a gallant gentleman whom his friends, and they are many, will long regret.

NURSING SISTER MARY L. HOCKING

Mary Louisa Hocking was born on 19 November 1887, daughter of Rev. Richard Hocking, Rector of Pillaton in Cornwall, and Frances Rodd. She was one of seven siblings with three sisters and three brothers. She trained as a nurse at the Devon & Exeter and Tunbridge Wells Eye & Ear hospitals before joining the Queen Alexandra's Royal Naval Nursing Service. She initially served at the Royal Naval Hospital (RNH) Haslar whilst conducting her initial naval training. On 17 June 1914 she was confirmed as a nursing sister. At that time, her maternal uncle Montague L.B. Rodd was a senior fleet surgeon also serving at the hospital in charge of the wards in B Section.

The Royal Navy Hospital Haslar (RNH Haslar) began as a Royal Navy hospital in 1753 and has a long and distinguished history in the medical care of service personnel in peacetime and in war. The hospital was the biggest hospital and the largest brick building in England when it was built and had an asylum for sailors with psychiatric disorders. Dr James Scott, a member of the influential Edinburgh Phrenological Society, was an early superintending psychiatrist. James Lind played a large part in discovering a cure for

The crest of the RNH Haslar. (Courtesy John Mules)

scurvy there, through his pioneering use of a double blind trial of vitamin C supplements (limes). He was known as a clinical observer and experimentalist, but also a nosologist (a specialist in a branch of medicine that deals with the classification of diseases), pathologist, laboratory researcher and epidemiologist. In 1902 the hospital became known as RNH *Haslar*.

After the loss of the *Rohilla* Mary had a short period of 'survivor's leave' before being appointed to RNH Chatham on 23 November 1914. During the Great War, RNH Chatham would appear to have been Mary Hocking's base hospital as it is here that she returned between hospital ship appointments. During these periods she would have nursed casualties from both naval engagements and the battlefields of northern France.

HM King Edward VII opened RNH Chatham on 26 July 1905 using a gold key which had been presented to him in a silver casket. He then toured the hospital's day rooms, operating theatre, offices, men's wards and kitchens. The hospital was in operational service with the Royal Navy until 1961. It passed out of service control in the 1960s and became a NHS establishment, now known as the Medway Maritime Hospital. Little of the original structure is left.

On 17 December 1914, Mary Hocking was posted to HMHS *Garth Castle*, which had only been commissioned as a hospital ship on 4 November. Her service on *Garth Castle*

Survivors from HMS *Strongbow*. (Courtesy John Mules)

would have coincided with the Gallipoli Campaign, a conflict during which an estimated 141,113 Allies were either killed or wounded. She remained with the *Garth Castle* until 22 November 1915 before returning to Chatham Hospital.

In 1916 Mary's family suffered a devastating loss when Flight Sub Lt William Hocking, the eldest of the siblings, was killed in a training accident.

Her next posting was to HMHS *China* on 26 February 1917. Her time on the *China* would have put her in support of the Grand Fleet during a period when there were no major naval engagements, but Germany was conducting unrestricted submarine warfare and the convoy system had been instituted. During this period there were smaller engagements such as the 'Action off Lerwick' in which nine (neutral) Scandinavian merchant ships and two British destroyers were sunk by German light cruisers. The survivors of this action passed through the Grand Fleet hospital ships, evidenced by an image of some of those from HMS *Strongbow*. Mary's posting to the *China* was completed on 18 March 1918 and she returned to RNH Chatham for the last time.

The QARNNS Service Register records that during her last period at this hospital, Nursing Sister Mary Louisa Hocking was specifically 'Recommended by the Surgeon General at Chatham for consistently meritorious and conscientious performance of her duties' in 1918 and then recommended for the associate award of the Royal Red Cross Medal in January 1919. The British *Journal of Nursing* of 17 May 1919 carried news of Mary Hocking having been awarded the Associate Royal Red Cross Second Class, which was presented by the King at Buckingham Palace on 4 December 1919 .

The Royal Red Cross (RRC) was instituted on 27 April 1883 by Queen Victoria, who wanted a special award for distinguished service by nursing sisters. The Royal Warrant said that the RRC medal be bestowed:

... upon any ladies, whether subjects or foreign persons, who may be recommended by Our Secretary of State for War for special exertions in providing for the nursing of sick and wounded soldiers and sailors of Our Army and Navy.

The second-class Associate Royal Red Cross grade was added during the First World War in November 1915 with bars to the first-class RRC being introduced in 1917. Bars are awarded in both classes to those nurses who perform further acts of devotion or bravery. Those awarded the Royal Red Cross Medal First Class are known as members whilst those awarded the RRC Second Class are known as associates.

On 21 October 1920, Mary was posted to another land-based hospital at Plymouth, where she remained until 22 February 1922, at which point she experienced a somewhat radical change to her usual appointments. Just two days later, on 24 February, she sailed on an international transit bound for foreign duty. On 17 April 1922, she took up her post at a Hong Kong hospital. It was during her time there that she was courted by her future husband Roderick John Mules, a civil engineer attached to the Admiralty. Her marriage to Roderick was a precursor to her resignation.

The 14 June 1924 saw Mary Hocking retracing her steps on transit from foreign duty (having embarked on the *Kashgar* to Tilbury). She found she had come full circle when she arrived home and was allocated back to RNH Haslar on 23 July, in an administrative appointment to cover foreign service leave prior to her discharge. The 22 September 1924 effectively marked Mary Louisa Hocking's resignation after a varied and distinguished nursing career with the Admiralty.

Roderick and Mary had two children, Frances and Roger. The family moved dependent upon Roderick's postings, which included Gibraltar, Trincomalee and finally Plymouth. Roderick, fourteen years her senior, passed away in 1964 aged 91, whilst Mary survived a further twenty years of peaceful retirement and died aged 97 on 12 September 1984.

Mary Hocking never spoke of her QARNNS service to her grandchildren and the only details that have been passed down within the family came from her son, who told two specific stories, one from each end of her service: one about *Rohilla*, the other from her time in Hong Kong. She always smiled as she spoke about being courted by Roderick, when during swimming parties he, not normally prone to frivolous activities, would sit in a boat pouring cherry brandy into her mouth as she swam.

Certainly no mention was ever made of where she served or what she saw during the main part of the war, and what is known has had to be drawn from official records and analysis of the many photographs she left behind, of which few are annotated.

APPENDIX III

MARY KEZIA ROBERTS

Mary Kezia was born in Liverpool on Wednesday 19 October 1870. She married David Roberts on 2 December 1896 at the age of 26, although her marriage certificate lists her age as 24 and her name as Mary Kezia 'Dooley' Humphreys.

Mary served on the *Adriatic*, the last of the White Star Line's turn of the century 'Big Four', and the only one that never carried the title of 'the world's largest ship'. The *Adriatic* was built by Harland and Wolff, Belfast, and launched in 1906 the same year as the *Rohilla*. She signed onto the RMS *Titanic* aged 42 at Southampton on 6 April 1912, listing her address as 9 Chestnut Grove, West Bridgford, Nottingham, the address she used for a letter to her husband from the ship. She wrote about her charge requesting the full menu for breakfast and the distance to carry things up and down stairs as so cruel that she was paying a youth 4s a trip to carry all her soiled dishes away as she was finding it hard enough to get through as it was.

After learning of the *Titanic*'s fate David and his family had an agonising wait for a definitive response from the Admiralty or the White Star Line. Whilst awaiting news of his wife's status, the *Nottingham Daily Express* carried the following on Thursday 18 April:

Mrs. M. K. Roberts, one of the stewardesses, is the wife of the principal of the West Bridgford Motor Company, and has been in the service of the White Star Line for some years. She was recently transferred to the Titanic and was at home with her husband and family only a few weeks ago for a brief stay prior to proceeding to Southampton.

This was followed a few days later with this:

Mr Roberts received a telegram on Saturday 20th April announcing that she was indeed safe. During the loss of the grand liner, Mary was fortunate enough to have been placed into one of the many vacant lifeboat seats and later picked up by the Carpathia before finally disembarking at the Titanic's intended destination of New York.

Having survived the terrible loss of the *Titanic*, Mary Roberts continued her career as a stewardess, leaving Southampton just six weeks after her return on the RMS *Majestic* for the remainder of 1912. Extracts from the Registrar General Agreements show the *Majestic* as departing from Southampton on 22 May, 12 June, 24 July, 14 August and 4 September. Sometime between 1912 and 1914 Mary Roberts left the White Star Line for the British

Mary Roberts and her family relax on a day out after her ordeal on the *Rohilla*.

India Steam Navigation Company and was assigned to the SS *Rohilla*. The moments after the *Titanic* struck the iceberg pale in comparison to her experiences on the *Rohilla*, which were truly horrific.

One would have thought that having survived two catastrophic maritime wrecks she might have chosen another career. However, Mary Roberts served her last commission on another of Harland and Wolff's vessels, the SS *Rajputana*, official number 146361, this time one built at the River Clyde shipyard. Embarking from London on 14 February 1929, the *Rajputana* was bound for Bombay, where Mary was discharged on 8 March after a short service.

The details of the *Rajputana* are below:

Name:	RAJPUTANA
Builder:	Harland and Wolff Greenock, Yard No 661
Port of Registry:	London
Propulsion:	Steam quadruple expansion
Launched:	Thursday 06/08/1925
Built:	1925
Ship Type:	Passenger Cargo Vessel
Tonnage:	16568 gross tons
Length:	547ft
Breadth:	71ft
Owner History:	Peninsular & Oriental Steam Navigation Company
Status:	Torpedoed and Sunk – 13/04/1941

The SS *Rajputana* was a British passenger and cargo carrying ocean liner built for the Peninsular & Oriental Steam Navigation Company at the Harland and Wolff docks on the River Clyde near Glasgow in 1925. She was one of the P&O 'R' class liners much of whose interiors were designed by Lord Inchcape's daughter Elsie Mackay. Named after the Rajputana region of western India, she sailed on a regular route between England and British India. She was requisitioned into the Royal Navy at the onset of the Second World War and commissioned in December 1939 as the armed merchant cruiser HMS *Rajputana*. The installation of eight 6in guns gave her the firepower of a light cruiser without the armoured protection. She was torpedoed and sunk off Iceland on 13 April 1941 in position 65,50N 27,25W, after escorting a convoy across the North Atlantic.

Mary Roberts passed away on 2 January 1932, a year before her husband David Roberts, who died in a motorcycle accident. They are buried together in the church of St Mary the Virgin, Ewell. They left behind four children Frank (Francis), Keziah Norah, Daisy Bell and Kathleen.

Mary Roberts' headstone, which identifies her as a *Titanic* survivor.

Within the confines of the church there lies a memorial reading:

In memory of Mary Keziah Roberts 1870–1932 David Roberts 1875–1933 and
Daisy Bell Roberts 1906–2003. Keziah Norah Matthews (Roberts) 1901–1984.

Some years later, Mary's daughter Norah Keziah wrote to the BBC about the telegrams
she had confirming her mother's survival after the wrecks of the *Titanic* and the *Rohilla*.
The letter was typewritten when Norah was 64, and there is a brief mention of a book her
mother wrote, but its whereabouts remain unknown.

C / O 111, The Chase,
Clapham, S.W.4
22nd January, 1965.

Dear Miss Anderson,
I have just rung up the B.B.C. and asked them if they will very kindly forward these
very lovely copies photographed from my Mother's Ship Seafaring Book ...
    The Photographers who took them for her Book a few weeks ago were ... The
Re-Avis of the Clapham Park Road, S.W.4.
    There are copies of her telegrams saying she was saved ... both on the TITANIC
AND ROHILLA SHIP too. She was on both, of course. Her Seafaring Book here that I
have must be about 40 years old.
    I was 11 years of age when she sailed on the fateful Titanic as I said. My old
address was c / co 1, Eaglewood Road, S.W. 12 but I left there on the 19th October,
1964 ... recently. I do thank you for putting that nice piece in the Sketch on the 27th
April, 1964 about what I said. I was then living at the old address at Eaglewood
Road, Clapham South ... but my new address now is 111, The Chase S.W.4
    Please keep these lively photos copies genuine copies from my dear Mother's
Book. Her name was Mrs Keziah Mary Roberts she died at the Epsom Cottage
Hospital, Epsom Hill, Epsom, Surrey, in 2nd January 1933 aged then ... Her
birthday was 19th October, 1870.

Bless you. Will you please let me know what you think of these.

Mrs Norah Keziah Mathews
(Nee Roberts)

I am most fortunate in having contact with three of Mary's descendants, each of a
different generation, and all very helpful in supplying me with a great deal of private
and privileged family history, that I might be able to piece together what you have
before you.

Francis Humphreys, pictured left, Mandy with son Paul in her arms and her daughter Tara, and Alice Humphreys. (Courtesy Mandy Harvey)

Kathleen was the first child born to Mary Roberts, preceding Frank, the only son, Nora, Daisy and Jean. My early source of information was Mandy Harvey, whose mother Anne was a daughter of Frank.

In January 2014 I received an email from Mrs Fiona Kilbane, a lady I had tried to open a dialogue with some months previously when her local newspaper carried a story about Mary Kezia Roberts. I sent all my contact details to the newspaper asking them if they would be so kind as to forward them to Mrs Kilbane, but the passage of time seemed to indicate that I had failed. It was therefore very pleasant to receive an email from Mrs Kilbane and then her auntie, Kathleen (Katy) Pennock, who lives in Australia.

I was very surprised to learn that Mary and David actually had five children: Kathleen, Frank, Keziah Norah, Daisy Bell and Jean (Katy's mother). Katy informed me that there is often very little mention of her mother when people talk about Mary Roberts, something I am happy to put right here. I feel most fortunate in having contact with three of Mary's descendants, each of a different generation all of whom have been very helpful, sharing private and privileged family information with me.

Fiona and Katy in particular have provided me with a wealth of information, both documents and photographs. Three large sheets of detailed family tree information have enabled me to learn far more about Mary's background especially Jean who was the youngest of Mary's children. She was born 3 August 1907 and later married Walter Williams, with whom she had four children: Walter Samuel (born 1936), Barbara (1939), Margaret (1942) and Kathleen (1945).

I have only scratched the surface of the information I have been given and know there is far more to learn, but that's for another day.

For now I must contend myself with Frank (Francis) who was born on 9 April 1898 he followed his father's footsteps as an electrical engineer. Frank also had a son, John, although there is no information about what happened to him.

I was so pleased to have had the opportunity of meeting Ray and Mandy Harvey, having exchanged many emails before the run-up to the filming of the *Coast* episode.

BBC *Coast* presenter Ian McMillan with Mandy and Ray Harvey in September 2011 during the filming of the Coast episode, which featured the loss of the *Rohilla*. (Copyright BBC)

APPENDIX IV

CASUALTIES & SURVIVORS

Died	Name	MM / RN	Rank / Rating
✝	Ambrose, Alfred Charles	MM	Laundryman
✝	*Anderson, Thomas	RN	Pte RMLI
✝	Anderson, William Edward	RNASBR	Senior Reserve Attendant
✝	Barron, William	MM	Saloon Pantryman
✝	Barter, Henry James	RNASBR	Junior Reserve Attendant
✝	Birtwistle, Milton	RNASBR	Senior Reserve Attendant
✝	Bleakley, John	MM	Storekeeper
✝	Brain, George	RN	Carpenter's Crew
✝	Brown, John	MM	3rd Engineer
✝	Burney, Albert Howard	RN	Shipwright 2nd class
✝	Cameron, Duncan	MM	General Servant
✝	Cowie, James	MM	Greaser
✝	Cribb, Herbert J.	MM	Able Seaman
✝	Currell, James	MM	Fireman & Trimmer
✝	Daly, William John	RNASBR	Senior Reserve Attendant
✝	Dawson, Fred	MM	General Servant
✝	Dawson, William	MM	Firemen & Trimmer
✝	Duffy, Matthew James	MM	Quartermaster
✝	Dunkley, Frank	RNASBR	Junior Reserve Attendant
✝	Elsworth, Alfred Carr	RNASBR	Senior Reserve Attendant
✝	Fogarty, John J.	MM	General Servant
✝	Gibson, Colin B.	MM	General Servant
✝	Gibson, William	MM	Ship's Cook
✝	Gillies, Alexander	MM	General Servant
✝	Gover, George	MM	Assistant Troop Storekeeper
✝	Graham, John	MM	General Servant
✝	Hare, John	MM	Troop Cook
✝	Harrison, Frederick William	RNASBR	Senior Reserve Attendant
✝	Henderson, Stewart	MM	Fireman & Trimmer
✝	Hodkinson, Harry	RNASBR	Senior Reserve Attendant

✚	Horsburgh, John Alex	MM	General Servant
✚	Horsfield, Thomas	RNASBR	Junior Reserve Attendant
✚	Horsfield, Walter	RNASBR	Junior Reserve Attendant
✚	Kane, John	MM	Fireman & Trimmer
✚	Kelly, James	MM	2nd Donkeyman
✚	Kerr, John	MM	General Servant
✚	Kinsella, John	MM	Fireman & Trimmer
✚	Kirk, George	MM	General Servant
✚	Macdonald, Donald	MM	General Servant
✚	MacKenzie, James	MM	General Servant
✚	Mardell, Charles Henry	RN	Sick Berth Attendant
✚	McBride, Henry Thomas	RN	1st class Ship's Corporal
✚	McCallum, Andrew	MM	General Servant
✚	McDonald, William	MM	Fireman & Trimmer
✚	McGlashan, Albert	MM	General Servant
✚	McLeod, Norman	MM	General Servant
✚	McMillan, Alexander	MM	Fireman & Trimmer
✚	MacNaughton, Donald	MM	General Servant
✚	MacNaughton, John	MM	General Servant
✚	Milner, Charles William Montgomery	RN	Sick Berth Attendant
✚	Moore, Philip Cuthbert	MM	3rd Officer
✚	Morgan, Frederick William	RN	Master-at-Arms (Pensioner)
✚	Morris, Sidney	RN	Sick Berth Steward
✚	Muir, William	MM	General Servant
✚	Murphy, John	MM	Greaser
✚	Neville, Maurice Alfred	RNASBR	Senior Reserve Attendant
✚	Nicolson, Laurence	MM	Quartermaster
✚	Nisbet, David	MM	Able Seaman
✚	Ogilvie, William	MM	2nd Butcher
✚	Page, Alfred	RN	Sick Berth Steward
✚	Parsons, George Edgar	RN	Sick Berth Attendant
✚	Paton, Daniel	MM	Fireman & Trimmer
✚	Paton, James	MM	Fireman & Trimmer
✚	Perrin, William	MM	Electrician
✚	Petty, Arthur	RNASBR	Senior Reserve Attendant
✚	Petty, Tom	RNASBR	Senior Reserve Attendant
✚	Pickles, John Thomas	RNASBR	Senior Reserve Attendant

✝	Queenan, James	MM	General Servant
✝	Rafferty, Philip	MM	2nd Cabin Pantryman
✝	Reid, Archie	MM	General Servant
✝	Reid, John	MM	2nd Cook
✝	Reid, William	MM	Fireman & Trimmer
✝	Robbins, Harry	RN	Master-at-Arms
✝	Rose, Charles Edward	MM	Carpenter's Mate
✝	Ross, George Inglesby	RN	Sick Berth Attendant
✝	Scott, Andrew	MM	Fireman & Trimmer
✝	Scott, Robert D.	MM	General Servant
✝	Sellars, James	RNASBR	Senior Reserve Attendant
✝	Shute, Albert Edward	RN	Sick Berth Steward
✝	Smith, John	MM	Fireman & Trimmer
✝	Stewart, Archibald	MM	General Servant
✝	Stewart, James	MM	Fireman and Trimmer
✝	Tarbet, Mathew	MM	General Servant
✝	Tinney, John	MM	Fireman & Trimmer
✝	Torrance, David	MM	Assistant Saloon Pantryman
✝	Watson, Robert B.	MM	Sculleryman
✝	Watts, Henry	MM	1st Donkeyman
✝	Weatherstone, Henry Wilson	MM	General Servant
✝	White, William	MM	General Servant
	Allen M.A., Rev. Roland	RN	Chaplain
	Armstrong, John	RN	Yeoman Signaller
	Ashcroft MB, Lionel Spence	RNVR	Surgeon
	Beckman, F.	MM	Ordinary Seaman
	Benington, Miss Margaret	RN	Nursing Sister
	Bennett, Miss Mary Barbara	RN	Nursing Sister
	Bigwood, Frank Albert	RNASBR	Senior Reserve Attendant
	Bond, Frank Albert	MM	1st Mate
	Braidwood, Tom P.	MM	4th Engineer
	Brennan, Thomas	MM	Able Seaman
	Brewer, Reginald	MM	Ordinary Seaman
	Brittain, James	MM	Troop Storekeeper
	Bruce, Robert	MM	Sailor
	Bunyan, John	MM	Greaser
	Burns, Michael	MM	Fireman & Trimmer

Coventry, Alexander G.	MM	Fireman
Craig, John	MM	Greaser
Crawley, John R.	MM	General Servant
Cresswell, Thomas Hungerford	RN	Surgeon (Temp)
Cribb, Arthur	MM	Boatswain's Mate
Cunnian. J.A.	MM	Able Seaman
Curtis, George	RN	2nd Writer
Davis, D.T.	MM	Able Seaman
Davis, George J.	MM	Able Seaman
Dick, William	MM	Greaser
Dickson, Robert	MM	Fireman & Trimmer
Dickson, Thomas	MM	Fireman & Trimmer
Doe, George	MM	Able Seaman
Eastwood, Robert William	RN	Senior Reserve Attendant
Edwards, Walter Charles	MM	Butcher
Evans, Lloyd	MM	Able Seaman
Evans, T.	MM	Boatswain's Mate
Farquhar, Joseph	MM	Sailor
Farquharson, William	RNASBR	Junior Reserve Attendant
Ferguson, Peter	MM	Able Seaman
Forbes, William	MM	Fireman & Trimmer
Foreman, Alexander	MM	Able Seaman
Fox, Alfred	MM	Ordinary Seaman
Fraser, John	MM	General Servant
Gallon, Sidney	MM	Deck Boy
Gavin, John	RN	2/Sick Berth Steward
Gay, George	MM	Storekeeper
Giuliani, Luigi	MM	Chef
Gordon, Robert	MM	General Servant
Gow, Joseph	MM	General Servant
Graham, Duncan C.	MM	4th Mate
Gray, William	MM	Fireman & Trimmer
Guthrie, Duncan	MM	Sailmaker
Gwydir, Rev Robert Basil	RN	R.C. Chaplain
Gwynn, Colin Campbell	MM	2nd Mate
Hare, Thomas	MM	Ship's Cook
Harrison, Arthur George	RN	2/Sick Berth Steward
Haste, George Pearce	MM	Able Seaman

	Hebdige, Thomas	MM	Deck Boy
	Henry, John Alexander	MM	Sailor
	Hicks, William John	RN	Chief Sick Berth Steward
	Hird, Alfred Ernest Wilson	RNVR	Surgeon
	Hocking, Miss Mary Louisa	RN	Nursing Sister
	Holland, William	MM	General Servant
	Hookey, F.	MM	Able Seaman
	Horscroft, Wallace William	RN	Shipwright II
	Huddy, J.	MM	2nd Mate
	Hughes, T.	MM	Able Seaman
	Johnston, Andrew	MM	Sailor
	Jones FRCS, Thomas Caldwell Littler	RNVR	Surgeon
	Jukes. Walter J.	MM	Troop Baker
	Kerr, Horatio N	MM	Assistant Clerk
	Knight, Frank	MM	Able Seaman
	Knight, John Thomas	RN	Master-at-Arms
	Legg, Edward	MM	2nd Steward
	Lindberg, William	MM	Fireman & Trimmer
	Lindsay, Angus S.	MM	Sculleryman
	Lock, Abraham	MM	Fireman & Trimmer
	Lomas, Ernest Courtney	RN	Fleet Surgeon
	Long, Leonard	RN	Sick Berth Attendant
	Mackenzie, E.	MM	7th Engineer
	MacKintosh, James	MM	General Servant
	Martin, Thomas	MM	Fireman & Trimmer
	Mascoll, Robert	MM	Able Seaman
	Matthews, Walter	MM	General Servant
	McBean, Samuel Leslie	RN	Surgeon
	McCormick, Michael	MM	Leading Fireman
	McLeod, Malcolm	MM	Fireman & Trimmer
	McMahon, T.	MM	Fireman & Trimmer
	Moffat, William	MM	Greaser
	Moncrieff, Joseph	MM	Sailor
	Morgan, Charles William Fairfax	MM	Junior 2nd Mate
	Murray, David	MM	Ordinary Seaman
	Murray, Herbert Leith	RNVR	Surgeon
	Murray, Thomas	MM	Sailor
	Neilson, David Landles.	MM	Master

Nicol, James	MM	Fireman & Trimmer
Nugent, William	MM	Greaser
Oram, Richard Goodhart	MM	Surgeon
Ovens, John	MM	Able Seaman
Paddock, Thomas H.	MM	Signalman
Parker, Ernest	MM	Deck Boy
Parker, William	MM	Deck Boy
Parrott, Ernest Frank	RN	2nd class Sick Berth Steward
Paterson, Miss Margaret Brand	RN	Nursing Sister
Patterson, William	MM	General Servant
Paul, Frederick William	RNVR	Dental Surgeon
Pocock, John Ford	MM	Baker
Powell, William Martin	MM	Chief Steward
Rennie, John	MM	Fireman & Trimmer
Reddiough, Fred	RNASBR	Senior Reserve Attendant
Robb, James	MM	Fireman & Trimmer
Roberts, Mrs Mary Kezia	MM	Stewardess
Robertson, James	MM	Fireman & Trimmer
Rodd, William Henry H.	MM	Clerk
Rogers, John	MM	Fireman & Trimmer
Rutherford, Robert	MM	Fireman & Trimmer
Sampson, Frederick Arthur	RN	Ship's Corporal 1st Class
Scott, L.L.	MM	Quartermaster
Scott, Thomas	MM	General Servant
Shewin, James	MM	Able Seaman
Simpson, Alexander	MM	3rd Cook
Skelton, Angus	MM	General Servant
Skinner, George	RNASBR	Junior Reserve Attendant
Smith, George	MM	Head Waiter
Smith, H.	MM	Able Seaman
Smith, Harry	MM	General Servant
Smith, Herbert Oliver	RN	Shipwright
Steen, Hugh	MM	Fireman & Trimmer
Skyrme, James Thomas	RN	Leading Shipwright
Sullivan, John James	MM	Sailor
Sumner, George H.	MM	6th Engineer
Sutherland, Walter	RNVR	2nd Shipwright

Taylor, Graham	MM	5th Engineer
Tennant, Robert	MM	Able Seaman
Thomson, James Hamilton	MM	2nd Engineer
Turley, Patrick	MM	Fireman & Trimmer
Turnbull, Matthew	MM	1st Engineer
Utting, Robert Thurlo	MM	Chief Marconi Operator
Waterworth, Anthony	RNASBR	Senior Reserve Attendant
Watt, John	MM	Greaser
Way, E.	MM	Quartermaster
White, Joseph	MM	Fireman & Trimmer
Wilkin, Herbert	MM	2nd Baker
Willis, Horace H.	MM	Barman
Wilson, Frederick Edwin	MM	Junior Marconi Operator
Winstanley, Archibald	MM	Senior 2nd Mate
Wood, William	MM	Sailor
Wootten, C.	MM	Boatswain
Young, Archibald	MM	Carpenter

MM = Mercantile Marine
RN = Royal Navy
RNSBR = Royal Navy Auxiliary Sick Reserve
RNVR = Royal Navy Volunteer Reserve

Accurately identifying those who survived the loss of the hospital, has proven to be a most difficult task, those who survived were accommodated throughout Whitby, the injured were taken to the Cottage Hospital whilst any survivors not requiring immediate treatment were transported to private dwellings, in the chaos that ensued it would have proven difficult to keep track of exactly who was sent were. As the Admiralty received notification from Whitby, the information was used to create lists of survivors or those whom perished, the information though went through many hands just to reach this point. The lists were released to governing bodies and newspapers but it was not long before an updated one was released, it must have been repetitive manually reproducing long lists of names, it would take just a short lapse of concentration for one of the casualties to be added to the wrong list. This was more demanding when one considers there were numerous cases of crew members who shared the same surname or a slight variant such as Ross or Rose. Thereafter the mistakes would simply be duplicated resulting in someone considered to have survived or perished.

After many months working through all manner of documents, gathered over almost three decades I needed a fresh perspective in a hope of confirming a more accurate identification list. I have been fortunate sharing information with Mr John Wilson, a grandson of Frederick Edwin Wilson, the Junior Marconi Operator on the Rohilla. John and I agreed that the figure of eighty-four/eighty-five souls who perished was always in question and that any change in the mortality rate is likely something which will spark some debate as the previous figure has been widely accepted over the years.

Following extensive research John and I now believe the names listed above are considered to be as accurate as can be derived for those onboard the Rohilla on 31 October 1914 in which a total of eighty - nine persons were officially recorded as having died in the disaster.

Mercantile Marine crew	173
Royal Navy crew	61*
Total	234

* Pte Thomas Anderson, RMLI was the Rohilla's only hospital patient when she left Leith and who was not strictly part of the RN compliment onboard.

The names of those onboard the Rohilla have been taken from official sources. The primary source were documents from the National Archives ADM 1/8402/423 and ADM 1/8401/401 which list survivors and those who perished. The documents are by no means small documents consisting of 138 A3 pages and 330 A3 pages respectively. The latter document also contains detailed information about the ship's crew home address and next of kin. There are a number of individual sheets titled "EXPORT of the death, of an Officer, Man or Boy, in accordance with Article 571 of the King's Regulations," and copies of "EXAMINATION ON OATH," sworn testimony from some of the key officers including Captain Neilson, however despite the huge amount of information they held there were still some inconsistencies, therefore, where possible other sources have been consulted. another National Archives document, BT 99/3051 was used to ensure the names of the Mercantile Marine are accurate.

There are two Crew Lists which cover the initial voyage from Southampton to Leith and the subsequent voyage from Leith destined for Dunkirk, which ended when the vessel was wrecked at Whitby. The Rohilla left Southampton with a partial crew, sufficient to man the ship for the voyage to Leith, before her departure from Leith additional crew members would have signed on for the coming voyage.

The 'Account Of Changes In A Crew Of A Foreign Going Ship' identifies those crew members who had left the ship or didn't join the ship for each voyage. It was important to reconcile these against the actual crew lists in order to identify the crew members who were on board during her fateful voyage. The crew lists also give a clear indication of those members of the Mercantile Marine who were drowned.

The lists do not include the Royal Navy personnel and the one patient who sailed on the ship from Leith. Other sources such as RN personnel records have been checked to compile a comprehensive and accurate list of Royal Navy personnel who were on the ship and reveal their fate and verify the accurate spelling of names.

Whilst allowing us to compile the list and fate of those on the Rohilla the official sources allowed us to resolve the correct spelling of surnames and identifying first names where in the past only initials were available. The use of newspaper lists was primarily used to confirm existing information rather than as definitive sources for names due to the large number of repeated errors of those reported as lost or saved.

John Wilson's help in identifying the number who perished has proven invaluable and I am indebted for his assistance.

As the survivors were brought ashore, they were conveyed with all possible speed to local hospitals and nursing homes, to some of the hotels, and to private residences, where everything possible was done for them. The list of the survivors and the places where they were received is as follows:

Peter Ferguson and Peter Dixon, 3 Crescent Terrace.

M. Lomas and M. Holland, 2 The Pier.

Quianlins and Eastwood, The Baths, Pier.

M. Nugent and Mr Brooksbank, Church Street, Rord.

Mr Lund, Sandgate.

F. Bigwood and A. Young, Mr W. Burn, Church Street.

Bond, Chief Officer, Mr W. Seaton Gray, St Hilda's Terrace.

W. Powell, Purser and Mr Trattles, West Cliff.

J. Moncrieff, C. Evans, T. Sampson, G. Gay, E. Parker, F. Parker, J. Rogers, W. Moffatt, J. White, D. Guthrie and A. Cribb, Custom House, Skilton.

Sampson, Brewer, Brennen and Rennie, Custom House Hotel.

F.H. Pocock, T. Hare, I. Bunyan, M. Burns, J.T. Skyme, W.C. Edwards, H. Steen, R. Rutherford and A. Lock, Seaside Home.

Turnbull and S. Gallon, Mr R.W. Milburn, 'Glenora'.

Angus Lindsay, James Bobb, H. Wilkin, F. Knight and Dr Kerr, Mrs Tracy, 'Fairlawn'.

A. Fox, G. Haste, W. Sutherland and Gray, Convalescent Home.

J. Craig, Dr Pern, Bagdale.

J. Crawley, T. Scott, T. Martin and Captain Nielsen, Angel Hotel.

J.T. Knight, G. Smith, 'Five Ladies', C. Wootten, F. Evans, E. Way, T. Paddock, T. Davis, E. Hookey, J. Farquahar, T. Hughes, Evans, Cummeau, R. Massot, W. Foster, A. Johnson, T. McMahon, D. Murray, A. Formain, W. Woods, M. McCland, Angel Hotel.

J. Addey, G. Skinner, J. Clark, J. Shewin, S. Leon, L. Scott, R. Tennant, Rev. R. Allan, T. Braidwood, G. Doe, H. Smith, G. Davis, A. Coventry, W. Limbery, W. Harrison, W. Smith (second steward), West Cliff Boarding House.

Crain and Mr Pierson, Grape Lane.

Frayer and Sullivan, Pier Hotel.

Pattison, Armstrong. Hebdidge and R.T. Uttery, 'Morgan'.

H. Willis, J. Macintosh, A. Coventry, W. Linberg, G. Smith, W.J. Hicks, F. Reddiough,

F. Bigwood, P. Turley, B. McKenzie, W. Hicks, John Caom, C.F. Morgan and W. Farquharson, Cottage Hospital.

Winstanley, 90 Church Street.

Murray Waterworth, 9 Sandgate.

Horcroft and Surgeon Hird, Market Hotel.

J. Brittain, J. Evans, Royal Hotel.

McBean, The Rectory.

Dixon, Watt, Lee, Dr Baines, Beckman and Robertson, Mrs Baines, 23 St Hilda's Terrace.

Ashcroft, Matthews, Graham, L. Murrey and Mr E.H. Chapman, 17 St Hilda's Terrace.

M. Wilson, M. McCormack and Dr G.B. Mitchell, Skinner Street.

E. Parrot, G. Curtis, and F.W. Paul, 5 Victoria Square.

Thompson, Jukes and Mr Jefferson, Prospect Hill.

Dr T.C. Littler-Jones, Hanover Terrace.

BIBLIOGRAPHY

British Newspaper Library:
Daily Mirror
Lancashire Evening Telegraph
The Suffolk Chronicle and Mercury
Middlesbrough Evening Gazette
Northern Echo
Nursing Times
Scarborough Evening News
The Times
The Town Crier, Barnoldswick
Whitby Gazette
Yorkshire Herald
Yorkshire Journal
Craven Herald and Pioneer
Pendle Today

Bradford, Sarah, George VI (London: Penguin, 2002)
Cox, Barry, Lifeboat Gallantry (London: Savannah, 1998)
Elder, Michael, For Those in Peril on The Sea: The Story of the Lifeboat Service (London: J. Murray, 1963)
Hancock, H.E., Wireless at Sea: The First Fifty Years (London: Marconi International Marine Communication Company, 1950)
Humble, A.F., The Rowing Life-boats of Whitby (Whitby: Horne & Son, 1974)
Johnstone, Tom, and James Hagerty, The Cross on the Sword: Catholic Chaplains in the Forces (London: Geoffrey Chapman, 1996)
Macvicar, Angus, Rescue Call: The Story of the Life-boat Men
Morris, Jeff, The History of Whitby Lifeboat Station
Taylor, Gordon, The Sea Chaplains: A History of the Chaplains of the Royal Navy (Oxford: Oxford Illustrated, 1979)
Wake Walker, Edward, Gold Medal Rescues with paintings by Tim Thompson (David & Charles, 1992)
Wilson, Ken, The Wreck of the Rohilla (Barnoldswick: Carrprint, 1981).
Craven's Part in the Great War
Maritime Wireless Telegraphy
The Lifeboat Journal – 1 February 1915
The Original RNLI Service Return Record for Tynemouth Lifeboat Station
The Original RNLI Service Return Record for Whitby Lifeboat Station

The following establishments proved to be most valuable assets. Some were approached directly, many via their websites, others by mail, and in some cases I engaged professional researchers to sift through the many thousands of documents to find what I was after.

Imperial War Museum London
National Maritime Museum Greenwich
Maritime History Archive (Memorial University of Newfoundland)
War Times Journal
Scarborough Maritime Heritage Centre
Royal Engineers Museum, Brompton Barracks, Prince Arthur Road, Gillingham, Kent
    ME4 4UG
Belmont Abbey and Douai Abbey Records
Commonwealth War Graves Commission
General Register Office
Lloyds Register
Public Record Office
The British Library